D1294631

WORLDS OF REFERENCE

WORLDS OF REFERENCE

lexicography, learning and language
from the clay tablet to the computer

Tom McArthur

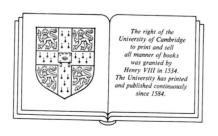

The right of the
University of Cambridge
to print and sell
all manner of books
was granted by
Henry VIII in 1534.
The University has printed
and published continuously
since 1584.

CAMBRIDGE UNIVERSITY PRESS

Cambridge
London   New York   New Rochelle
Melbourne   Sydney

Published by the Press Syndicate of the University of Cambridge
The Pitt Building, Trumpington Street, Cambridge CB2 1RP
32 East 57th Street, New York, NY 10022, USA
10 Stamford Road, Oakleigh, Melbourne 3166, Australia

© Cambridge University Press 1986

First published 1986 *September 5, 1986*

Printed in Great Britain at the University Press, Cambridge

British Library Cataloguing in Publication Data
McArthur, Tom
  Worlds of reference: lexicography, learning and language
  from the clay tablet to the computer.
  1. Information storage and retrieval system – History
  I. Title
  025.5'2'09 Z699

Library of Congress Cataloguing in Publication Data
McArthur, Tom
  Worlds of reference.
  Bibliography: p.
  Includes index.
  1. Dictionaries and encyclopedias – History.
I. Title.
AE1.M33 1985   030'.9   85-7860
ISBN 0 521 30637 X

Contents

THE MODERN WORLD

List of figures

Acknowledgements

My debt to the many researchers and sources listed in the notes and references is immense. In particular, however, I would like to acknowledge Robert Collison, Elizabeth Eisenstein, Richard Gregory, John Lyons, Karl Popper, Allen Walker Read and De Witt Starnes as seminal influences at important stages over the 12 years during which this work has developed from a compelling but amorphous idea to its present – albeit interim – stage. I would also like to thank David Abercrombie and John Sinclair for their personal encouragement when the project was still gestating, part of a thesis in lexicology at the University of Edinburgh in the early seventies. Particular gratitude is also due to A.J. Aitken, R.R.K. Hartmann and Roland Hindmarsh for their invaluable comments on various drafts of the material in recent years. Finally, I am also grateful to Susan Glendinning, Catherine Devillers, Feri McArthur and Betsy Stockdale for service beyond the call of duty as guinea pigs testing the general readability of the material. In covering such a vast area of human thought and effort I have been conscious throughout of the impossibility of one person adequately handling even one line of argument. I am very much aware of the gaps in my knowledge and the help I have received in reducing those gaps to manageable proportions. As a consequence, I am happy to share the virtues of the work with many, and to keep the vices to myself.

The author is most grateful to the following organizations and individuals for permission to reproduce their illustrations.

Bodleian Library: 85,86; The British Library: 12, 28 (*bottom*) (BL.Or.6902; BL.Or.8210), 30 (BL.Or.8210), 92 (*left*); Reproduced by courtesy of the Trustees of the British Museum: 27(BM 2496.4 Rm56; BM 99014 Rm62), 28 (*top left, top right*) (BM 122869 Rm56; BM 22505 Rm56), 34(BM 1514 Rm63); British Telecom: 175; By permission of the Syndics of Cambridge University Library: 42(MS Rm Dd.viii 22, Plinius MS folio 67 recto), 52, 53, 92 (*right*) (Ely.C.134), 99 (CUL Reading Rm Ant.b.89.5; CUL Ant.b.89.5), 113 (CUL Acton.c.51.24), 115 (Rare Books Bb.4.59 (F)), 116 (Rare Books Bb.4.59(F)); French Government Tourist Office: 18, 48 (*below*); Kings College, Cambridge, Dr Halls: 61; Kings College, Cambridge and Jarrolds of Norwich: 60; Longman: 149, 150; Mansell Collection: 66; Chris McLeod: 164 (*left*); Multimedia Publications (UK) Ltd: 151; Reproduced by courtesy of Oxford University Press: 128, 129, 132; Trustees of the Science Museum (London): 164 (*below*); Turkish Embassy: 48 (*above*).

Foreword and forewarning

Where is the Life we have lost in living?
Where is the wisdom we have lost in knowledge?
Where is the knowledge we have lost in information? ★

T.S. ELIOT, *Choruses from 'The Rock'* (1934)

T.S. Eliot asked these questions in the third decade of the twentieth century, well before the electronic age and the information explosion had come upon us. The sentiment behind these three questions, however, amply expresses the tensions (religious, cultural, social, educational) that have accumulated over the centuries as our species has struggled to live less brutishly, think more wisely, amass more knowledge, and make more and more information available to more and more people for more and more purposes.

Today, in hard technological reality, we are creating a new world of finger-tip information. In the process, some would say, we are losing our souls. It is all too big, and the simpler truths of quill-and-parchment times can look very attractive in a wasteland of words, books, printouts, facts, and figures.

How did it come to this? How did we reach this state of doubt for some, delight for others, and overload for everybody? Did it begin with the Victorians or with the Puritans, or can we push the blame back to the ancient Greeks? Is it indeed a unique experience, or has it all happened before to earlier societies, and if it did can we learn anything from what happened to *them*?

This book seeks to provide at least a provisional answer to these questions, and to promote further discussion. It suggests that the fault (if fault there is, which I doubt) lies within the species *Homo sapiens* itself. However, this very name offers a clue to what is going on: the creature that is sapient, that needs to know, that must make sense of things if it can, and expand its horizons all the time. *Worlds of Reference* is an account of the long effort involved in knowing, and struggling to retain what we think we know.

In writing this survey, I have not tried to plumb the depths of any one of the many subjects on which I have touched. It would have been good to study ancient Sumer in the original clay and cuneiform, to have read Thomas Aquinas *in toto*, and to have become thoroughly versed in information theory, artificial intelligence and the microprocessor. To have tried to do all that and more, however, would have been (as Samuel Johnson once put it) 'to lash the wind' and be guilty of the sin of pride. The old adage *ars longa, vita brevis* is even truer today than when it was coined.

I am content therefore to have written an overview which draws together strands from many disciplines that I am convinced *ought* to be drawn together. If this should lead in due course to fuller research in, and a better understanding of, the same areas and the patterns I have tried to delineate, I shall consider the work to have been well worth while.

To Feri, inevitably

Mind, word and world

Ion: And what is there that Homer speaks about which I don't know?

Socrates: Why, does not Homer speak often enough about arts and crafts? For example, driving a chariot – if I can remember the verses, I will repeat them.

Ion: Oh, I'll say them, I remember.

PLATO, the *Dialogue of Ion the Reciter of Homer*★

Genesis, in the 15th-century Gutenberg Bible. In the beginning, however, Homo sapiens had no such visual aids – only mind and voice.

1
Knowing, referring and recording: storing information beyond the brain

According to current estimates, the species *Homo* has been in existence for about two million years, although it may not have become properly *sapiens* till around 100,000 years ago.[1]

If we take the second figure as providing a rough time scale for 'true' humanity, then what we call *civilization* (a complex of organized agriculture, cities, central authority, armies, some kind of literacy, and facilities for keeping records) occupies only about the last 5% of the scale. In its turn, the period during which civilized humankind has had recognizably modern reference systems like catalogues, directories, maps, encyclopedias, and dictionaries is less than 1%. In terms of the experience of the race, therefore, what we have stored in our libraries and computers today – no matter how solid it seems, no matter how inclined we are to take it for granted – is late, brief and fragile.

The history of civilization is more than a tally of our dynasties, governments, wars, class struggles and cultural movements; it is also the story of how human beings have learned to develop and operate systems of reference and information retrieval that are external to the brain.[2] If the above estimates are reliable, then for some 99.75% of the existence of the species *Homo*, and for some 95% of the time that it has been *sapiens*, there were *no* external systems at all. The brain with its erratic memory was the only apparatus available for knowing, referring and recording – and that was the natural state of things. The bulk of our ancestors would have found anything else unimaginable, and for some aboriginal peoples today, in remote areas, this statement still holds true.[3]

The species *Homo* has created over two million years a sociocultural chasm between itself and the other living creatures that inhabit the earth. The taming of fire, the making of tools, the possession of sophisticated shelters, the growth of social ritual and the evolution of speech have all contributed to the widening of the chasm, but until breath-takingly recently in terms of geological time humankind shared with cats and chimpanzees one similarity: whatever events they experienced and observations they made blew away like smoke on the wind. Whatever they passed on to future generations was done either through the genes or immediate personal contact, leaving no consultable record.

At some imprecise point, however, *Homo* reached a take-off point, a kind of critical mass after which a whole chain reaction of achievements became possible – including the storing of information elsewhere than in the brain. Our present civilization is both a result of – and a stage in - that chain reaction. As Richard Gregory observes,[4] 'It now appears that there were some two million years of slow but distinct progress in tool-making, before the explosion of technology . . . The change in conceptual understanding is then so rapid that we are forced to attribute the way we think very largely to our tools *and what has been created by them*' (my italics). In that explosion, I would add, novel ways of containerizing information figure largely.

For Gregory, in his study of mind, the interplay of artifact with intellect, the effect of percept on concept, and the way in which 'real' tools have served as models for 'tools of the mind' have been as crucial in the development of our species as its basic biology. The equipment that we handle in our daily lives has contributed to the enrichment of our minds, and this enrichment has further contributed to the enrichment of the equipment that we handle in our daily lives.

Just as, long ago, we learned to cut up the carcasses of animals and name the varieties of plants, just as we acquired the ability to make shapes out of pieces of skin sewn together, so we transposed 'ideas' from the physical world and 'cut up' and 'stitched together' parallel artifacts inside our heads, creating mental dissections, mental classifications, mental frames and mental bags or containers. Language was the midwife in this transfer from worldscape to mindscape; it was the natural mediating element because it is both a public and a private matter. We share it when we communicate, but we do not directly share it when we engage in the soliloquies of the mind. In general terms, our minds all operate in comparable ways, but within our various cultures the frames of reference are different, and within each culture for every individual the structures and systems of the mind are unique and closed off, each one from every other one.

Despite this, however, certain evolutionary developments that shade from biology into technology are detectable. Commentators in recent years have drawn attention to them in various ways, distinguishing one, two or more of four distinct stages, jumps or shifts in the way *Homo sapiens* has developed communication, system-building in the mind, language, reference and the keeping of records. Elizabeth Eisenstein discussing the impact of the printing press, Walter Ong describing orality and literacy, and Anthony Smith describing newspaper technology, among others, have drawn attention to such shifts, which I would present as follows[5]:

- The consolidation of *speech and gesture* into firm language systems and oral traditions. This took many millennia, but what looks at first sight like a slow process was indeed a 'jump' in terms of the even longer and slower evolutionary processes that preceded it.

- The far more rapid development of *writing*, the analogue of organized speech and gesture. We can say with reasonable certainty that this development is just over five millennia old – nothing at all in terms of geological and biological time scales.

- The very recent explosion of *print*, occurring only in the last five centuries, a mere eye-blink from nature's point of view.

- The current burst of activity in terms of *electronic computation* hardly yet measurable in decades. It is, however, already transforming the technical and managerial élite of our civilization, and affecting our children so strongly and obviously in certain nations, that to make this statement in the 1980s is to commit a cliché.

Grasping these four stages, jumps or shifts is not difficult intellectually, but to appreciate their inner dynamic and their psychosocial force is much harder, and might best be approached by considering the barriers that they – inadvertently – create. The first of these is the barrier – I called it a 'chasm' a few paragraphs earlier – between ourselves and all other living creatures. We have speech and imagination, but we cannot think ourselves into the mental states and modes of communication of chameleons and cows.[6] Chimpanzees may serve us as research associates and learn unchimpanzee tricks, but even the alertest of them will never appreciate why we train them to do certain things and make certain signs.[7] The barrier is too great.

More disturbing, however, are the barriers that occur within our own species. With regard to the second shift, towards systems of writing, the attitude of the literate to the pre-literate is striking. It is hard for people who acquired the ability to read and write in childhood to understand and even tolerate the lifestyles of truly non-literate peoples – regularly classed and disdained as 'savages', 'heathen', 'barbarians', or simply 'illiterates'. For a literate person, pre-literacy is a kindergarten condition. In tandem, it is hard for people living in a print culture, with all its standardized lettering, to imagine life in the now-vanished scribal cultures (Eisenstein 1979). The print revolution has obliterated all such cultures, and it is difficult to appreciate – truly appreciate – the worlds of clay tablets, papyrus rolls, parchments, and manuscript copying.

In addition, it is also hard for people who are passably literate by the standards of a print culture to understand and be patient with those of their fellow citizens who cannot read and write (for whatever reason). These 'sub-literates' feel their inferiority every day of their lives, often going to great lengths to conceal their deficiency. It is only quite recently that our societies have begun to acknowledge that there are millions of citizens in the industrialized world with literacy problems. It is only quite recently that self-help programmes have developed in order to do something about their plight.[8]

Finally, and quite soon at that, it is going to be hard for computerate generations to imagine a pre-electronic world. We are already dividing into those who accept and understand, and those who are uncertain, confused and even resentful. Luddite tensions already exist between those who embrace the 'micro millennium' and those who will resist it to the last, with the rest of us strung out between the two extremes.

Crossing a divide like these is bound to exact its toll. At least one social commentator in recent years has described such a toll in terms of a quasi-psychological illness – 'future shock'. Alvin Toffler sees the human race at the end of the twentieth century as falling into three types:

- 'yesterday's people', effectively those still bonded to the neolithic farming revolution that created our civilizations
- 'today's people', those who are bonded to the civilization that arose after the Industrial Revolution (but which I would prefer to relate to the Renaissance and the invention of printing)
- 'tomorrow's people', a 'third wave' who relate to a new 'worldwide superindustrial society now in the throes of its birth'.

Toffler is concerned about the collision of past, present and future in our individual psyches and across the communities of the world. He writes vividly and with a taste for the sensational; and yet the subject *is* sensational, and the picture he offers is a recognizable one.[9] The old, the older, and the very new *are* in collision and *do* cause stress and anxiety. However, intense and magnified as they may be in our time, this is not to say that they are unique to that time. As Gregory indicates, the explosion began long ago, and humanity has been struggling to adapt to change for at least the last five millennia.

Collision and conflict occur, but they are not necessarily total and apocalyptic. One can point to the accommodations and compromises as well as to the dangers and divisions – especially in the area of communication, information and reference. In each of the instances that I have listed, the old can and does co-exist with the new, and the new has tended to buttress and give fresh impetus to the old.

Thus, the emergence of writing systems has not damaged speech (although it has profoundly influenced educated speech in many cultures in terms of the social graces, logic and rhetoric, grammar and elocution, and orderly academic discourse). Print has not done away with hand-writing and hand-copying, although it has done away with the copying and distribution of manuscripts; more people today engage in letter-writing by hand and even in calligraphy (in Japan and the Arab world, for example, if not in the West) than ever served as scribes in days gone by. It is also highly unlikely that computers (or television) will do away with the printed word and the bound book (although they will certainly amend our traditional conceptions and practices in interesting ways).[10]

I would now like to look at a universal feature in the shifts or jumps that we have been considering, a feature that can be expressed by means of the terms 'primary' and 'secondary'. Thus, the first jump from sounds and gestures to organized vocal language was the development of a *secondary* use for a *primary* system. Speech is imposed upon, or develops from, a primary apparatus that evolved for other more basic purposes: lungs, larynx, pharynx, mouth, nose, teeth, and lips were the apparatus of breathing, eating and drinking (Abercrombie 1967:20; O'Connor 1973:22). When the secondary set of skills emerged, they did not seriously interfere with what was already going on: we still breathe, eat and drink as well as speak, and often manage all four more or less together, although it can pose risks.

The second shift, however, was radically different in one unique respect. The first shift had made use of pre-existing organs of the body and head, but the second shift moved language right away from the body and its essential activities, and changed the focus, as it were, from mouth and ear to hand and eye. The new analogue of speech – making marks on surfaces, then reading them again as often as you wanted without them ever changing – was nonetheless a *secondary* system, as linguists seldom fail to point out.[11] Speech is the primary form of language. Of the secondary system, however, Christopher Evans says, in the *Micro Millennium* (1979:104):

> The invention of writing was the most revolutionary of all human inventions, for in one great blow it severed the chains which tied an individual and his limited culture to a finite region of space, to a restricted slice of time. Through the act of writing, one human being could express ideas or facts which were communicated to another individual. These facts could then remain as a permanent record after the originator had forgotten them or had passed away into dust. The significance of permanent data storage is the principal and perhaps the *sole* reason why Man is so absolutely the dominant creature of the planet. All non-human animals carry their knowledge and experience with them when they die. Man can preserve the richest fruits of his brain power, and stockpile them indefinitely for his descendants to feed on.

A container other than the brain had been found for information and a particular kind of reference; from this new system it was possible to see that certain kinds of data were better off outside our brains and mouths than inside them. Just as for millennia we had been putting physical objects like food and tools in bags and carrying them around or leaving them be, so we now began to put mental objects in the new equivalent of bags, fossilizing the achievement in such expressions as 'the contents' of a book. In doing this, we ceased to be the slaves of transience; it was, in fact, the intellectual equivalent of storing up the harvest for later consumption.

Writing, however, requires considerable skill and powers of concentration; it is also often a solitary craft that requires a kind of monastic dedication. For much of its history it has been in the hands (both literally and figuratively) of professional élites who have been willing to give it the attention it requires in return for certain social privileges that it bestows. Such élites have often had ties with ritual and religion, with the result that we retain nowadays something of the accumulated veneration that our unlettered ancestors felt for their scribal élites, while our children at school still experience the pain and the pressure mandatory in the crafts of reading and writing.

The third shift, upon the invention of the printing press, moved us from the primary manuscript to the secondary (or derivative) printed page. Our attitudes to writing and writers did not necessarily change much, but the dissemination of the written word did begin to pass beyond the control of the scribal hierarchies. More people than ever before became involved in the manufacture, writing, printing, binding, publishing, distributing, buying, selling and reading of graphic materials; indeed, in due course Western society at large was even persuaded that every single citizen of every single state in the world could become more or less literate (a dream that is still far from fulfilment).

The fourth and most recent of the shifts is so new that we are still debating it, but like the others it is also a secondary adaptation of a primary activity. Electronic computation is as derivative of print as print is derivative of script and script of sound, and sound in its turn of breathing. Its potential, however, for the further democratization of knowledge is staggering. Like the printing press, the hand-gun, the radio and the telephone, it is one of history's great equalizers.

2

Information and World 3: in the beginning was the Word

Christopher Evans proposes writing as the fundamental means by which we have created a 'stockpile' of the 'richest fruits' of human brainpower. Like bees, we have created something of immense worth that is both collective and yet separate from all of us.

He is not alone in this view, which has been taken further by the philosopher of science, Karl Popper. For him, there are three distinct 'worlds' available to us: World 1 of material things, World 2 of what has developed in our minds, and World 3, the result of their interaction.[1] The first is what *Homo* has always had to contend with: the storms, heat, cold, teeth, claws, sticks and stones, flesh and bone of 'reality'. The second is the mental analogue of all that, our inner landscape of images, sounds and unspoken words, collective and yet unique to each of us, sensing, responding to and seeking to interpret World 1. The third is our honey-store, all the ideas and information that have become a kind of public domain as a result of what World 2 has concluded about World 1. As Bryan Magee puts it (1973:61): 'World 3, then, is the world of ideas, art, science, language, ethics, institutions – the whole cultural heritage, in short – in so far as this is encoded and preserved in such World 1 objects as brains, books, machines, films, computers, pictures, and records of any kind.'

The lines that you are reading belong in World 1, part of the general worldscape. How you process them is World 2, your mindscape.[2] Their message or content, however, is part of World 3, which has independent value and, in Magee's view, make libraries and databanks far and away more important than the knowledge that is in any one person's head at any one time. What we may call the 'oratures' of pre-literate peoples belong also in World 3, but they are far less efficiently housed and safeguarded than the 'literatures' of literate societies.[3] This is because the containers used – the finite and wasting brains of bards and genealogists – are less secure than other containers, and the delivery systems – human mouths – less dependable.

The Western world nowadays uses a single term for the most significant aspect of Popper's World 3 – the aspect that makes it a commodity or resource. That term is 'information', a word which came into general use around the time of the invention of the printing press.[4] In recent decades, a great deal of thought has been given to this aspect of World 3 and to how it can be manipulated in World 1: experts now consider how this commodity is shaped and transmitted (in 'information theory'), and how it can be handled (in 'information processing').

Indeed, some theorists have gone so far as to extend the concept of information into physics and cosmology, alongside 'entropy' and 'the second law of thermodynamics'. In a recent work entitled *Grammatical Man*, Jeremy Campbell asserts that 'nature can no longer be seen as matter and energy alone . . . To the powerful theories of chemistry and physics must be added a late arrival: the theory of information. Nature must be interpreted as matter, energy, and information' (1982:16).

Such intriguing new trinities, however, are not central issues in this review, although they are by no means irrelevant. This is made abundantly clear by the following observations of the information scientist Merrill Flood:

> All of these technological advances (the computer, etc.) together have made information a new basic resource that supplements the familiar natural resources of matter and energy. Accumulated world knowledge takes on an entirely new meaning and significance as techniques for mining, storing, sharing, and using information in new ways are learned. Knowledge in the form of newly stored information is not degraded or destroyed with use.

> Stores of information represent a new kind of transactable commodity, ranking in future human importance alongside material and energy resources. Control of information stores and processing facilities may well become more important than material and energy resources as a source of social and economic power. This situation may lead to a wider dispersal of human power, as suggested above, and to a reduction in importance of the few specialists who hold power merely because of special knowledge.

In the same series of articles,[5] David Kronick divides what he calls the 'information media' into two broad categories – primary and secondary – much as in figure 1 (my diagram). Kronick's main professional interest is

Fig. 1 David Kronick's division of the information media

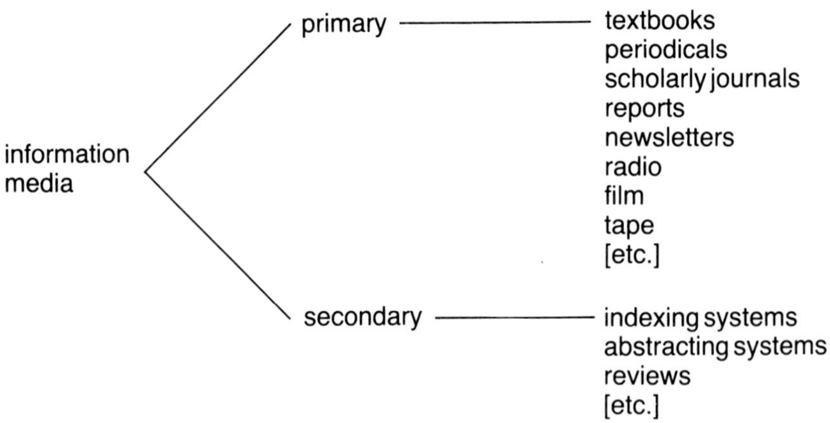

information media

primary —————— textbooks
periodicals
scholarly journals
reports
newsletters
radio
film
tape
[etc.]

secondary —————— indexing systems
abstracting systems
reviews
[etc.]

communication within the medical profession, but it is clear from his categorization that any comprehensive secondary system must also contain works of lexicography and general reference. Indeed, dictionaries and encyclopaedias are classic examples of how we abstract information from primary sources of various kinds and marshal that information in terms of some kind of indexing or 'pointing' system.

It is equally clear from Flood's remarks that information as such can only exist as a usable resource *if* it is properly accessible, and it is only properly accessible *if* all the appropriate procedures of the secondary media are in place: numbers, letters, alphabetization, thematization, contents lists, correspondences between indexes and locations of data, and so forth. Without these vital 'secondary' procedures, 'primary' material, however valuable in itself, may be rendered functionally worthless.

Library science illustrates this point. A large number of books may be worth having, however stacked. It is not, however, until that pile is sorted out (in terms of shelf arrangement and perhaps something detailed like the Universal Decimal System) that the pile becomes 'informed' (to use an archaic but relevant sense of the word *inform*). The essence of information handling is that by imposing shape it banishes randomness. The possibility that such-and-such a book is on such-and-such a shelf is good, the probability is even better, but the *certainty* that it can be traced to that shelf every time is best of all. In terms of information theory, 'noise' (chaos) is thus transformed into a decently coded 'message' (order) – whenever a suitable system of ordering, *however arbitrary*, is introduced. The greater the certainty of finding what you want when you want it, the better the system.

A loosely structured system like a library is always at risk, of course. The processes of entropy invade it constantly, as books are shifted around, taken away, brought back, put in holding piles (till they can be replaced on their shelves), misplaced, damaged, lost and stolen. The guardians of the system have to be vigilant in its defence and maintenance, seeking all the time to restore the classical perfection of its form without impeding the user – although some librarians grow so obsessively concerned with classical perfection that they appear in principle to be anti-user.

A tightly structured system like a book, on the other hand, faces the opposite problem. A printed and bound dictionary, for example, is like a fossil; the moment it is complete and published, it is dated and rendered imperfect by the continuing flow of the language beyond what it has described. Revision and adaptation are both expensive and laborious. New usages are therefore put into holding files, then perhaps added in special lists to a later impression of the work, until at length there is enough new material in the appended lists and further holding files to justify a fully revised edition (this usually after the passage of about 10 to 20 years).

Neither the loosely nor the tightly structured system is ideal, yet we have become accustomed to both in our struggle with the World 1 of containers and the World 3 of information contained. It is probable, however, that our ideas on what can be done about such imperfect systems will be shaken up

The great domed Reading Room of the British Library in London and its tiered shelves of wordbooks.

by such things as information science and the attendant technology of the computer. These could very well help in various ways to make both libraries and books more flexible and efficient. In the process, however, they will probably make both libraries and books behave rather differently from what we have been used to.

Ordering is at the heart of much of World 3. Language is a serial phenomenon and the mechanisms we use for arranging information – numbers and letters – can only be used for this purpose because they are basically invariant series, however much we shuffle them about. Orderliness is also inherent in other areas of World 3, such as music, art, mathematics, literature, drama and cinema. Order is everywhere in such matters, from the arrangement of scenes in a drama or opera to the sequences in which films are taken and shown and tapes are recorded and played back. Such order, as Campbell implies, reflects a deeper and wider order in the atoms, molecules, crystals, bodies, planets, and stars around us. In other words, 'order' here means the codes that make all things possible.

If order is inherent in World 3, what however is ordered? Nature in World 1 has its patterns for atoms and molecules, but what is the currency of information as arranged by our minds?[6] There would appear to be something like three currencies available to us, two relating to our sensory systems and one to language. The first two are images and sounds, while the third is 'words'.

Although one might say that images, sounds and words are rather obviously the coinage of the mind, there is nothing simple about them. They operate the way they do because they are capable of existing in all three of Popper's Worlds and can appear in an infinite range of patterns. There is no end to the films we can take or the cartoons we can draw and appreciate; there is no end to the rhythmic sounds we can compose and call 'music' or 'song'; and there is certainly no limit to the combinations of words we can produce or the number of words we can invent.

There is, however, a fundamental difference between images and sounds on the one hand and words on the other. In crude general terms, images come to us first via our physical eyes from a world 'out there'; the images of our mind's eye derive from them, and can shape through art further physical images for our physical eyes to see. Similarly, sounds also come to us via our physical ears, and the sounds we hear in our mind's ear derive from them, and can shape through art further physical sounds for our physical ears to hear.

Words, however, did not initially come to us from the world out there beyond the human race. Our remote ancestors existed before words existed, though they knew images and sounds. The species *Homo* did not invent images and sounds, though we have augmented them; we did, however, invent words.[7]

Additionally, words make use of both the ear and the eye. For the bulk of the time that language has been used, 'words' have been borne to and from us as elements in a stream of sound; after the invention of writing, they have also been borne to and from us as elements in a stream of visual signs. As a consequence, they *are* sounds and images while being *beyond* sounds and images. This paradox is a crucial factor in their nature as units of language. If we see the phonic and the visual as mediums for language, then we must also agree, as the linguist John Lyons puts it, that elements of language are 'medium-transferable'. They can swim in both kinds of water.[8]

Words are the products of the human brain in seeking to come to terms with and communicate in the real world. As such they are psychophysical tools that correspond to purely physical tools like spades, and psychophysical containers that correspond to purely physical containers like bags and boxes. A 'noun' is as much a tool of the mind as a saw or an axe is a tool of the world; in that it 'contains' or classifies an enormous number of other words, it is also as much a container as a handbag or a suitcase.

Many words relate to things in the world ('That is a *church*; this is a *mosque*'), but they should not be confused with what they point to. Additionally, in 'pointing' or referring to elements in the world they enable us to see and hear those elements more precisely; without words we would not distinguish colours in the way we do or varieties of animals and plants. This does not mean, however, that words are always by nature precise; they are, as any lexicographer knows all too well, slippery creatures that seem to have *one* shape and reference but usually prove to have more than one, with all sorts of nuances and shades thrown in (perhaps, ultimately, as many such nuances and shades as there are individuals using a particular language). Words have common cores of meaning for us all as users of a language, but they also have penumbras that make them fuzzy-edged. Thus, a 'cat' can be small and cuddly if it is domestic, but large and savage if it is in the jungle; 'cat' can refer to animals, but it can also refer to women, whips and young men in urban ghettoes. It can, if you follow a few rules, refer to almost anything you want (assuming you can persuade enough other people to accept the extension you want to give it).

Words are homely, and yet they can be sources of fear and vehicles of mysticism. Beyond the everyday casual use of language lie areas of oaths and curses, spells and enchantment that are as viable today as they ever were; the voodoo aspect of words, their propaganda power, their suasive qualities are all still vigorous. I can 'give you my word' and you will hope I don't then 'break it'. I won't of course, because 'my word is my bond'. I can 'have a word with you' and we chat; I can 'have words with you', and we quarrel. These idiomatic expressions in English indicate the social potency of the concept. How much more potent still when Christians consider that 'in the beginning was the Word, and the Word was with God, and the Word was God', or when a Muslim says 'it is written' and we know that what was written is words that are not in any earthly book?

The professions of the word have always excited a measure of awe: shamans, poets, actors, playwrights, orators, magicians, preachers, philosophers, teachers, lawyers and authors – and now computer programmers with whole new 'languages' like a BASIC that isn't basic and a COBOL that sounds like a medieval German demon.

Containers for knowledge: the human brain alongside some of its analogues and adjuncts –
tablet, parchment, books and discs.

The species to which we belong virtually defines itself by the words it has invented – *Homo loquens*, the talking animal.[9] Today its words are everywhere, on walls, on pages and on display screens. How did they get there? What processes of history have led to the reference and information systems that we use today, and in particular the systems in which words are central – encyclopaedias, textbooks and dictionaries?

When I first started the work that led to this book, I thought I was engaged in outlining the history of lexicography and its related disciplines. It took some time and frustration before I realized that I was in fact toying with a distinct way of looking at human history. An account of this kind can, however, only be attempted now, because its own shape and terminology are dependent on concepts and procedures that have emerged in recent decades in such areas as linguistics, information theory and library science, computer studies and artificial intelligence.

These developments suggest new angles from which we can look at old familiar artifacts and systems of arrangement – from the cave paintings of our prehistoric ancestors to such present-day publishing institutions as the *Encyclopaedia Britannica* and the *Oxford English Dictionary*.

We can start with the cave paintings.

The ancient world

They pull up the annual crop of papyrus-reed which grows in the marshes, cut the stalks in two, and eat the lower part, about eighteen inches in length, first baking it in a closed pan, heated red-hot, if they want to enjoy it to perfection. The upper section of the stalk is used for some other purpose.

HERODOTUS, *The Histories,* Book 2, in Egypt*

Places and objects of reference: Cro-Magnon man not only drew beasts on the walls of his cave galleries, but used their horns and antlers for the world's earliest memos.

3

Containers of knowledge: the first reference technologies

Some 30,000 years ago the Cro-Magnon peoples[1] of Europe developed a skill that (as far as we know) had not existed before. They began to create on rock surfaces shapes that were analogues of other shapes that lived and moved in the actual world.

This is not simply a devious way of saying that they began to draw pictures of animals; rather, saying that they drew animals is simply a convenient shorthand for what they achieved. For the first time ever they re-stated perceptions of three-dimensional creatures in terms of outline alone; they made the mobile immobile and in so doing 'tamed' it, and tamed it in a pretty permanent way. The results of their achievement can still be seen and admired today, on the walls of caverns like Lascaux in France and Altamira in Spain. We have no idea, however, whether Cro-Magnon artists also drew on rock walls *outside* caverns (as other later societies have done), or why they went to so much trouble to paint their great beasts in awkward subterranean corners.

Their pictures may have served as magico-religious focuses, linked with the hunt or with the powers of animal 'spirits' . The animals may have been drawn or studied as parts of seasonal, initiation or other rites; or they may even have been antediluvian graffiti, of the type 'Red Buffalo was here'.

Their motivations, however, are not the central issue in this review. It is the *fact* of their existence that matters. The people involved could 'read' these paintings and relate them to objects elsewhere. They were, therefore, public centres of reference, however many or few the people who were involved with them. The pictures made the walls and tunnels where they were drawn different from all other walls and tunnels; they served to create a gallery, a *place of reference* to which people could come for specific kinds of experience.

In tandem with these ancient galleries there developed something smaller but no less significant. Human beings have presumably, since time immemorial, used their fingers for pointing and listing, two primary modes of referring and organizing. They could draw attention to a distant stranger, count heads, or make rhetorical 'points'. Although the languages we have used in the last two or three millennia do not date back directly to Cro-Magnon times, it is still worthwhile noting that we use the term 'index' for both the pointing finger and a list of a certain kind that also figuratively points, and that the term 'digit' (so useful in mathematics and computation generally) derives from the Latin word for a finger. (Indeed, it can be argued that we favour decimal arithmetic over duodecimal or binary because we have been blessed with 10 fingers to count on, and not 12 or 2.)

At some stage our ancestors made a secondary shift from fingers to other things like sticks, stones and bits of bone.[2] With these, their pointing and listing could take on greater permanence and referential value. Evidence of this shift dates from about the same time as the cave paintings; items of bone and antler have been found with grooves or dots on them, expressing patterns of an apparently serial type.[3] A line of 50 such marks might, for example, consist of 5 marks made with one tool, 12 with another, 7 with a third, and so forth. The same person might have done all the work at different times with different tools, or different people might have shared the work at various times with various tools. They might have done it in order to record the tallies for hunts, the cycles of the moon or certain rites, or some other statistical matter of interest to the community. Again, however, that is not the central issue here. What matters is that the tallies were made, and that the bones appear as a consequence to have been used as *objects of reference.*

There are many examples of the use of parallel tallying devices among non- and semi-literate peoples in historical times. Among the Maoris of New Zealand, for example, the reciting of genealogies was helped along by using notched sticks. Each notch indicated an ancestor, and the reciter worked along the notches much as a Roman Catholic works along the rosary while praying. Such devices are aids to memory; they cannot be 'read' as such for separately existing information, but they are the beginnings of externalized data.

The evidence is scant but compelling. It suggests that our remoter ancestors had two crude modes of recording and reference: the *place of reference* and the *object of reference.* The place was large and awesome and its displays could be gazed upon in more or less serial fashion, and in a way that is markedly like wandering inside a medieval cathedral or a modern museum. The object, however, was small and relatively homely, and was conveniently portable; its displays were also serial, whether scratched on wood, cut in bone, strung as beads on thread, knotted in rope or arranged with paint. Interested people had to travel to the place, but the object could travel to *them,* or move around with them as part of their luggage. In this it markedly resembles a medieval scroll or a modern book.

This is because, in both the place and the object, surfaces had been compelled by the mind to become containers of knowledge, although such surfaces bore no physical resemblance whatever to 'proper' containers like holes and bags. They are the archetypal extremes in the arrangement of reference materials, and we have yet to transcend them.

When the human race passed its take-off point or time of critical mass, the first peoples for whom everything came together and accelerated appear to have been the inhabitants of ancient Sumer and Egypt. By any yardstick they were innovators, and yet each innovated along very distinct lines: the Sumerians of what is now southern Iraq developed a clay-based civilization, while the folk of the Nile Valley worked with reeds and stone.[4]

Between 5,000 and 6,000 years ago, both communities created complex cities, developed agricultures that used irrigation, grew cereal crops, and kept herd animals, used the wheel, worked metals, formulated systems of measurement, studied the sky – and invented writing, record-keeping, scholarship, and bureaucracy. How much the one owed to the other is not clear, but apparently Sumer was slightly earlier by a margin of a few hundred years. Both societies existed for millennia, and bequeathed us much of the cultural conditioning that operates in, around and upon us. Theirs were such institutions as the seven-day week and the signs of the Zodiac; our clocks still use their time schemes with sets of 60, and our children go to adaptations of their schools. We live within the social and intellectual geometry that they created, and think of it as natural and eternal.

In Sumer, almost everything basic was made of clay, from pots to houses. When something convenient was needed for tallying, the soft-to-hard quality of the argillic mud in the ubiquitous irrigation ditches proved literally 'handy'. One scooped up a handful, shaped it for holding in one hand, flattened the upper surface, then made various pictographic marks on it with the end of a cut reed. Thus, clay made all the basic containers, from realia to reading, that ancient Mesopotamia wanted. The simple clay extension of the tally stick ushered in a recording-and-reference technology that spread across West Asia and lasted for more then 3,000 years, for we know that clay tablets were still in use as late as the first century AD.

The simple marks pressed into clay when it was wet evolved in due course into the complex style of writing now known as 'cuneiform' or wedge-shaped. With the passage of time, signs became stylized and lost their primary pictorial values, to become a secondary system of ideograms ('idea signs', as in Chinese traditional writing) and syllabograms ('syllable signs', as in traditional Japanese adaptations of Chinese writing). Along with the linear or serial ordering of the signs, at first vertically, then horizontally, there also developed as incidental extras a range of conventions that are ancestral to such present-day conveniences as pagination, margins, white space and punctuation, without which scannable information would be impossible.

The Sumerians evidently started with the portable object of reference and in due course moved on to adorning large places of reference. The Egyptians, however, appear to have done things the other way round. Wherever they had walls – whether the public walls of temples or in the cave-like privacy of their tombs – they cut and painted pictures in serial masses. Much of this activity was linked with religion, and as a result their primary sign system is called 'hieroglyphic' (that is, 'dealing in sacred carvings'). Like the Sumerians, the Egyptians made use of mud and reeds, but the mud did not become a medium for information. Instead, they did something with their reeds that had never occurred to the inhabitants of Sumer. Abundantly available in the Delta of the Nile, the reed *Papyrus cyperus* served as a staple of their civilization: its pith was a common foodstuff, the roots were used as fuel, and the stems could be used for making boats, sails, cordage, mats, a kind of cloth, and a kind of writing surface.

One use for the reed sheets was great banners, decorated with hieroglyphs, that were hung on the walls of buildings. These banners had one
enormous advantage over putting pictograms on the walls themselves: they
could be taken down, rolled up, put away, taken out again, sent off somewhere else, unrolled and re-hung. In a word, although they were large, they
were *portable*. In essence, however, they were objects for hanging in galleries,
to be gazed upon by pilgrim-like visitors. In early Egypt indeed, whether the
hieroglyphs were cut or painted on the walls or placed on banners, they were
read by people who walked into a book and strolled from page to page.

In due course, however, the Egyptians learned to miniaturize, by
adapting their vertically hung banners into horizontally held rolls. Sheets of
papyrus, glued together end to end, formed rolls that were convenient to the
hands, about eight inches (20 centimetres) high and anything from 15 to 40
feet (5 to 13 metres) long. For us the result seems clumsy, but these rolls
should be understood in terms of the great banners that preceded them. They
had spindles at both ends, and one read them by winding the papyrus from
one spindle to the other, which is precisely the same procedure as is used
nowadays with magnetic tape and film. The papyrus roll also shared the
strengths and weaknesses of tape and film: easy continuity, but problems in
checking back and forward to precise points, and always a risk of breakages.
Patching up rolls was no doubt as common then as the repairing and splicing
of tape and film are today.

What did it mean, in the third millennium BC, to be able to read such
things as clay tablets and papyrus rolls?[5] It was certainly different from reading today. Firstly, no one supposed then that the population at large would
have anything to do with such matters. For a Sumerian to know that a clay
object was a tablet for writing on and not a brick for building with was an
achievement; for an Egyptian to appreciate that pictograms were not just pictures was much the same. To know which way was 'up' on a cuneiform tablet
and which the direction of flow meant sophistication; to be able to separate
the proper gods and pharaohs from their representations was not always easy
for the average Egyptian.

It was by no means obvious even to the literate that *any* good smooth
surface would do as well as clay in Sumer and papyrus in Egypt – neither society used the other's system. Nor was it obvious that *any* agreed system of
marks would do the job. Lastly, it could not have been in the least apparent
that the only limit upon the *quantity* of information that could be recorded and
stored was the limitations in *quality* of the technologies themselves – the
limitations imposed by wet clay that had to be baked hard, and by split and
spread reed-bark that had to be pasted into sheets. We are the possessors of
much more elaborate systems, but we are still limited by the kinds of display
surfaces we can command, the sizes we prefer, the means available to us for
actual inscription, the survivability of the materials used, the kinds of
language and script currently favoured, and the storage chambers that we can
afford.[6]

It was – and is – difficult to make a distinction in such matters between the *contingent* and the *universal*. Clay, for example, is *contingent;* it just happened to be there in abundance in the right place at the right time, and people used it. Similarly, papyrus reeds were contingent, as are all writing surfaces and all the tools we have ever used for making marks on those surfaces. The clay-and-cuneiform technology was contingent upon the way things developed in Sumer, and the reed-and-hieroglyph technology was contingent upon the way things developed in Egypt. They were only two from among all the possible technologies that might be set up for the same purposes. Each technological medium imposed its own special limitations and had its own special cultural 'flavour', and is therefore interesting; what is of greater interest, though, is everything that lies behind the contingent, the *universal* factors common to all such technologies: ordering, listing, display, hierarchy of arrangement, edge and margin, sectioning, spacing, contrasts – these transcend the contingent world of clay and reeds.

Our awareness, however, of the universal and our ability to benefit from that awareness have only emerged after centuries of struggling with such things as bits of wet clay, pieces of gummy papyrus, scraped animal skins and oddments of adapted rags and wood pulp. It was hard work to get nature to provide the containers of knowledge.

4

Systems for knowledge: school and letter, book and library

Around the year 2350 BC, the dominion of Mesopotamia passed from the people for Sumer in the south to the people of Akkad in the north. The passage was a violent one, one after which nothing was ever quite the same again (Claiborne 1974; Edzard 1976).

The Akkadians were an uncultured Semitic people, and as usurpers of an ancient civilization were ambivalent about its values and institutions. However, as is often the case, in the process of conquest they assimilated much of what was already normal for the Sumerians, and this included the scribal bureaucracy by means of which their complex society was maintained. A scribe in those remote days was far more than a medieval clerk or a Victorian lackey. He belonged to a professional élite who possessed skills which later civilizations have apportioned among diverse successor occupations: archivist, chronicler, surveyor, mathematician, accountant, teacher, compiler, and author. Scribes were the literal right-hand men of rulers and merchant princes, engaged in the work of law and civil administration, and seldom far from the ritual and myth of the temple-ziggurats. They were the key people in their society.

The Akkadians had to make use of the scribal training institutions if they were to understand and maintain the society they had usurped. In the scribal schools their sons learned the arts of reading and writing, but they had to learn those arts *in Sumerian*, for they were accessible only in that language. Sumerian, however, was a non-Semitic language, for which no cognate language has ever been found anywhere, and this factor proved crucial not only for events in Mesopotamia but for the history of education and reference materials at large.

Eventually, because of the everyday pressures of Akkadian, the Sumerian language died out as a vernacular in its own right, but it lived on for centuries as the language of scribal education, administration, scholarship, and social prestige. It was, in other words, the 'high' or 'classical' language of the Sumero-Akkadian complex.

Fortunately for us, large quantities of débris survive from the scribal schools in which the sons of Akkad settled down with the traditions of Sumer. By fitting together pieces of broken practice tablets, archaeologists have learned that the schools engaged in two linked activities:

- They compiled, and taught from, bilingual lists with Sumerian word-forms in one column and their Akkadian equivalents in another.
- Whenever a text was rendered from Sumerian into Akkadian, they retained the original on the same tablet with the new version, a line of Sumerian first, then a line of Akkadian translating it, then another line of Sumerian, and so on, an intricate piece of contrastive language work.

The ancient world possessed many public inscriptions where the same statement or proclamation was made in two or more languages side by side. Such inscriptions as the Rosetta Stone have, for example, proved useful to palaeographers in their efforts to decipher previously unknown scripts, by comparing the unknown with the known. Such parallel texts, however, though interesting as multilingual displays of information, are quite distinct from the artifacts just described.

The publicly displayed texts were not organized for the purposes of explaining one language in terms of another. They were strictly utilitarian; you read the one you *could* read, or a scribe read out the appropriate one to the appropriate audience of unlettered citizens. With the new practices in the scribal schools, however, something unique had developed: scholarly work intended to sustain a tradition in difficult times while transferring skills from one language group to another. This was the beginning of the translation method of language teaching and also the beginning of the art of definition by synonym. In the orderly columnar manner of its listing, it is also the beginning of lexicography.

During the millennium that followed the cultures of Mesopotamia and Egypt were consolidated, the people thanking their gods for the benefits of civilization that had been bequeathed to them and seeking to keep such crafts as writing unsullied and unchanged.[1] Despite the pressures to conserve and conform, however, changes did begin to occur, especially in the region of Phoenicia-Canaan, midway between the two great cultures. In Ebla, scribes became skilled in cuneiform and the listing of languages side by side (using identical first syllables as a means of listing words, as in *ni-gu, ni-ba, ni-gal*). The real breakthrough however appears to have occurred in Ugarit, around 1400 BC, for there a proto-alphabet of 30 signs arranged in fixed order has been found, used on clay tablets for a Canaanite dialect. Both its precise origin and its fate are unknown, however, and there is a gap in the archaeology until around 1000 BC, when there emerged in the Phoenician city of Byblos an alphabet of 22 signs.

The advantage of an alphabet over the Mesopotamian and Egyptian systems lay in its startling economy and flexibility; as an achievement, it ranks with the invention of the wheel and the domestication of the horse. Instead of hundreds of distinct *pictograms* (picture signs), *ideograms* (idea signs), *logograms* (word signs), and *syllabograms* (syllable signs), between 20 and 30 quasi-phonetic symbols could be used to portray an infinity of words. Such an economical system could also transfer more easily from language to language than its cumbersome predecessors.

A third advantage that seems kindergarten to us now is the value of an alphabet as an invariant series, like numbers, but the virtues of invariant series were not widely apparent at that time. It is no surprise, however, that even in the face of the conservatism of the scribes of Babylon and Egypt the new invention began to eclipse both cuneiform and the hieratic scripts while leaving tablets and rolls unaffected.

The heyday of the papyrus roll was the first millennium BC, the period during which the Greeks rose to importance in the eastern Mediterranean. It is to the Greeks that we owe much of the vocabulary of recording and reference, just as we owe them much of the vocabulary of philosophy and science. They called the Egyptian reed *pápyros* and its inner bark *bíblos*. A roll was understood in terms of where it stopped or was 'cut', so they called it *tómos* ('a cutting'), whence our idea of weighty 'tomes' and the French *un tome*. For the Romans a *tómos* was a *volumen*, whose plural form is *volumina*. Long works of the imagination, the law or religion needed more than one roll, so they were indeed 'voluminous'.

The Greeks also gave us a fundamental word for the containers of papyrus rolls. Such a container was a *bibliothéke*; this concept, however, was flexible in terms of size, for it could refer to either a box or a room, a cupboard or a building. English has not inherited this idea, for today we put books in 'bookcases' in 'libraries'. The French, however, have kept the original flexibility in *bibliothèque*.

With the proliferation of scribal schools, temples and other community institutions, enormous *bibliothékai* came into existence, containing thousands of tablets or rolls. By the fourth century BC such *libraria* (to use the Roman word) were common in Greece, Asia Minor, Egypt and West Asia. The two most famous collections of the ancient world were in the Greek cities of Alexandria and Pergamon, the first founded around 300 BC, the second just under a century later.

Competition between the libraries of the two cities was fierce, part of a greater competition for domination of the Hellenized world.[2] This rivalry has marked the world in various ways, one of which was the inadvertent invention of the book. The story is as follows.

King Ptolemy Philadelphus of Egypt, eager to weaken the influence of the Pergamites, placed an embargo upon the export of papyrus to Asia Minor. As a consequence the Pergamites were forced to look elsewhere for the materials they needed for writing things down. Their ruler, Eumenes II, encouraged experimentation with animal skins, which from time to time had been used as writing surfaces. The result was the development of a material that the Romans in due course called *charta pergamena* ('the leaf or sheet from Pergamon'). Improved methods of stretching, cleaning and scraping the skins of young sheep, goats and cows led to a fine new material that could be used on *both* sides – an unheard-of luxury.

Stitched together, the pieces of pergamena made passable rolls, with the advantage over papyrus that they could fold without cracking. Although not given immediately the same status as papyrus, the new material was a

*A Sumerian survey
tablet with prototype lines
and columns (c. 1980 BC).*

*A fragment from the Egyptian papyrus 'Book of the Dead' of the Royal Scribe Hunefer
(c. 1310 BC).*

Some reference styles that failed: *TOP LEFT a Mesopotamian cone-like tablet to be held and looked down at (c. 1760 BC) TOP RIGHT an Assyrian nonagonal prism to be read by rotation round the page-sides (c. 720 BC) CENTRE a Mahayana Buddhist 'loose-leaf' palm-leaf 'book' (c. AD 1142), BOTTOM its short-lived metal derivative.*

success; its name was also a success, and survives in such forms as *pergamino* in Spanish, *parchemin* in French, and 'parchment' in English. The Romans particularly favoured the use of the skins of new or still-born calves (*vituli*); this kind of parchment they called *vitulinum* ('calf-stuff'), whose present-day English form is 'vellum'.

Ptolemy's embargo therefore proved counter-productive, encouraging an alternative medium that in due course eclipsed Egypt's ancient asset. Although for several centuries parchment remained no more than a substitute for papyrus, the Pergamites continued to experiment with it, and by the beginning of the Christian era were blending the use of parchment with an old idea of tying waxed wooden tablets together with thongs. Such collections of tablets were known in Latin as *codices (codex*, 'a block of wood', from *caudex*, 'a tree trunk'). What was now done, however, was to use parchment's excellent propensity for folding. Sheets were folded in two across the middle to make an arrangement in which one could write on all four sides (in Latin *quaternio*, English a 'quire'). Folded sheets were placed one on top of the other and then stitched together, not however along the edge but along the central fold. The whole folded set was then placed between thin boards as covers and bound together with those covers. The result might look to us like a Neanderthal attempt at making a book, but once again has to be seen in terms of what had gone before.

The new parchment-based codex was mainly used as a notebook or a ledger. For a long time it lacked social prestige, and was not used for 'high' purposes, but with the spread of Christianity this state of affairs radically changed. The new religion spread at a lower social level than that of the copyists and librarians, and the proselytizers of Christianity were therefore familiar with the codex and came to prefer it for their own purposes to the roll (even though 'the Bible' as a name fossilizes the name for such rolls). The Christians may well have appreciated one advantage of the new ledger-like format: it was much easier to refer back and forward from page to page between covers than inside a 30-foot roll on spindles.

By the third century AD, the codex was the regular form for the recording of Christian materials, and rose socially as the new religion rose. By the fourth century, it was the accepted medium for non-Christian materials as well, a state of affairs that was to prevail in the West for the next thousand years.

At the same time, however, as the codex was beginning to become attractive in the West, a series of significant events was taking place in China. Chinese writing, a system of thousands of ideograms, had been in existence since about 1500 BC. Whether these were a separate invention or the result of stimulus diffusion from Sumer, ideograms were – and have remained into this century – a central feature of Chinese civilization. No alphabet emerged, and though the Japanese adapted the Chinese system into syllabaries, the Chinese themselves showed no inclination to follow suit.

The surface first used for these ideograms was a kind of bamboo tablet, which was displaced around 200 BC by sheets made from silk waste. In

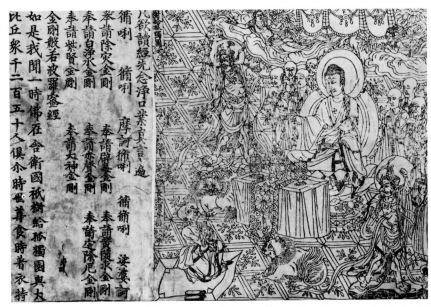

A page of the Chinese Buddhist Diamond Sutra, *the earliest blockcut-printed 'book' (AD 868).*

AD 105 an official of the Imperial Court named Ts'ai Lun developed a new kind of surface not unlike this by using mulberry and other fibres, pieces of old fish net, hemp waste and other rags. The end-product of this odd amalgam was the first true 'paper' (quite irrespective of the derivation of the English word from *pápyros*). In due course linen and cotton rags provided the base for the making of paper, and this state of affairs lasted until around 1800, when wood pulp became a serious alternative source.

The art of paper-making spread and developed exceedingly slowly. It reached West Asia in the late eighth century and did not enter into common use in Europe until the fourteenth century, when the demand generated by printing machines proved too great for the makers of parchment.

China was also the ultimate source of printing, whose development was also slow. As early as AD 175 Confucian texts were being cut in stone, from which rubbings on silk or paper could be taken. Some centuries later wooden blocks and a lamp-black ink were in use, so that whole pages could be reproduced quite speedily by means of making inked impressions from the wood on paper. The thousands of ideograms of Chinese writing, however, were not amenable to development as movable type, and so the whole technology remained dormant until well into the Middle Ages.

By the second or third century of the Christian era, however, the technologies of recording and copying had taken on a shape that modern observers can recognise and feel comfortable with. In the West a parchment-and-alphabet technology was ousting both its great predecessors and was set for a long innings during which it too would become hallowed and hard to challenge. Its time of dominance over scribal culture at large was not to be as long as either of the previous systems, but it was to bridge a particularly troubled and confused period of human history, at which we will look shortly. In the meantime, however, we can turn aside from considering technology to look at what was happening to another universal in the contingent world – taxonomy.

5

The taxonomic urge:
class, classic and classification

Writing and the kind of work for which writing is the principal tool make considerable demands on the human brain – and made as many demands in the ancient world as they do today. On this point, Robert Claiborne observes (1974:90): 'The physical skills involved – in Mesopotamia managing a stylus of reed or wood on clay, and in Egypt wielding an inked brush on papyrus – were modest, but the mental skills were enormous.'

Hundreds of signs had to be mastered and put to use in a variety of complex activities. The scribe was a clerk and calligrapher, but he was also of necessity a polymath; his interests took in the whole sweep of his civilization (a side of his life that has been inherited by present-day encyclopedists and lexicographers). His training was long, hard and, from the point of view of the mass of his fellow citizens, esoteric. Indeed, his basic training was so complex that for many years, unlike other apprentices, he was of little practical value to his guild.

The numerous signs that early scribes needed for their work had to be memorized, and for this mnemonic aids were essential. The signs had no fixed ordering (as with numbers and the later alphabet), and were so numerous that some kind of overall shape had to be given to them so that they could be acquired in manageable groups. This shape was provided by the original pictorial associations of the signs; no matter how far in practice a sign might have moved from its first referent, it still had links with the real world, and so trainees could memorize in terms of animal signs, plant signs, signs for people and places, and so on (Claiborne 1974: 89–92; Matoré 1968: 40).

There was nothing magically new in this. Classification and thematization were already inherent in society at large. Then as now, society and its view of the world were replete with order, system and stratification.[1] Communities had their ranks, castes and guilds, armies their divisions, priesthoods their hierarchies, merchants their inventories, farmers their fields and boundaries, architects their various structural conventions, and the gods their pantheons. It is no surprise, therefore, that the grand themes of life could carry over into the scribal classrooms as systems by which signs closely tied to life could be memorized. Indeed, both in society at large and in the categories of signs we can see at work a basic human impulse that can be called 'the taxonomic urge'.

Bilingual proto-dictionaries: *LEFT animals' names from the 14th tablet of a series RIGHT a section of tablet 7 of a legal glossary. In both, Sumerian is on the left, Akkadian on the right.*

    This urge has its physical and its mental embodiments, and those that float between the two. Thus, military ranks can be physically observed both in badges and in behaviour, as well as understood in terms of an abstract hierarchy (with attendant linguistic realizations in words like 'sergeant' and 'captain'). Such social and mental arrangements as a military or priestly hierarchy are as much artifacts as a pot, a pan or a pyramid: a rank or a caste cannot exist until it has a system within which to exist, just as a pot, a pan or a pyramid cannot exist until the need for it is clarified. Pots and pans, palaces and pyramids, ranks and castes, groups of signs, 'fields' of learning, and so forth are all equally exercises in containerization, and the interplay of what is first *per*ceived and then *con*ceived.

The civil servants of ancient Egypt, scribes jealously preserved their privileges and looked down on other men. This statute shows Pes-Shu-Per, a scribe from the city of Thebes c. 750 BC. His kilt, stretched tight, acts as a support for the papyrus on which he is shown writing. Scribal equipment hangs on his left shoulder and an ink palette rests on his left thigh.

Classification and thematization have many forms, but the key forms appear to be only two: first, the making of categories or groups, and then the creation of a hierarchy (a pyramid shape or tree diagram, to express the matter by means of two convenient and common metaphors) through which to systematize the categories or groups. We see this in society, in terms of such social constructs as military ranks, and we see it in language in terms of such relationships as 'hyponymy'.[2] Essentially, hyponymy refers to the arrangement whereby certain *super*ordinate terms are said to 'contain' or sub-sume certain other *sub*ordinate terms; that is, there are groups, and some are ranked 'above' and others 'below', but only because they are conceived in some kind of container/contained or controller/controlled relationship. Thus, ANIMAL is a superordinate term or semantic container in English for such other subordinate terms as CAT, CAMEL, CHAMELEON, HIPPOPOTAMUS or HORSE, while in modern armies GENERAL is a super-ordinate term set above COLONEL, CAPTAIN, SERGEANT, etc., because of a relationship through which authority is seen to flow downward. In all such metaphors, a higher position indicates a greater capacity, control or ability to contain; indeed, the metaphor of 'high' against 'low' figures strongly in the social and semantic history of the civilization to which we belong, and there-fore in the history of that civilization's artifacts, whether these are religions on the one hand or works of reference on the other.

This is not an easy area to chart, in part at least because language and awareness are not always conscious activities: the hyponymies that we use in language and the stratifications that we register in society are often subliminal matters, to be brought into conscious focus only with difficulty, and often resisting precise focus. Many of our attempts at classification in the natural world, for example, are fuzzy at the edges and are in effect provisional under-takings; it is easier to be precise about the ranks of a man-made army than about the proper species and sub-species of animals, and anthropologists have demonstrated cogently how differently human groups organize such apparently basic matters as kinship groups and immediate family relation-ships.

In addition, simple 'classification' is hard to achieve without the impos-ition of special value judgements of 'better' and 'worse', not far removed from judgements like 'higher' or 'lower'. Although there might not have been preferred or specially favoured signs or groups of signs among those that the ancient scribes memorized, there have certainly been many preferred elements in other social taxonomies. A good example of this can be found in the history of China, although China is by no means the only culture in which such value judgements occur.

For a long time, the Chinese people considered the period from 600 to 200 BC paramount in their culture; it was when all the elements that are quin-tessentially Chinese came together, and so in English this period is termed 'classical', a word which nowadays primarily implies elegance, quality, simplicity and prestige, rather than simply describing one 'class' among others, as it once did. It suggests a golden glow from the past, and certain ideals of the good life associated with that past. A 'classical' period, however, only *has* classical value because it is 'classed' or classified in terms of epochs and ideas that are judged (for whatever reasons) as better or worse. A classical period is pre-eminently the 'best' of times, and usually everything since the end of that epoch has been a struggle to maintain its (assumed) standards. In diagrammatic terms, we have a line sloping down from a 'high' past point to 'lower' later points – not a hyponymous or hierarchical shape, but something similar, and certainly similar enough for English-users at least to use words like 'class', 'classy', and 'classic' together as terms that distinguish between what is better and what is worse.

During the period that later Chinese scholars deemed classical a number of works of reference were produced in the bamboo-and-ideogram technology of the time. These works were seen as in various ways contributing to a proper ordering of life, and are as a consequence known as 'classics'.[3] They are associated, rightly or wrongly, with the culturally central name of Confucius (Kung Fu Tse, 551–479 BC), and their usual order is shown in table 1.

Table 1 *The Confucian classics*

	Title	Translation	Nature
1	*I Ching*	The Classic of Changes	divination and fortune-telling
2	*Shu Ching*	The Classic of History	a collection of official documents
3	*Shih Ching*	The Classic of Poetry	a collection of temple, court and folk songs
4	*Li Chi*	The Record of Rites	a collection of instructions for rituals
5	*Ch'un Ch'iu*	Spring and Autumn	the annals of the feudal state of Lu where Confucius was born

These works served China for centuries as guides, precedents and standards against which later things could be measured,[4] much as the Vedas and the great epics have served the Hindus[5] and the collection known as the Bible ('the Papyrus Roll') has served Christianity.[6]

Were the Chinese classics, the four Vedas, and the books of the Bible rationally planned, however, as sociocultural guides for whole civilizations? Many people who are culturally and emotionally involved with such collections will say yes, and will offer as their justification social or theological arguments drawn from within the body of such works themselves. In objective terms, however, there is no hard evidence of original planned coherence or reasoned internal consistency, in the Chinese works just listed, in the Vedas or in the Bible. What happened in ancient China and elsewhere is probably much the same as what happened when the groups of signs were set up for trainee scribes to memorize: such works had been created by various people for various purposes, were then collated for other newer purposes, and given a new shape, as it were, *after the event*. Classification of this kind is by nature retrospective and therefore often retroactive. Ancient works, whether secular or scriptural, simply accumulated, their authorship unknown or uncertain. They grew into togetherness and were then suitably classified (and 'classicized'), even creatively edited to fit their perceived classifications better. Once together long enough, they then acquired a patina of rightness, so that they have continued to remain 'right' even when people no longer shape their lives by their standards and admonitions.

Retroactive 'legislation' of this kind may well be what our scribal ancestors first consciously understood as classification when they organized texts: You took what tradition had accumulated, imposed order of a sort on it in terms of the worldview of your time and place, and got a council to sanction what you had done. In time, that council would also become part of the classical tradition. *Post-facto* editing of this kind appears to lie at the heart of many 'canonical' compilations, rendering it hard for later generations to look at classicized and sanctified materials objectively and comparatively. As a consequence, such works are moved out of discussions of, say, how humanity has developed its works of reference.

Yet the issue is important, because most of the early efforts of the human race at compiling guidebooks (dare one loosely call them 'encyclopedias'?) have been classicized, canonized, sanctified or divinized virtually beyond discussion, while works that have been excluded from the proper canon have been labelled 'apocryphal' or otherwise classified as invalid, false or heretical. The Vedas represent an oral-cum-literary foundation for Hindu civilization and religion, valued by many as revelation; they could also be called an ancient 'Encyclopaedia Indica', organized thematically in four books with a different kind of brahmin officiating over the rituals listed in each book. Later important Hindu works have been classed by some as a 'fifth' Veda, rejected however by the orthodox. The Bible is comparable, an 'Encyclopaedia Hebraica' (Old Testament) and 'Christiana' (New Testament), edited into its present shape through the efforts of various groups at various times in its long history. Apart from the natural interest of its content, it is relevant here because it is organized chronologically, largely by means of the names of people ('Samuel', 'Daniel', 'Matthew', etc.), and in terms of two revelations (that of Moses and that of Jesus), as well as having (latterly) chapters, verses and concordances that figure importantly in the history of aids to easier reference. It is the classified book *par excellence*.

However, because works like the Chinese classics, the Vedas and the Bible are not conventionally seen as kinds of works of reference (and are instead viewed as too classical or too divine to be tampered with), many people find it difficult to live with the evidence of historiographers that such works *have* been consistently tampered with down the centuries, and that they are as syncretic and imperfect (while as fascinating and wonderful) as any other largescale human compilation. Even where painstaking scholarship has pointed out external sources, borrowings, influences, derivations, interpolations, adaptations and re-writes, it is not easy even for the scholars themselves to live with the implications (because of emotional involvement in the belief systems that such works serve to define and sustain).

Looked at simply as artifacts, however, works like the Chinese classics, in their context and ordering, tell us a great deal about the concerns and priorities of those who did that ordering and of the culture and period to which they belonged. From within a culture, such classical orderings look safe, eternal, inspired and absolute; from outside, especially when compared with the works of other cultures, they can look limited, relative and transient. They are recognisable as culture-bound and period-bound.

As a consequence, there is a tension between the classical and canonical on the one hand, and the comparative and provisional on the other. As we shall see, this tension runs through the whole history of reference materials, which often have a religious or quasi-religious tinge to them. An interim Bible is unthinkable, even though one may know and accept that from time to time its translated version (on which one entirely relies) has to be 'revised'. Often and curiously, the interim nature of dictionaries and encyclopedias in the modern world has also tended to be unthinkable or unacceptable, people responding to certain established works as if they were Mosaic tablets handed down from on high. This classical and scriptural 'height' appears indeed to be one of the enduring elements in the approach of the human race to the works through which it classifies the world around it.

In the last few paragraphs I have been trying hard to exercise a kind of tactful logic, but even that 'logic' is not an absolute thing. It too had to be invented, and its inventors, or systematizers and clarifiers, were the ancient Greeks whom we still tend to think of as the 'classical' Greeks. They were also the coiners of the term 'taxonomy' that figures so importantly here, which meant in their language 'the rules or laws of ordering'. Like the Chinese, they had their own classics, the works assigned to Homer, but in the heritage of the Westernized world the classicism of ancient Greece rests peculiarly upon a series of individuals, philosophers who were not at all anonymous, as were the bulk of the Sumerian and Egyptian scholar-scribes who preceded them. From Pythagoras in the sixth century BC through Plato, Aristotle and the scholars of the Hellenistic Age, their ideas still echo in every literate Western, Westernized and Islamic mind, while the mental coinage that they used is still negotiable throughout the civilized world.[7]

Socrates (c. 470–399 BC) taught freedom of inquiry in a world driven largely by unquestioned and unquestioning tradition. He proposed reasoned argument in place of simple acceptance or careless rationalization. He was committed to unbiassed observation and open debate, and was put to death by his fellow citizens of Athens for corrupting the young. His disciple Plato (c. 428– c. 348 BC) recorded what we know of the words of Socrates and enlarged upon his theories and practices, using dialectic and dialogue as techniques for analysing the constituents of 'ultimate good'. He sought to synthesize all Greek thought up to his time, and as a consequence Robert Collison, the historian of encyclopedias, observes: 'If there were a father of encyclopaedias whose claim would be generally acknowledged, it would almost certainly be Plato.' Although he wrote many treatises, he did not produce anything that could be considered to be an encyclopedia by modern standards, but he clearly sought to catch all knowledge in a single taxonomic net. To help with this objective and to train others, he founded the Academy in 388 BC, in Athens, an institution which lasted nine centuries and bequeathed the words 'academy' and 'academic' to later civilizations. The subjects that particularly interested him were:

- *politiké*   the study of how best to run a *pólis* or city state
- *aisthetiké*   what we perceive through our senses, particularly in terms of what we consider beautiful
- *philosophía* the love and pursuit of wisdom and knowledge rather than the assumption that one already possesses them
- *philía*   human relations such as love and friendship
- *paideía*   'the raising of the young'; training, discipline, education.

Like his master, Plato was interested in clarifying the principles of reasoning, and propounded a theory that has been enormously influential ever since: that there exists – somewhere pure – a list or pattern of perfect and eternal Forms behind the kaleidoscopic imperfections of the perceived world. These Forms he called 'Ideas', abstractions beyond our reach that are only even indirectly approached by the trained and sensitive mind.

His disciple Aristotle (384–322 BC) moved away from his master's '*idea*lism' towards what we have come to call 'realism', an acceptance and proper understanding of things as they imperfectly are. As Edouard Delebecque (1976:373) puts it: 'Where Plato opened up the lofty road of the idea, Aristotle opened up the earthly track of the fact.' In our sense, he was more of a scientist and empiricist than his master, concerned as much with observation as with speculation. He wrote treatises that discussed and developed his master's interests in logic, ethics, politics, poetics, rhetoric, biology, and metaphysics, virtually creating and defining such subjects for future generations to accept and sustain. Who today would dare to doubt the legitimacy of 'politics' and 'biology' as proper intellectual containers? In 335 BC, he founded the Lyceum as a rival school to the Academy, where the teachers walked around as they talked and were therefore known as 'peripatetic'. Both the Academy and the Lyceum had libraries, which served as models for the later great library of Alexandria, the *Mouseion* ('place of the Muses') or, in Latin, the Museum.

Alexandria was of course one of the cities founded by Alexander of Macedon, who in *his* turn was a disciple of Aristotle. In his brief career, Alexander carried his intellectual master's doctrines across West Asia and into Egypt, with incalculable results.[8] One immediate and reasonably calculable result was, however, the spread of the ideals of Greek education itself. Basic schooling in the Hellenistic Age, among the sons of the better-off, included the erstwhile scribal arts of reading, writing and arithmetic. At about the age of 14, however, the boys were introduced to something more elaborate – the *enkýklios paideía* ('the rounded-out training', 'the circle of learning', 'all-round or general education'). The purpose of this training was to create a civilized Hellene, the 'gentleman' of the ancient world, who stood apart from but could work for the betterment of the barbarians all around. This approach balanced literature and mathematics, and was revolutionary in its implications. Henri-Irénée Marrou says of it (1976:324):

This ideal was no longer social, communal in character, as had been that of the city state; it now concerned man as an individual – or better, as a person. This civilization of the Hellenistic age has been defined as a civilization of *paideia* – which eventually denoted the condition of a person achieving enlightened, mature self-fulfilment but which originally signified education per se.

The *enkýklios paideía*, however much honoured in the breech or unimaginatively pursued, derives directly from the Greek philosophical tradition, and has served as the basis over more than 2,000 years for what is still known as 'a liberal arts education'. For the entirety of the Middle Ages in Christendom it was the dominant theme of non-scriptural education, when it was known as 'the seven liberal arts'. These seven arts were divided into two levels (the *trivium* and *quadrivium*) whose names became virtually synonymous with all that was worthwhile in general education (see figure 2).

Fig. 2 The seven liberal arts

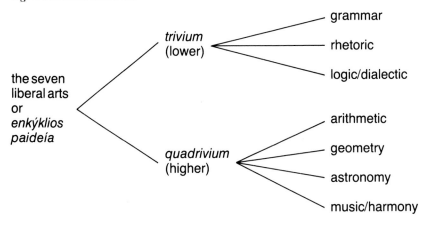

Like the Chinese classics, the taxonomy of the liberal arts tells us a great deal about the mentality of Western educators from the days of the Hellenistic scholars through Rome and Byzantium to the Middle Ages and modern times. The student was required to move from language to the higher abstract beauties of mathematics and music, and the route was via rules, models and exercises rigorously pursued. One can almost feel the music of the spheres in the closeness of astronomy and harmony.

This pagan Hellenistic scheme survived all the strife and confusion of the centuries after the fall of Rome, to become the educational jewel of the Christian Age of Faith. In that Age of Faith, the seven arts of the *enkýklios paideía* were indeed so revered that the first set of three was taken to symbolize the Holy Trinity, while the second set represented the four rivers of Paradise.[9]

6

Missionaries and monasteries: reference and reverence

The Romans had a different view of the world from the Greeks: they were engineers rather than philosophers. Indeed, it is virtually a cliché to suggest – as I believe was the case – that a well-built aqueduct had far more inherent appeal to them than a well-framed syllogism.

Nonetheless, their leaders admired the Greeks and adopted wholesale their theories of nature and culture, their basic educational values, and much of their technical and philosophical vocabulary. The *enkýklios paideía* had a strong natural appeal because it was a coherent system, and the Romans had nothing that could compare or compete with it. A number of practical Romans who were also administrators or soldiers continued the treatise-making inclinations of Plato, Aristotle, Speusippus and other Greek polymaths, and it was one of these in particular who turned the *enkýklios paideía* from a general curriculum into a certain kind of compilation. The process that he initiated was to take more than 1,000 years to complete, but it began in the first century AD in Rome.

The compiler in question was Gaius Plinius Secundus (AD 23–79), more commonly known to posterity as Pliny the Elder. He was an administrator and soldier who died on active duty at the age of 56, suffocated by the fumes of the same volcanic eruption that destroyed the towns of Pompeii and Herculaneum. He was, in Collison's words, 'a spare-time anthologist . . . accustomed to seeing the world in terms of divisions and sub-divisions'.[1] His dedication, organizational style and willingness to list his sources makes him the first of the 'modern' compilers. Of his work, Jerry Stannard, the historian of science, says: 'The history of early science cannot be understood properly without recognizing Pliny's role, both in establishing a new type of scientific literature – the encyclopedia – and in supplying the content that would be accepted for over 1500 years.'

This is not to suggest, however, that Pliny's major work bears much of an immediate resemblance to what we now know as 'encyclopedias'. Rather, his work has much in common with the enormous essays of 'the father of History', the Greek traveller and observer Herodotus (c. 485– c. 425 BC). Pliny, however, typifies what we could call the 'taxonomic' or 'lexicographic mentality': everything went into his compilation, whether large or small, fact

Pliny and his translators: first, a brief excerpt from the original, Pliny, Book VIII, on *elephanti et dracones,* then Philemon Holland's rendering of the passage in 1601 (where the troglodytes and dragons survive), then Rackham's Loeb translation in 1942, where we now meet serpents and cave-dwellers.

> Elephantos fert Africa ultra Syrticas solitudines et in Mauretania, ferunt Aethiopes et Troglodytae, ut dictum est, sed maximos India bellantesque cum his perpetua discordia dracones tantae magnitudinis et ipsos ut circumplexu facili ambiant nexuque nodi praestringant. conmoriuntur ea dimicatione, victusque conruens complexum elidit pondere. (Pliny)

Elephants breed in that part of Africke which lieth beyond the desarts and wildernesse of the Syrtes: also in Mauretania: they are found also amongst the Aethyopians and Troglodites, as hath beene said: but India bringeth forth the biggest: as also the dragons that are continually at variance with them, and evermore fighting, and those of such greatnesse, that they can easily clasp and wind round about the Elephants, and withall tye them fast with a knot. In this conflict they die, both the one and the other: the Elephant he fals downe dead as conquered, and with his heavy weight crusheth and squeaseth the dragon that is wound and wreathed about him. (Holland)

Elephants are produced by Africa beyond the deserts of Sidra and by the country of the Moors; also by the land of Ethiopia and the Cave-dwellers, as has been said; but the biggest ones by India, as well as serpents that keep up a continual feud and warfare with them, the serpents also being of so large a size that they easily encircle the elephants in their coils and fetter them with a twisted knot. In this duel both combatants die together, and the vanquished elephant in falling crushes with its weight the snake coiled round it. (Loeb)

Pliny's Historia naturalis: *excerpts in* MS *form, in Latin, in Elizabethan and in modern English.*

or fiction, reality or myth, personal advice or borrowed counsel. He had perused some 2,000 sources and collected some 20,000 noteworthy 'facts', to which he then added additional information from his personal experience. The result was his 37-volume collection the *Historia naturalis* (which is usually translated straightforwardly as the *Natural History* but could just as easily be interpreted in modern terms as *General Knowledge*).[2]

The work is methodical, but not rigorously so; it rambles as it informs, and does not always keep to the specific topics assigned to particular books. The structure does not bear a strong direct resemblance to the ordering of subjects in the *enkýklios paideía*, but a curious scribal error made in later centuries has enabled us to see it as though it closely followed the Greek pattern. This error was to convert the phrase *enkýklios paideía*, as found in the manuscripts of such classical writers as Pliny, Quintilian and Galen, into a single compound form *enkýkliopaideía*, which then passed through the copyists' slip into medieval Latin as *encyclopaedia*.[3] At no time was there in the ancient – or even in the medieval – world of reference a set of papyrus rolls or codices actually *called* an 'encyclopedia', but if there had been, Pliny's *Natural History* would probably have been that set.

Equally, however, it could be argued that Pliny was the father of the scientific treatise, the monograph, and even the textbook. The general arrangement of the *Historia naturalis* pre-echoes many later conventions: it is clearly divided into subject sections or themes, openly states where the information comes from, and tries – however oddly to us now – to be objective and comprehensive. In general terms, the arrangement of the 37 books is as follows:

1   preface, table of the contents in detail, and acknowledgement of sources
2   the world, godhead, the stars, planets, meteors, the sun, climate, the tides, volcanoes and fire
3–6 physical and historical geography: places and people around the Mediterranean, in Northern Europe, in Africa, West Asia, India and China
7   the human race, birth and death, oddities and freaks, women, bodily capacities
8   land animals
9   sea creatures
10   birds
11   insects
12–19 trees, vines and wine, crops and agriculture
20–32 medicines and drugs, obtained from flowers, herbs, trees and animals
33–4 metals
35   painting
36–7 minerals, mountains, gems and jewellery

Pliny incorporated elements of Aristotle and other classical sources and, without ever knowing that it would be so, served to pass them on to centuries that would later be called 'the Dark Ages' (when the direct link with ancient

Greece was lost in Western Europe). Whether he was writing of fact or
wild fancy, his work became the basis for whatever general non-religious
education there was and its authority extended right through what we now
call 'the Middle Ages', going virtually unchallenged until Niccolo Leoniceno's
De erroribus Plinii ('On Pliny's Mistakes') appeared in 1492 in Ferrara, Italy –
the year in which Columbus stumbled upon the New World.

Western Europe went through considerable turmoil, however, before a
time arrived when men could consider doubting the authority of Pliny.
Indeed, it is interesting to ask how a state of affairs could arise in which Pliny
– and Aristotle – could become so unquestioned and unquestionable. The
answer has much to do with both the particular course of European history
over the next thousand years and the general way in which our species
responds to its great taxonomists and to *post-facto* decisions about what is classical and absolute.[4]

The Roman Empire, with its potent mix of good order and imperial
savagery, declined through the middle centuries of the first millennium AD,
leaving the West in thorough disarray. Society at large, from the fifth to the
tenth century, was pulled at from three directions at once, by what were at
the time known as *Barbaria, Romania* and *Christianismus*.

Barbaria was the impact and influence of the hordes from the north:
Goths and Vandals, Huns and Alans, Burgundians, Alemannians, Franks,
Angles and many others. *Romania* was what remained of the old imperial
order, including the profound prestige of Rome itself. *Christianismus* was the
growing social and spiritual dominion of the new salvationism that slowly
coalesced into a *Roman* Catholic church – universal, and yet tied to the Eternal
City. These forces worked on the West while South-Eastern Europe continued in the relative stability of the Romano-Greek empire of Byzantium,
and all of North Africa and West Asia became the preserve of Islam and the
Arabs. By the year 1000, when many expected the end of the world, the
sociopolitical map of the whole area was so changed that no Babylonian,
Egyptian, Greek or Roman would have recognized it. A world had indeed
ended.

Certain forces, however, were operating to prevent the total disintegra-
tion of the West. Some Church Fathers, for example, turned away from the
single-minded fundamentalist desire among many Christians to reject the old
'pagan' world and all its Satanic artifacts. They sought instead for a compromise between Christianismus and Romania.[5] Their reason was
straightforward enough: Christianity was endangered by its own success in
converting both the civilized world and the heathen world of the barbarians.
It could not wage spiritual warfare on two fronts; to avoid sliding into
barbarism itself, it needed to accommodate the forms of the Greeks and
Romans.[6]

There had always, of course, been an element of Hellenism in Christianity, as we can see from the language and style of the New Testament itself.
Indeed, as early as the first century the formula *en Khristō paideía* was in use as
a kind of rival to or adaptation of the *enkýklios paideía*: here, the Christian man
of God would replace the civilized Hellene as the true ideal to aim at.[7]

The intelligentsia of the Church made their compromise with consider-able style; what happened looks more like a baptism of paganism than a sociopolitical concession. The leaders of the move toward controlled synthesis were Saint Augustine of Hippo (354–430) and Saint Jerome (347–c.419). Both were reconcilers and bookmen in their own right: the former synthesized Christian dogma and Platonic thought in his *De civitate Dei* ('Concerning God's City State'), while the latter accepted secular litera-ture as worthwhile and translated the Bible into Latin, a move which acknowledged the importance of this language as a means of consolidating Christendom.

A third significant figure was Flavius Aurelius Cassiodorus (c.490–c.585), whose long life covered the period of greatest turmoil. He was cast in the same mould as Pliny, but with the difference that he was Christian and served the Gothic kings of Italy. In about 551, however, he gave up the life of statesman and civil servant in order to found his own monastic community, the Vivarium ('game park' or 'fish pond', evidently a kind of animal reserve). There he sought, for the benefit of his brother monks, to bring together both Christian and classical learning, and encouraged the brothers to copy out manuscripts from both backgrounds in order to preserve them all, an exam-ple that became standard monastic practice from then on, with great social and scholastic consequences. He was also a prolific compiler himself, creating sets of model letters for bureaucrats to follow, a Christian history of the world, a treatise on the soul and the afterlife, a grammar, and a large compen-dium on both scripture and the liberal arts.

The outstanding proto-encyclopedist, however, was Isidorus Hispalensis, or Saint Isidore of Seville (c.560–636), a father of the church, an archbishop, and an even more prolific compiler and pedagogue than Cassiodorus: some 10 major compendia – on language, natural history, gen-eral history, Biblical figures, ethics and theology, church organization, medi-tation, monastic practice, and the greatest of all, the *Etymologiae*. This was itself in 20 parts and had the full title *Originum sive etymologiarum libri* ('Books of Origins or Etymologies'). The whole is a Pliny-like composite that includes the seven liberal arts alongside such other subjects as architecture, history and agriculture.

Isidore's intention was to provide basic guidance on every imaginable subject for the newly converted people of Spain to follow. He was rigorous as regards religious orthodoxy, but at the same time valued the pagan educa-tional tradition (the only properly formulated model available to him). For many centuries his *Etymologiae* were major sources of educational inspiration.

The intentions of these Christian scholar-guides were not unlike those of the Chinese classicists; both were interested in establishing standard collec-tions that would found and maintain cultures of a specific kind. The Confu-cians and the Christian Fathers were both determined that a certain ethos would triumph over a barbarous world. China built a Great Wall for its phys-ical defence during its classical period. Christendom's walls were less spec-tacular; they surrounded only its cities and monasteries, but with them, perhaps inevitably, went a mentality that was also walled. The immediate milieu out of which developed works of reference that we can recognize as 'modern' was not one of expansion and optimism, like early Sumer or Classical Greece, but one of defence, containment, conformity and conservation: the circle of learning was as embattled as any citadel.

This fact explains much. The works of Cassiodorus and Isidore looked back towards a doubly golden past: the Calvary of Christ and the secular achievements of Greece and Rome. They and works like them served to affirm a certain kind of residual society, part at least of whose remit was to keep the faith and await the Millennium. There was no urge to explore and expand; quite the contrary, there was every reason to conserve and to meditate in cloistered calm on the wonder and wisdom of earlier times, when God walked the earth and inspired men wrote the truth on fine parchment.

Additionally, where the materials were specifically in the care of monks, men dedicated to worship under a stern other-worldly rule, engaged in compartmentalized activities of self-discipline and prayer, preparing for both personal and universal salvation, there was a natural tendency to imbue *all* written material with some of the awe that surrounded sacred scripture itself. As we have already noted, the written word has always been in itself a source of awe for the un- and semi-lettered. Many people, finding both divine and secular guidance coming from the fathers of the church and their monasteries, preserved by the pious labours of monks in their scriptoria, must have seen *all* the written materials emanating from such sources as equal in revelation.

Thus was a special authoritarianism born and a kind of divinization of books fostered. The mystique made all such writings as hard to challenge as the Bible itself, and has served to add an element of *reverence* in our civilization to works of *reference*.

The medieval world

Adam scriveyn,
    if ever it thee bifalle
Boece or Troilus
    to wryten newe,
Under thy lokkes
    thou must have the scalle,
But after my making
    thou wryte trewe.
So ofte a daye
    I mote thy werk renewe,
Hit to correcte
    and eek to rubbe and scrape;
And al is through
    thy negligence and rape.

GEOFFREY CHAUCER, *words to his scribe*★

Aspiring to different heavens: the Blue Mosque in Istanbul and the Cathedral of Rheims.

7
Faith versus reason: summations of truth

Christendom and Muslim Arabia were co-inheritors of the Greco-Roman world, and as such have always had much more in common than their respective protagonists would like us to believe.

First, in the sense in which the word 'barbarian' was used by the Greeks and the Romans, both these successor cultures were barbarian. Curiously enough, however, the ruling classes of both to a considerable extent accepted the label, and did something about redeeming themselves. Like the ancient Akkadians who inherited the glories of Sumer, they were ambivalent about the cultures that they had replaced, but in large measure that ambivalence allowed them to assimilate towards the standards of their precursors, despite, in both cases, the existence of a forceful, proselytizing creed that on the face of it brooked no rivals.

Secondly, and as a consequence, the leaders of both new societies were impelled to attempt some kind of compromise between their religious dogmas and the techniques of secular reasoning inherited from Greece.[1] Both needed large numbers of organizers of various kinds – public officials, teachers, lawyers, clerks, court retainers and the like. These organizers required a standard education within a coherent worldview, and in terms of one culture-wide language. The only models available for such educational programmes were those of the Greco-Roman world as it in turn had built upon the Sumero-Egyptian experience. Each of the new civilizations, however, had its own universal scholarly-cum-bureaucratic language: 'classical' Arabic for Islam, and 'classical' Latin for Western Christendom. Without being at all aware of it, the two cultures were repeating, each in its own distinctive way, the experiences of the Akkadians; in their school systems men learned to read, write and think in a special 'high' language that was not usually the language of the home, and had to engage in complex contrastive exercises between that language and whatever other vernaculars they might know.

Thirdly and finally, the two civilizations possessed similar feudal–imperial social systems, and throughout the Middle Ages were fairly evenly matched in technological and military terms (with if anything a slight tilt in favour of Islam). In the year 1100, no one could have safely prophesied which would ultimately gain dominance over the other.

Despite these similarities there were of course certain fundamental differences that have proved of lasting importance. In Western Europe, for example, the barbarians were seeking to accommodate themselves to an essentially alien system of thought (the compromise of Christianity and Greco-Roman 'paganism'); their experience was likely to make them stressed and split-minded. The Arabs largely lacked such a sense of the inferior inheriting the superior; they were engaged in exporting a home-grown revelation that they *knew* to be better than anything else in the world.[2] Where the Western European was often in cringing awe of his inheritance, the Arab was in awe only of God and His Prophet. Additionally, learning survived patchily in the West, while it was available like goods spread in a bazaar to the conquering Arabs.

Tensions, however, inevitably arose in Islam between the Quranic revelation on the one hand and the legacy of Greek humanism on the other. Such was the certainty of the Muslim leaders in their own role and revelation, however, that a compromise on the scale of the Christian Fathers' did not take place. That there was nevertheless a progressive impact of Greek secularism on Islamic ways of seeing the world is evident from the changes in the ways in which various works were thematized between the ninth and fourteenth centuries. In his studies of the evolution of the encyclopedia, Robert Collison draws our attention to three particular works of reference (although with emphases rather different from my own).[3]

The first of the three cogently demonstrates the austerity of early Islam. It is the *Kitab 'Uyun al-Akhbar* ('The Book of the Best Traditions'), compiled by the teacher and language scholar Ibn Qutayba (828–89). In much the same spirit as the ancient Chinese classics, this work was intended to establish standards, and its priorities and worldview are clearly stated:

1 power	6 asceticism
2 war	7 friendship
3 nobility	8 prayers
4 character	9 food
5 learning and eloquence	10 women

The starkness of Ibn Qutayba contrasts sharply, however, with the themes and structure of the work of the Persian scholar and statesman Al-Khwarizmi who, around a century later (c.975–97), compiled the *Mafatih al-'Ulum* ('Key to the Sciences'). This work divides 'science' into two distinct and culture-related compartments, the 'indigenous' and the 'foreign' (see figure 3).

Al-Khwarizmi's approach to indigenous values is very different from Ibn Qutayba's, and suggests that a certain amount of foreign matter had penetrated here too. His foreign list, though not a precise catalogue of the Greek arts, is Greek-based. It is a kind of halfway house, and more thought-provoking still is a vast 9,000-page treatise compiled by the Egyptian scholar An-Nuwairi (d. 1332). His work, the *Nihayat al-'Arab Fi Funun al-Adab* ('The Aim of the Intelligent in the Art of Letters'), has the following themes:

1 geography, geology, meteorology, astronomy, chronology
2 humanity – its anatomy, folklore, conduct and politics
3 zoology
4 botany
5 history

The secular, naturalistic and essentially 'scientific' quality in this taxonomy is strongly reminiscent of the Greeks and has a distinctly modern look about it. It comes as no surprise to learn from Collison that the work was still in circulation as recently as 1923.

It is clear from this cursory look that scholars of Islam were compiling 'encyclopedic' works at an early date. It does not appear to have been common practice, however, for the secular disciplines that interested Al-Khwarizmi and An-Nuwairi to get into the curriculums of the *madrasah* or Muslim colleges. The custodians of Islamic orthodoxy were suspicious about anything that did not emanate from or harmonize precisely with the teachings of the Quran, and this has remained a potent element in the fabric of Muslim society right to the present day.

Christendom of course also had its ultra-orthodox who suspected everything that did not emanate from or accord with the Bible and the Papacy. Their leaders were often forceful too, but they did not occupy positions of over-riding strength and, in any case, the essential compromises had been made much earlier by Churchmen whose evangelical and hierarchical credentials were beyond question. Additionally, in response to the need for a standardized training for priests and scholar-administrators, there arose in the West a movement – Scholasticism – that was fully in favour with the

Fig. 3 Al-Khwarizmi's sciences

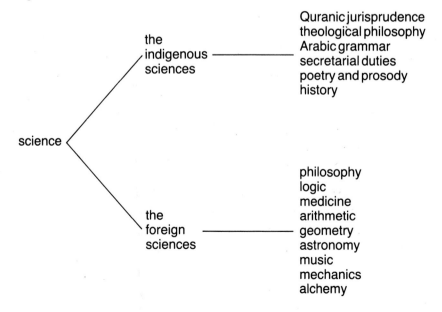

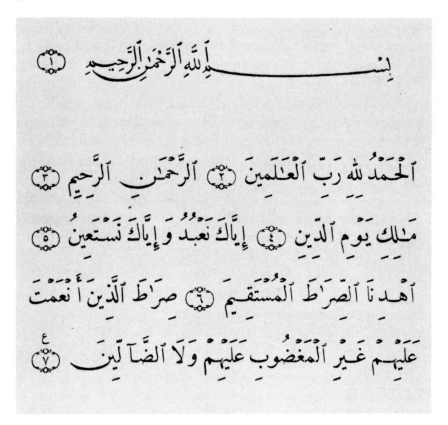

بِسْمِ اللَّهِ الرَّحْمَٰنِ الرَّحِيمِ ۝١

الْحَمْدُ لِلَّهِ رَبِّ الْعَٰلَمِينَ ۝٢ الرَّحْمَٰنِ الرَّحِيمِ ۝٣

مَٰلِكِ يَوْمِ الدِّينِ ۝٤ إِيَّاكَ نَعْبُدُ وَإِيَّاكَ نَسْتَعِينُ ۝٥

اهْدِنَا الصِّرَٰطَ الْمُسْتَقِيمَ ۝٦ صِرَٰطَ الَّذِينَ أَنْعَمْتَ

عَلَيْهِمْ غَيْرِ الْمَغْضُوبِ عَلَيْهِمْ وَلَا الضَّآلِّينَ ۝٧

The Word of God in the hands of men: *the opening* surah *or chapter of the Quran: 'In the name of God, the Compassionate, the Merciful'*.

Roman Catholic élite. Indeed, in due course, this movement provided a special synthesis of pagan and ecclesiastical that became official theological doctrine, thereby entrenching among the custodians of information and works of reference the dual heritage that was both a source of strength and a cause of doubt and confusion.

The Schoolman who achieved the great synthesis was the Dominican friar Saint Thomas Aquinas (c.1225–74). He was a controversial figure in his lifetime and his views have met with opposition within the Church. For many, however, he has been for centuries the successful reconciler of faith and reason and the quintessential encyclopedist of Roman Catholic thought.

By the time Aquinas was ready to embark on his magnum opus the Scholastic movement had paved the way well for him. The name suggests exactly what the movement was. As Josef Pieper puts it:[4] 'Scholasticism above all was an unprecedented process of learning, literally a vast "scholastic" enterprise that continued for several centuries. Since the existing materials had to be ordered and made accessible to learning and teaching, the very prosaic labour of "schoolwork", or organizing, sorting, and classifying

The Word of God in the hands of men: *the Book of Genesis in the medieval manuscript of the Vulgate Bible: 'In the beginning God made heaven and earth'.*

materials *inevitably acquired an unprecedented importance*' (my italics). At least within the Church the barbarian élite was determined to learn and to impose learning where it was deemed necessary. Men like Aquinas stood at the peak of all this effort, while below and around them laboured countless copyists, summarists, teachers and makers of scholastic nets in which – some day – the *omne scibile* ('all that is knowable') might be caught.

Hugues de Saint-Victor, a Scholastic of the twelfth century, summed up the general approach to knowledge when he advised his students: 'Learn everything; later you will see that nothing is superfluous.' To this end the Schoolmen massed their sentences and their texts and attempted their *summae* (syntheses or summations of knowledge). Their taxonomic enthusiasms were the crowning of Saint Isidore's work, turning this Age of Faith into a new golden age for many Roman Catholics.

Saint-Victor expresses the taxonomic urge as developed by the Scholastics most compellingly in his discussion of the seven liberal arts, where he says:

> Philosophy is divided into the theoretical, the practical, the mechanical, and the logical. Theory is divided into theology, physics, and mathematics. Mathematics includes, arithmetic, music, and geometry. Practical philosophy is divided into the solitary, the private, and the public. The mechanical arts include spinning, arms-making, navigation, agriculture, hunting, medicine, and the theatrical art. Logic includes grammar and expression; there are two kinds of expression, probable and sophistical demonstration. Probable demonstration is divided into dialectic and rhetoric. In this division, only the chief parts of philosophy are contained; there are still other subdivisions of these parts, but the parts can suffice for now. As to these, if you have regard only for number, there are twenty-one; if you wish to compute stages, you will find thirty-eight.[5]

The listing and categorizing has a numbingly inexorable quality about it, and must have been impressive to the student. Saint-Victor described his own attempt at a *summa* as *brevis quaedam summa omnium* ('a specific brief summation of everything that exists'). This breath-taking lack of humility in the face of a complex universe is only explicable if we accept that the Schoolmen sincerely believed that all knowledge *was* within reach or, as Hugues evidently believed, had already been in the possession of the ancient masters.

Thomas Aquinas evidently began his great work, the *Summa theologiae* or *theologica*, in a comparable frame of mind to Hugues de Saint-Victor. It consisted of three parts, which can be examined today in no less than 60 separate small volumes, and was written (in Italy and France) to help novices understand the nature of theology.[6] The work is characterized by a certain dry and impersonal rigour which was evidently not central to Thomas's personality; he is said to have been a kind and exemplary friar, and an enthusiastic preacher who, towards the end of his life at least, developed a mystical bent. This may, indeed, account for the fact that the third part of the great *Summa* is unfinished. On this point, Copleston notes:[7]

> In December 1273, after an experience while saying Mass, he suspended work on the third part of his *Summa theologica*, telling his secretary that he had reached the end of his writing and giving as his reason the fact that 'all I have written seems to me like so much straw compared with what I have seen and with what has been revealed to me'.

What he had written, however, was to stand as one of the great achievements of the medieval Church, and something that Copleston considers is wrongly overlooked nowadays by philosophers as they leap straight, in their studies, from Aristotle to Bacon and Descartes. Certainly, we cannot overlook it in a review of how our species has tried to cope with the world of facts and ideas. The three divisions of the *Summa theologiae* are:

1 theology, God, the Trinity, the Creation, angels, cosmogony, man, human intelligence, divine government, and world order

2 the human race, morality, emotion, virtue, sin, law, and grace; faith, hope, charity, mysticism and miracles, and the religious life

3 the Incarnate Word, Christ, mediation, the Virgin Mary, the Passion and Resurrection, the sacraments and penance.

As Aquinas himself points out, human reasoning is not used in the *Summa* in order to prove faith, but to manifest some of the implications of its message. Whatever his later thoughts on the worth of his own work, Aquinas has made it possible for a Roman Catholic of the twentieth century, George Brantl (1961:21), to say that 'one of the distinguishing marks of Catholicism is its refusal to invalidate reason or to exile it from religious belief. It is maintained that although Christian faith far exceeds the powers of reason, it does not destroy reason. On the contrary, Catholicism maintains that the preconditions for the commitment of faith may be validated by reason.'

This is no small achievement, given that there always has been and probably always will be a tension between revealed truth (as understood in any religion) and truth arrived at by argument and experimentation. Ultimately, the leap of faith and the dialectic of rationalism belong in different areas of human experience (and may even belong in different departments of the mind and brain). As regards the great synthesis, however, Roland Bainton (1966:207–8) is right when he sees Aquinas as integrating Christian salvationism with the other European heritage from secular Greece:

> The distinctive genius of Aquinas was that he effected a new synthesis of Christian and classical traditions by incorporating into his theology arguments from the writings of Aristotle and of ancient Arabic scholars. Aquinas assumed a middle ground between the extreme positions of contemporary scholastics. In his theology faith and reason were distinct but complementary, rather than antithetical . . . He rendered compatible the mysteries of Christian faith and the truths observable from man's natural experience.

The tension that Aquinas sought to resolve – but did *not* resolve to the satisfaction of later generations of Western thinkers – is very much in evidence among compilers of works of reference, for these must always come to terms with the worldviews dominant in society at any time, or may need to seek a compromise among worldviews that conflict. Just as compilers have often been torn between a Platonic perfectionism and a sense of Aristotelian realism, so they can also be caught between dogma and doubt. In approaching even such apparently prosaic works as encyclopedias and dictionaries, editors face some five distinct options:

> – They can openly found their work on dogma. They can insist that there is no God but God and Muhammad is His Prophet, or they can present the Roman Catholic Church as the sole repository of religious truth (or any other absolute belief system). Users of the work may then agree or disagree, and find the compilation useful or useless. *This is the path of faith.*

- They can openly found their work on rationalism. They can try to avoid making assertions that they cannot substantiate through the reasoned marshalling of 'facts' or good logical arguments. They can deal in data, scientific consensus, statistical probability, and various kinds of relativity. *This is the path of reason and of secular humanism.*
- They can claim neutrality, and seek for 'fairness'. They can offer their users a menu of various viewpoints, allowing contenders for Position X and Attitude Y to have their say. Here, the concept 'God', for example, could be approached from both the angle of faith and the angle of rationalism. *This is the path of would-be even-handedness, hopefully giving offence to none.*
- They can seek some kind of compromise. This compromise might be open or concealed, comfortable or uneasy. It could assert, for example, that the work is based on Belief System A, but that it will allow for certain admixtures from Belief System B. The concept 'God' might then be handled one way if the basic system was Islam or Communism, and compatible elements culled from elsewhere if they suited the main case. *This, as a path of compromise, is also often the path of propaganda and expediency.*
- They can just get on with the compilation and not worry about cosmic underpinnings. They might do this because it seemed unnecessary or even silly to raise such issues or state the obvious. Such compilations are often the most period- and culture-bound of all (like Ibn Qutayba and the Chinese classicists). *This could be the path of naivety, but it is also often the path of self-deception and intellectual dishonesty.*

Here we have more than a problem for compilers of works of reference. It is a fundamental human issue, whether we should consent to work within parent-like systems of guaranteed (but restraining) truths, or try and test everything as we go along. The dichotomy here can also be expressed in terms of a continuum, with the hierarchical and authoritarian at one end, and the libertarian and individualistic at the other – allowing us to look for 'reasonable' compromise positions at various points between the two. Whether, however, we go for a container model or a continuum model of the problem, there is a strong link between this dichotomy and our earlier remarks about *post-facto* classicization on the one hand and the relative and humanistic on the other.

The strict position of faith and classicism is an honest position. The strict position of reason and sceptical humanism is also an honest position. Most of our problems arise in the conflict between unyielding alternative faiths and classicisms, or in the tug-of-war between what is prescribed and what our knowledge of life tells us is possible. We have not yet transcended such matters in our lives at large, and it is therefore not surprising that we have trouble transcending them while trying to compile honest reference books.

8
The élites of knowledge: *universitas*

Schooling is built into the very brickwork of our civilization. If the collective and compulsory instruction of the young were to come to an end, we would feel that something as fundamental as August or tap water had gone out of our lives, and would be deeply disturbed. *That* is the measure of the success of the movement initiated by the Schoolmen of the Age of Faith.

The roots, of course, go back to Sumer, Egypt, Greece and Rome, but the scale on which the Schoolmen operated and their degree of organization had no precedent in those earlier cultures. With the development of the monastic and episcopal schools, the trickle of education that survived the fall of the Western Roman Empire turned first into a stream, then into a river.[1]

The aspiring scholar (and we can note how today this word has two levels of meaning: 'school pupil' and 'learned inquirer') had a clearcut progression to follow. With a career in the Church in mind, he learned the Latin language in the first 'cycle' of instruction, along with a general knowledge of scripture and training in the basic church services. If he passed into the second cycle he embarked upon first the *trivium* then the *quadrivium*. If, finally, he was selected for higher things (in the service of Church or state), he could move into a third cycle of advanced studies centring on philosophy, logic and theology. In general terms, this three-tier system of circles of knowledge still continues, especially in our institutions of higher education, where the diligent young can pass through the grades of 'bachelor', 'master' and 'doctor'.

What we are describing here, in practical functional terms, is the system of school, text and teacher. It is still largely honoured (although it is even more widely simply taken for granted, like brickwork). Many modern and not so modern educational critics have, however, castigated it as cramped and stultifying and not unlike a prison. No doubt such criticism has often been justified; certainly, the basic psychology of the system has been irrevocably shaped by the rules, order, timings, bells and structures of the medieval religious life. That same system did, however, also have its Peter Abelards[2] and other inspirers of students. Then, as now, it could be dull or stimulating, suffocating or liberating, depending on what the masters were like. Its success or failure has always been predicated upon openness or closedness of the societies and the minds that operated it.[3]

Because of our familiarity with later forms of this system, we tend to assume (if we think about the matter at all) that students in the Middle Ages had about as much contact as ourselves with 'books'. This, however, was not so, and is a crucial factor in our appreciation of how our legacy from those days has been shaped. Codices and manuscripts could not in the very nature of things be freely available; the cost of such materials and the time and effort needed for the accurate copying of texts militated against easy access and distribution. Written materials were therefore rare and precious, and as a consequence the mediation of the 'master' or (occasionally the 'mistress', for nuns) was of about the same importance as the direct instruction of the shaman, bard or genealogist in a pre- or non-literate culture. As Elizabeth Eisenstein puts it (1979:11):

> the texture of scribal culture was so thin that heavy reliance was placed on oral transmission even by literate élites. Insofar as dictation governed copying in scriptoria and literary compositions were 'published' by being read aloud, even 'book' learning was governed by reliance on the spoken word – producing a hybrid half-oral, half-literate culture that has no precise counterpart today.

In the schoolroom, the master was often no more than a *lector* or one who reads aloud, a function that is still reflected rather more than less in the English word 'lecturer' and fully sustained in the French *lecteur*. As Georges Gusdorf says of the system (1976:1175): 'Before the advent of the printed book, truth was established orally; it arose in conformity with fixed rules amid the exchange of arguments, of which Scholasticism defined the code.' Books, therefore, were still essentially supplements to speech and debate, and in the oral process 'truth was a truth of repetition and commentary' based on the canonical texts of long ago.

As a consequence, mnemonic aids were as important in medieval Europe as in ancient Mesopotamia. In their catechisms, choruses and staged disputations, scholars memorized everything from the conjugation of Latin verbs to the proofs of the existence of God much as one memorizes the gambits and strategies of the masters of chess.

Dependence upon repetitive mnemonic patterns and ancient authoritative texts has also been criticized in recent times as a mechanical and self-subordinating process that stifles creativity and forms obedient and conservative minds. There is truth in this criticism, but at the same time it would be wrong to forget the sheer size of the social adventure upon which the Schoolmen were embarked – as well as the dearth of alternative models for them to exploit. On the one hand, parchment was expensive, slates were clumsy, writing materials like pen and ink were delicate and messy if not carefully used, and mass production did not exist. On the other hand, the brains of the students were freely available as receptacles, and there was plenty of time and incentive to memorize. There were few social distractions for the students of medieval theocratic society, and the populace at large was just as impressed by the results of organized rote learning as by the ability to read and write. Indeed, the students came from backgrounds where the recitation of ballads and epics was a valued skill, and where incantation had much of the quality of enchantment – the two words having in fact the same origin in the Latin *cantare*, 'to sing'.

Within this tightly structured master-student-and-text, repeat-and-debate system, certain centres of learning such as Bologna in Italy and Paris in France became outstandingly successful. Such a centre of excellence came in the course of time to be known as a *studium generale*, a title that echoes the *enkýklios paideía* and can be translated as 'centre of general learning' or even as 'comprehensive school'. Such *studia generalia* were recognized by civil and religious authorities throughout Europe, and were often under the special protection of a pope or an emperor. They were places where clerics and others could be educated beyond the norm, and the vigour of their intellectual life drew to them teachers and students from far afield, making them far more independent-minded than the closely governed monastic and episcopal institutions, and far more socially and intellectually rigorous. Indeed, it was the common practice of students who attended them to carry their detailed lecture notes back to their home institutions and donate them to the libraries there, so that others might benefit from contact with the centres of excellence.

As the *studia generalia* developed, formal companies or guilds of scholars and students grew up in association with them. These groups came into existence partly for social and administrative convenience, partly for the legal protection of their members, because rights of local residence or of citizenship were not always automatically extended to the often motley crowds of intellectual incomers. Such a guild for scholars in a *studium* was known as an *universitas*. The basic meaning of this term at that time was 'totality' or 'all in one' (perhaps even with a hint of 'solidarity'). It was used both to denote a company or guild and to refer to the whole world. It was therefore particularly apt in this new setting, because the scholars and their students were both a guild like other guilds and a coming together of like-minded cosmopolitans.

In due course, by a kind of social osmosis, the name for the scholarly brotherhood was transferred to the institution in and for which they worked, and 'university' supplanted 'study' (which today refers in English at least to a smaller chamber or to the thing done, as in a Department of Islamic Studies). By this transfer of name and presumably also power, the scholarly élite was able to strengthen its position as guardian of knowledge and the vehicle through which the accreditation of further generations could be achieved. In this, the 'apostolic succession' was by means of conferring a parchment (and how significant that symbol is) upon a graduate of the university, in a ceremony as solemn as any mass or marriage. When a student had passed through the hands of the *universitas*, he was perceived by all and sundry as different in kind from the day he entered the cloisters of learning as a freshman.

The final seal of approval for a *studium/universitas* came in the form of a charter from the Pope. Institutions boasting such charters spread like a pedagogic rash across Europe, half inside and half outside the Church, just as the learning of the Schoolmen, for all the wit of Aquinas, was always half

Universitas in parchment: *The Charter of King's College, Cambridge.*

inside and half outside Christianity. Bologna, Paris and Oxford were flourishing by the end of the twelfth century, Cambridge was formed in 1209, Naples in 1224, and so on.

The universities inherited a shadowy tradition from the monasteries of the so-called 'Dark Ages'; they were seen as centres of guaranteed learning in a world of uncertain standards. What was in their codices and manuscripts and in the heads of their 'faculties'[4] (a word derived from the Latin *facultas*, in turn a translation of the Greek *dýnamis* or 'power') was the precious inheritance of civilization, and even hard-bitten kings and knights were careful how they dealt with it. Over the years a quasi-ecclesiastical architecture grew up to enshrine it appropriately, in the process lending new nuances to words like 'cloister' and 'spire'. In an age of pilgrims, the universities became centres for a new kind of pilgrimage, and their mystique was – and still is – profound.

Today, educational architecture derived from medieval college and classroom can be found everywhere in the world; it is now, whether of mellowed stone, red brick or concrete, part of the expected scenery of our cities. We accept this kind of physical setting for non-physical disciplines in a vague subliminal way (unless we are architects or art historians), and do not think too much about it, although we talk from time to time about 'dreaming spires' or 'places properly conducive to study', or even 'ivory towers' when

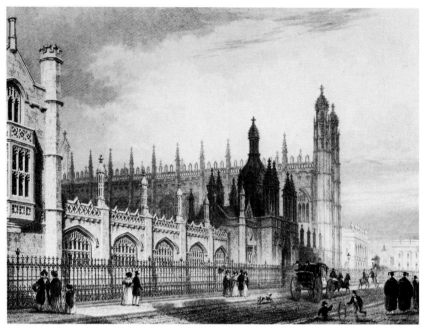

Universitas in stone and gown: *King's Parade, Cambridge.*

we have some doubt about the relevance of centres of higher learning. The basic containing-and-processing function of such architecture (as purpose-built as any pyramid, temple or cathedral) exerts its subtle influences quietly, especially on those who come for a period of years to circulate through the structures. The mind learns a certain significant geometry at the same time as it is prepared by the faculty for guild membership.

Stationers in the Middle Ages were generally attached to universities and copied out, like the old scriptoria, the texts that the guild told them to copy. The monopoly on learning was therefore complete: to have access to learning one co-operated with the Church and went to one of its schools, colleges or to a university, which was almost part of the Church. Books might travel out of the immediate ambit of the ecclesiastical and academic authorities, but the key to those books – literacy – was in their hands (and literacy largely meant literacy in Latin). Although an *universitas* was supposedly a totality and the circle of learning supposedly for all, in fact the totality was limited and the circle a closed one.

At this point one could move towards the language of the class struggle and the polemics of the disadvantaged against the privileged. This would, however, be rather an anachronism in the period before the first peasants' revolts, and in any case what interests me more specifically here is not equality of opportunity (which was an impossibility at that time) but rather the kind of mediation that animated medieval education. Because of the hybrid oral–literary system that Eisenstein has pointed to, the schoolmaster as mediator was a crucial figure. The text (or textbook) could not stand alone; like scripture and the priest, education needed a mediator between information and the informee. Materials were scarce, and in any case the master had already taken the path and knew the way.

Textbooks then as now, of course, were open to all who could read, but our civilization does not see a textbook as the same kind of thing as a novel or (importantly) as a reference book. Textbooks are text-based, and texts were the foundation of Scholastic education. Textbooks are therefore geared to supervised group use and not to individual self-governing study (even when they are advertised nowadays as self-study manuals). Such works do not communicate wholly in their own right with the student; it is the teacher who, as mediator, controls the use of the book – and without the teacher the book would not usually be read at all by most of the people for whom it was designed. Its justification is entirely in terms of the institution in which it may be used, the course into which it may fit, and the master or mistress who may use it.

General works of reference are not at all the same, and the attitude of educational systems is different towards them from the attitude to textbooks and course materials. Teachers may use them, and they may be present on shelves in the classroom, but they can be anywhere at all and still do their work. This is quite simply because they are seldom mediated by teachers and hardly ever seen as *needing* mediation by teachers. Just as the university was half outside the Church, so the reference book is half outside the educational systems we use. Schools and colleges do not normally give their students courses in how to use dictionaries, encyclopedias, gazetteers, directories, etc. Even the use of language is different for them: you 'read' or 'study' a textbook, but you 'consult', 'look things up in' or 'dip into' a work of reference.

Textbooks and reference books are therefore used and controlled in different ways. In a system that is largely geared to hierarchy and supervision (as Scholastic education was and as most of our education still is), the autonomy and motivation of works that lie out on the edge of things has often been a matter of concern – sometimes mild, sometimes massive – on the part of the traditional guardians of 'true' knowledge, who prefer to have the power of imprimatur over all educational works and strict control over the presentation and dissemination of anything that discusses fundamental issues. Saint Jerome's Bible, for example, was called the *Editio vulgata* ('the popular edition'), but a major element in the debate that brought on the Reformation concerned the *in*accessibility of such works. The Bible was not available for general consultation in the new vernaculars of Europe; the Church-based system guarded this and every other part of its heritage altogether too well, and in the opposition of terms like 'academic' and 'élite' (suggesting the 'elect' of God) on the one hand and 'popular' and 'vulgar' on the other we get a suggestion as to why. Knowledge was considered safer in the care of the properly sanctioned, who could then in a suitably paternal (if not paternalistic) manner apportion it and use it as they thought best.

Works of reference, however, even when compiled and distributed by members of the élite for their own purposes, had an independent flavour about them that could disturb the collegiate calm, while their vague 'teach yourself' quality could serve to encourage independence of mind and so undermine the proper edifice of truth and tradition. If guilds and other groups acquire a special mediating function, they will tend to treasure it, because it is part of their justification for existing. Members will point to the successes of the system, and shake their heads over the occasional injustices and failures of that system as matters which inevitably arise in an imperfect world. Mediation of this kind has often arisen out of technological or social necessity, because books could not be rapidly copied and widely distributed, or even properly interpreted without the in-group knowledge of a particular 'classical' language and 'high' training. The monopoly thus created, however, was not something that a priesthood or guild would lightly give up, and monopolies are generally accompanied by resentments and the potential for riot.

Although it did not cause large ripples in the calm of medieval collegiate life, the reference book, because of its special private nature, had the *potential* to cause ripples if the system ever changed, and in particular changed in the direction of the 'popular' as opposed to the 'scholarly'. With certain technological innovations emerging in the late fourteenth century, however, that is exactly what happened.

The early modern world

How long soever the matter, I hope in God for high words.
SHAKESPEARE, *Love's Labour's Lost*

*If Shakespeare had wanted to use an English dictionary, he would have
had to compile his own.*

McADAM and MILNE, *Johnson's Dictionary*, 1963★

The triumph of taxonomy and technology: an early printing press in operation.

9
All knowledge for all men: the *omne scibile* and the printing press

The Greeks wanted to know everything so that they could think better and the Romans so that they could act better, but the medieval Christians wanted it for the greater glory of God and the remission of their sins. To us today, faced with a knowledge explosion of truly staggering proportions, all three of our ancestor cultures may look thoroughly naive in their hopes. We should be cautious in our conclusions, however; as their descendants, we carry in the strata of our minds all sorts of fossil gifts from them.

All three cultures were interested in the improvement of the species (as they understood it); their contributions, however, have only served to heighten the age-old tensions between thought, action and belief. These tensions in their turn exert powerful influences over what we do in such areas as the organization of information in such things as books. A good example of this comes from the Middle Ages: the monumental *Speculum triplex* ('triple mirror') that was completed in 1244. It compiler was Vincent de Beauvais, a Dominican friar like Aquinas who was, however, more interested in the world and men's immediate needs than the great summarist. Vincent sought to hold up a mirror in which humanity could look at itself and its surroundings – and then do better both collectively and as individuals.[1]

Vincent's labour was enormous, producing a work with 80 parts and nearly 10,000 chapters. In size it had no rival until the eighteenth century, and its success can be measured by the fact that its last revised version came out in 1879. As its name suggests, the *Speculum* was arranged in three great divisions:

–	the *speculum naturale* ('the mirror of nature')	God, angels and devils, man, the creation, and natural history
–	the *speculum doctrinale* ('the mirror of learning')	grammar, logic, ethics, medicine, crafts, etc.
–	the *speculum historiale* ('the mirror of history')	a summary of the first two divisions and a history of the world

After Vincent's death a fourth division was added – a *speculum morale* or 'mirror of ethics', whose content was derived from the *Summa theologica* of Aquinas. Thus, the entire vast work contrived to blend the worlds of thought, action and belief.

The readers of this compilation and others like it were supposed to study it and become informed, enlightened and – hopefully – better human beings. Such works were not intended as tools to be used in the universities (that is, they were not textbooks); rather, in present-day terms, they could be called 'teach yourself' books or 'home university kits'. Importantly, therefore, they required no trained mediator between text and scanner of text; they represent in fact the start of an alternative to the school-book-and-master system: They inaugurate the broad populist tradition of self-help and self-salvation that was to burgeon so fiercely during the Reformation.

It is probably from about this time – under the impact of the *summae* and the *specula* – that we get the widespread and largely undiscussed conviction that, somehow, a 'good' encyclopedia does (or ought to) encompass all knowledge, and a 'good' dictionary does (or ought to) encompass all the 'proper' words of a language. This conviction is a vague thing – most often displayed negatively, when we cannot find something we are looking for in a book that we think *ought* to have it. The conviction has also been nurtured by a variety of developments since the Middle Ages that we shall look at here in due course. In essence, however, it is Scholastic, for it suggests that we really truly *should* know how many angels can dance on the head of a pin; it can be aligned with Platonic idealism and religious faith. Upon reflection we realize that it is not compatible with reality or reason, but part of us goes on insisting that in a good and proper state of affairs – in a truly *classically* ordered world – things would be so.

Any compiler of any kind of largescale reference work knows the mixed feelings that go with establishing the limits of that work. The cut-off point for the entries and the detail will define the work's imperfections, and lay it open to the rush of gentle or vehement accusations: 'You didn't include x, and you didn't say enough about y.' Of necessity, however, compilers and their publishers must approach their adventure in reference with certain assumptions about exhaustiveness and cut-off points. In this area, the options open to them seem to be four:

- General exhaustiveness is in principle *not* possible. It belongs, say, to God or in the realm of perfect Ideas, to which we have no direct access. It should not therefore be sought after. This was largely the view of orthodox medieval theologians in both Islam and Christendom, and, curiously enough, is largely the view of scholars and scientists today, although usually expressed in secular terms and in relation to the limitations of the human brain.
- General exhaustiveness *is* possible in principle, if only we go about things the right way. This appears to have been the view of many of the Roman and medieval compilers who had rational–secular inclinations, and has been evinced since then by many systematic natural scientists, especially in the nineteenth century. They have assumed that little by little, verifying as we go, we can put together the jigsaw of the cosmos. The *studium generale* of the Scholastics and the

scientific method of Bacon and Descartes are similar in that both imply that a net can be made to catch the *omne scibile*.

— *Limited* exhaustiveness is possible, if – right at the start of a compiling enterprise – the range is clearly specified in relation to explicit criteria of inclusion and exclusion. This is a popular viewpoint among scholars today; it has the virtue of appearing consistent and principled. Compilers who proceed on this basis protect themselves against charges of being dilettanti (whether or not they produce readable books).

— *Only an imperfect sampling is possible:* a better or worse cataloguing of a world that resists catalogues. This is considered true whether or not one has tried to make a compilation look properly principled. The work should consequently be done as well as one can do it, and then consulted by others for whatever light it may shed. Many compilers, wittingly or otherwise, are nearer to this position than any of the other three. Such compilers, however, lay themselves open (especially today) to charges of dilettantism and amateurism. Yet they often provide what the generally educated world wants, and are occasionally pioneers whose work can serve as a base for more 'rigorous' development by others.

Regardless, however, of the ultimate truth about exhaustiveness, the business of putting knowledge in better physical and mental containers proceeded briskly in the Age of Faith. Not only were manuscripts and codices beautifully illustrated and written, they were ever more efficiently laid out in terms of entitling, sectioning into chapters, and presenting on the page. Authors of all kinds, fiction as well as non-fiction, took the fluid stuff inside their heads and disciplined it in orderly visible compartments that we take for granted (although each of us at school has had to learn their conventions).

The structuring of books, however, is anything but 'natural' – indeed, it is thoroughly *un*natural and took all of 4,000 years to bring about. The achievement of the Scholastics, pre-eminently among the world's scribal élites, was to conventionalize the themes, plots and shapes of books in a truly rigorous way, as they also structured syllabuses, scripture and debate. What they and other élites like them have done marks us off forever from pre- and non-literate humankind, for the models of the world that we have in our heads have been conditioned by centuries of literacy and 'scribalism'. Our experience of books has served in fact to intensify what was already present in oral poems and epics. The safety of script and the greater clarity of its themes, plots and chapters reassure us and guide us so well, that – like our medieval predecessors – we cannot readily return to, or even understand, the mainsprings of a truly oral tradition.

Thus, the Scholastics helped 'literature' to supersede 'orature'. Indeed, since the tenth century, the triumph of organized written-and-depicted material over the great oral heritages has been complete – so complete that some writers talk of 'oral literatures' to describe the earlier state, and I have been forced to invent 'orature' as a distinct term for that state. In the tenth century the literate civilizations were still oases in a world of orature; today, oral heritages survive only on the very fringes of our lives.

Script triumphed, and even if the *omne scibile* could not truly be embraced a passable imitation could be offered to a civilization that was ready to accept it as the real thing. Medieval Christendom, at least until the coming of such upheavals as the Black Death in the fourteenth century, was largely willing to accept that its scribal élite knew whatever was worth knowing about the higher things of life.[2] It was also largely accepted that institutions like the universities were entitled, through their papal charters, to mediate both divine and secular truth – and a mélange of the two – to suitable students. There were ideological stirrings here and there, it is true, among such heretic groups as the Waldenses and the Lollards, but it was not ideology as such that precipitated the next great change. Rather, it was the technological union of an ancient Phoenician writing system with an ancient Chinese technique for reproducing words – and this on the banks of the Rhine.

It is hard to overstate the impact of the printing press on civilization at large, both in its own right and as part of the vast re-ordering of things that we see in retrospect as the Renaissance, the Reformation, the weakening of the Papacy, the fall of the Byzantine Empire to the Turks, the ebbing of Muslim expansion in the West, the Copernican Revolution in science, and the discovery of the Americas. Even so, however, Elizabeth Eisenstein can say with justification that – whatever our lip service – the arrival of printing has been 'the unacknowledged revolution'.[3] As she points out, 'almost no studies are devoted to the consequences that ensued once printers had begun to ply their trades throughout Europe'. Her own timely study, however, indicates that the consequences were epoch-making.

They were so vast, indeed, that they have virtually wiped out our ability to understand what life was like in the scribal cultures that preceded printing. Eisenstein (1979: 8–9) notes that

> even a cursory acquaintance with the findings of anthropologists or casual observations of pre-school age children may help to remind us of the gulf that exists between oral and literate cultures. Several studies, accordingly, have illuminated the difference between mentalities shaped by reliance on the spoken as opposed to the written word. The gulf that separates our experience from that of literate élites who relied exclusively on hand-copied texts is much more difficult to fathom. There is nothing analogous in our experience or in that of any living creature within the Western world at present. The conditions of scribal culture thus have to be artificially reconstructed by recourse to history books and reference guides.

In other words, the success of print has been so great and so ubiquitous that it has blotted out its own origins, if not intellectually and academically then psychologically. As I suggested at the start of this book, however, we are poised on the edge of another revolution that could be even more epoch-making than the arrival and application of paper-and-type technology. What comparable effect might not *it* have?

Be that as it may, however, the idea of printing made its appearance in Europe sometime in the late fourteenth century. There is no hard evidence that any actual *equipment* ever got to Europe from China (although the nomadic Uighurs appear to have taken it into the Muslim world); the idea may therefore have been the result of stimulus diffusion, where someone told someone else about something that worked in a particular way and produced a greater response than he bargained for.

By the turn of the fourteenth century, whatever its origin, movable wooden type (xylography) was being used in Europe. It proved to be troublesome, however, in that the letters were hard to carve and to standardize, and all too easy to break. Around 1430, therefore, attention turned to metal. Metallographic printing developed rapidly, using standardized dies to strike moulds in matrices of clay, onto which lead was then poured in order to create a text-bearing surface. This surface in its turn could then be separated from the matrices, inked, and pressed onto sheets of paper so as to produce copies of a printed page.

Although there has been some dispute as to who actually invented the printing press proper, the accolade has traditionally gone to Johannes Gutenberg, who built his press around 1436 and in the 1450s produced the first printed Latin Bible.[4] His invention combined the kind of press traditionally used at that time for binding codices with an adaptation of metallographic printing that used dies, matrices and re-arrangeable type. This moveable type was made of lead and could be set or 'composed' in blocks of varying lengths and widths in order to print whole columns or pages at a time. It could then be disassembled and used again in other combinations, the actual type being kept in trays organized alphabetically.

This was a novel triumph of taxonomy and technology together: The composed type was held together in special frames, inked, then brought rhythmically into contact with a surface that held a new sheet of paper every time the contact was made and until enough copies of that particular page or set of pages had been made. Over the succeeding centuries all sorts of refinements on this basic procedure have been developed, but it is this cyclical rhythm of sheet, ink and composed type that completely changed the worlds of information and education.

It is not possible here to go into detail on paper-and-type technology any more than I was able to describe in detail such earlier technologies as clay and cuneiform, reed and hieroglyph, bamboo and ideogram, or parchment and alphabet.[5] One reason is simply the size and focus of this book, in which we are considering the implications of technologies rather than their nature as crafts. Another and even more cogent reason is that the hardware of the reference technologies has grown almost exponentially more complex as the millennia have passed: difficult to circumscribe in a single large volume, leave alone in a few paragraphs. Sufficient to note here that print technology has been intricate in its hardware (the presses, etc.), fertile and flexible in the software that has been associated with it and produced by it (books, magazines, etc.), and utterly radical in its impact on all of us.

In a relatively short time, the painstaking labour of individual copyists in scriptoria and stationery workrooms came to an end, releasing many literate people for other kinds of clerical employment. The quiet scriptoria of the monasteries and stationers' enterprises were supplanted by noisy printshops in which, for the first time, reference technology became a recognizably *industrial* process comparable to the crafts of metalsmiths, cartwrights and other skilled artisans. Indeed, an era of mass production came into being for books and other printed items well before it began for such other things as clothing, tools, weapons, vehicles and food products. It was a foreshadowing of the Industrial Revolution by some 300 years.

This mass production, unlike the bulk of copying, was also beyond the control of both the Church and the universities. It was a 'trade' rather than a 'profession' and rapidly became commercial, something which had only been peripheral in the world of parchment and codex. Ecclesiastics and academics have never been entirely happy about this shift in control or indeed about the commercialization of the world of books. It is not so much that they have opposed so obviously useful a development, but rather that they regret its necessity and vaguely perpetuate a nostalgia for the scribalism that died during the Renaissance.

Where previously there had been relatively few people involved in the hand-copying of scripts, a whole array of occupations now burgeoned with the new technology: printers, compositors, binders, warehousemen, transporters, booksellers, publishers, critics, advertisers, salesmen, and a greatly expanded stationery trade. The growth of such an industry naturally intrigued the artisans and merchants who became involved in it. These groups were impelled through vested interest, and a parallel desire for more say in the running of their own lives, to become part of their own market. Knowledge was proving to be power. In setting out to acquire their knowledge more and more through books, such groups greatly increased the literate base of Western European society.

Church-based education for their sons, where it was available, still interested them; their own schools also interested them and became more significant as time passed, but it was the press itself that gave much greater impetus to learning – and to self-mediation – outside the colleges.[6] The vested interest of the traditional mediators of knowledge was undermined, but never so blatantly that they could inveigh with conviction against the books, pamphlets and newssheets that the presses produced so abundantly. A split-mindedness arose in the ranks of scholarship. Scholars used such things as works of reference, were glad enough from time to time to produce them or be associated with them, but have not always quite approved of works that served in essence to by-pass them. The self-educated are often admired, but are seldom legitimated by the group-educated. The processes through which they have gained their self-education – even the great encyclopedias of recent centuries – are often for the scholar caste ever so slightly tainted with what the French call *vulgarisation*. This is a point to which we shall return in due course.

The printing presses ruptured the educational monopoly of the Church and the institutions that were closely associated with the Church, encouraging both an interest in books and an independence of mind at a time when many people were questioning traditional Catholicism. It is, I suspect, no accident that the first Latin Bible was printed in German Europe in the 1450s and the first eruption of the Reformation took place there, under Martin Luther, in 1517.

At a different but equally important level, the standardization of the shapes and sizes of pages and of metal letters (so that printing might be made easier) encouraged standardization in other areas. Standardizing moved out, as it were, in waves: from spelling, punctuation and layout to styles of written language and, at length, to the officially acceptable forms of the newly emerging vernacular languages that had for so many centuries been in the shadow of Latin. In tandem, the increasingly rapid production and distribution of materials encouraged competition in styles of writing and presentation. Wider publics were reached faster than ever before, and critical feedback became for the first time a serious factor for writers, editors and publishers. The determining of truly efficient formats was made easier, and authors began to pay real attention to their public. Indeed, it was possible for authors and publics to develop at all, where in the past an author of significance had usually lived 1,000 years earlier than his readers and remained forever beyond reach. The printing press not only produced more of what had already been in existence for centuries; it also encouraged people to produce more material that was entirely new.

Finally, a civilization that had depended for the training of its intelligentsia on learning through the *ear* and committing a great deal of this learning to memory slowly began to change to one that increasingly depended on learning through the *eye* and external reference. Where books had been few and private, they became many and much more publicly available – sources for permanent easy consultation.

A whole way of life withered as the presses grew more active and added to the store of what was known and knowable. In an important way the presses answered the Scholastics, coinciding as they did with the fall of Scholasticism. They made it clear, for those who cared to think about it, that no single human being or any human system would ever catch the *omne scibile* in their net.

10

Theme versus alphabet:
the roots of lexicography

Most educated people today, if asked, would define lexicography as the business of making dictionaries, and dictionaries as books for words marshalled in alphabetic order. In this response they would be largely correct, but they would not be entirely correct, nor would they be describing the state of affairs out of which lexicography emerged. In addition, they would probably also be surprised to learn how recent an acquisition word-ordering by means of the alphabet is.

Given the great backcloth of philosophy, religion and disputation against which the 'encyclopedia' slowly emerged, its sister the 'dictionary' appears to have more or less crept into the classroom by a side door and crouched down in a corner. The strictly alphabetic wordbook (the dominant genre today) came into existence in a thoroughly casual and haphazard manner, and it would have taken a very reckless Schoolman to have predicted much of a future for it. The attention of the great Scholastics was elsewhere.

Interest in language teaching, however, was basic to the whole Scholastic programme, even if that teaching related only to one language.[1] The cement that held Western Christendom together was Latin,[2] a language that was simultaneously both 'dead' and 'alive'. It was dead in that no one now learned it as a mother tongue, but it was vitally alive as the medium of religious communion and scholarly communication. It was the spoken and written vehicle of the monastic and episcopal schools, and of the universities that were not quite inside and not quite outside Mother Church.

All aspirants to clerical careers everywhere – Basques or Burgundians, Catalans or Castilians, Gaels or Germans, Saxons or Swedes – all had to master this 'high' language as a foundation for everything else that they would do; there was *no* advancement in the universal church in one's own vernacular. The aspiring cleric became of necessity bilingual, and through his bilingualism acquired some measure of divinely sanctioned knowledge. The resemblance to the experience of young Akkadian scribes three millennia earlier is marked, even though the cultural climate was so different.

Nor does the parallelism end there: the young scribes of ancient Mesopotamia learned their cuneiform signs in thematic groups drawn from the everyday world, and the young clerics of medieval Western Europe learned their Latin wordstore in the same way. Bilingual grammatical and conversational primers were available, based on models used in the ancient world for Romans to learn Greek and Greeks to learn Latin; the acquisition of words, however, was handled generally in terms of special *vocabularia*. These were lists of *vocabula* ('words' or 'utterances') and are the originals of our present-day word 'vocabulary'.

A *vocabularium* was organized, not alphabetically, but in themes or conventionalized topics. One famous example of the type was compiled by the Anglo-Saxon scholar Aelfric, Abbot of Eynsham, near Oxford (c. 955– c. 1010). He was a well-known prose-writer and educator cast in the mould of Cassiodorus and Saint Isidore, and prepared not just a vocabularium but also a bilingual grammar and a conversational manual for his novices. An eleventh-century version of the thematic list that he developed is as follows, as expressive of the medieval Christian worldview as Ibn Qutayba a century earlier had been expressive of the worldview of Islam:

1 God, heaven, angels, sun, moon, earth, sea
2 man, woman, the parts of the body
3 kinship, professional and trades people, artisans
4 diseases
5 abstract terms
6 times of the year and day, seasons, the weather
7 colours
8 birds
9 fishes
10 beasts
11 herbs
12 trees
13 house furnishings
14 kitchen and cooking utensils
15 weapons
16 parts of a city
17 metals and precious stones
18 general terms (abstract and concrete)

The listed topics put the continuum of life into manageable containers and were eminently respectable in Scholastic terms: they belonged with the circle of what was traditional, acceptable and good. It had always been done like that. Another approach *did* exist, but it was much less justifiable and something of a chore.

Alphabetization has humble origins, much like the codex. To get at those origins properly, however, needs a slight initial aside. Manuscripts and codices, as we have noted, were scarce and valuable objects, but this scarcity and cost did not discourage many of their users from writing little notes on them, much as many people do today in the margins of their books. One popular annotation of this sort was a brief note to 'explain' a difficult or unusual word in the text. Such a note was most commonly placed above the target word, between the lines, or in the margin. A hard Latin word might be explained by an easier one, or by an assumed vernacular equivalent. It was, in fact, a casual application of the Akkadian approach, made possible, however, by a technology of pen and parchment rather than cut reeds and clay tablets that were soft when used but rock-hard forever after.

The Classical Greek term for a difficult or special word was *glossa* or *glotta*. This word's semantic evolution seems to have been from an initial meaning 'tongue' (as in *glossitis*) to 'language in general' (as in *polyglot*) to 'language not one's own' (as in *glossolalia*, 'speaking in tongues'), then to 'foreign language' and finally to 'difficult item in a (usually foreign) language'. The word passed into Latin and did a further semantic flip wherein it represented the activity done to explain an odd or foreign term. As a consequence we now 'gloss' difficult words and the results are 'glosses'. In sum, scholars refer to the medieval annotations nowadays as 'interlinear glosses' in manuscripts and codices.

Modern historians of lexicography, both for French and English, see the origin of the 'dictionary' proper in this cavalier yet practical way of adding snippets to copied texts.[3] Variously, throughout the early Middle Ages, *glossae collectae* began to appear, semi-formal lists that teachers and students could use to point up difficult expressions worth remembering. Many were ordered only in the sense that they were listed as they were lifted from the annotated texts; some, however, were re-cast alphabetically in terms of the first letter only. Progress was made from the eighth century onward, however, in moving to second- and third-letter ordering, but it is clear from the *glossaria* that survive that the progress was at a snail's pace, spanning some 300 or 400 years before all-through alphabetic ordering was common.

Nothing was certain or fixed in the early glossaries: not alphabetization or thematization[4], not vertical or horizontal listing, not glossing within Latin or bilingually. Spellings were not consistent and vernacular words were even from time to time Latinized. Even the one lexical compilation of any note that adopted alphabetization was not whole-hearted about it. This was the tenth century Byzantine work known as the *Lexicon* of Suidas, which could be called a prototype 'encyclopedic dictionary'. It was something of a maverick, however, and does not appear to have directly influenced any other work, whether encyclopedic or lexicographic.[5]

Why did alphabetization fail to catch on?[6] One reason must certainly be that people had already become accustomed over too many centuries to thematically ordered material. Such material bore a close resemblance to the 'normal' organization of written work: tables of contents and chapters that divide things up neatly and follow each other more or less logically. In such works, the numbering of chapters and pages was the only use of an invariant series of symbols.

Alphabetization may also have been offensive to the global Scholastic view of things. It must have seemed a perverse, disjointed and ultimately meaningless way of ordering material to men who were interested in neat frames for the containing of all knowledge. Certainly, alphabetization poses problems of fragmentation that may be less immediately obvious with word lists but can become serious when dealing with subject lists. Related items are scattered across the alphabet, and the effort to re-unite such items by cross-referring can be a frustrating task. It may even seem a foolish task to someone who wants to integrate rather than scatter our knowledge.

Although some properly alphabetic works appeared before Gutenberg printed his first book, the printing press seems to have been the factor that changed everything in favour of non-thematic ordering. Compositors were constantly re-shuffling the letters of the alphabet around as small hard metal objects in trays and in composites. They and their associates – which included many writers who were wont to frequent the print shops – became as a consequence increasingly at home with the convenience that the alphabet offers as an invariant series. Where scholars and copyists had previously been unaccustomed even to thinking of words and parts of words alphabetically, printers were now spending a great part of their time doing nothing else. Sheer familiarity with hard physical objects in a very practical craft appears, therefore, to have promoted interest in ABC order in other, related but more abstract fields.

Even so, however, it took more than 100 years after the advent of printing for alphabetization to establish itself as a serious and regular tool in the world of reference. Practices like the making of concordances, indexes and ABC wordbooks gained momentum slowly, but all appear to have established themselves firmly by around 1600, a date when the modern world of science and technology was beginning to take shape.

In the meantime, as regards works of language reference, all was a kind of creative flux, both in terms of format and in the titles used for such works. Format was now essentially an either/or matter: you went for a set of themes as Pliny, Aelfric and Vincent had done, or you contemplated the newly interesting possibility of ABC order. Titling, however, demonstrates the flux in men's minds more cogently, and is worth a little attention. In general, some five categories of titles had emerged:

- a simple direction description:
  Li Chi: The Record of Rites
  Historia naturalis: Natural History
  Editio vulgata: The Common Edition
- a simple description with a value judgement built into it:
  I Ching: The Classic of Changes
  Kitab 'Uyun al-Akhbar: The Book of the Best Traditions
  Chronica maiora: The Greater Chronicles
- the use of a short focusing device followed by the subject placed in focus:
  De lingua latina: On the Latin Language
  De Civitate Dei: Concerning the City of God
  De rerum natura: About the Nature of Things

– a description showing the number of containers needed to house the
work in question:
Differentiarum libri: The Books of Differences
Disciplinarum libri IX: Nine Books of Subjects
Sententiarum libri tres: Three Books of Sentences
– a description incorporating a generic term and often also a subtle
value judgement:
Institutiones divinarum et saecularum litterarum: Instructions in Divine
and Profane Matters
Summa contra gentiles: A Comprehensive Review in Reply to the
Gentiles
Speculum triplex: The Threefold Mirror

These classes are fairly easy to differentiate, and predominated into the
late Middle Ages. Here and there we can also find an analogical-cum-
figurative approach, already exhibited above with Vincent's *speculum*
('mirror') and popular from medieval times right up to our own. Some older
examples are:

Hortus deliciarum: The Garden of Delights, a twelfth-century work by
the abbess Herrad, which is probably the first lexicographic compilation by a woman
Ortus vocabulorum: The Garden of Words, an anonymous wordbook
printed in England in 1500
Liber floridus: The Flowery Book, a twelfth-century general miscellany
by Lambert de St-Omer
Li Livres dou trésor: The Treasure Books, a thirteenth-century vernacular treatise by Brunetto Latini, the teacher of Dante
Thesaurus linguae romanae et britannicae: Treasure-House of the Roman
and British Tongues, a fifteenth-century wordbook by Geoffrey the
Grammarian
Liber de nuptiis Mercurii et Philologiae: A Book Concerning the Wedding
of Mercury and Philology, a fifth-century compendium of the seven
liberal arts by Martianus Capella
Visio delectable: The Delightful Vision, a fifteenth-century work by
Alfonso de la Torre about a child receiving instruction from maidens
each of whom embodies one of the liberal arts

In the late Middle Ages and early Renaissance periods titles for
wordbooks proliferated as men sought to get the right coverall term or
stimulating metaphor for what they were doing:

abecedarium – an abecedary or absee, an ABC
alvearium – an alveary (a bee-hive or honey-store)
dictionarius or *dictionarium* – a dictionary, a book of *dictiones* (words and
expressions)
glossarium – a glossary (an explanatory list, usually collected from
other lists)
(h)ortus – a 'garden'

lexicon – a lexicon (a wordbook, a collection of *lexis* or words, often of a
  specialized or classical nature)
manipulus – a maniple (a handful)
medulla – the 'kernel' or 'marrow' of a matter
promptuarium or *promptorium* – a promptuary (a store-house)
thesaurus – a thesaurus (treasury or treasure-house)
vocabularium – a vocabulary (the words of a language, especially if listed
  in any way)
vulgaria – the 'common things' of life or a language

Of these dozen contenders, only three have survived in modern English
as regular generic terms for wordbooks: *dictionary, lexicon* and *thesaurus*. One
has survived as a term for a word list (*glossary*), and one as a general term for
the words of a language or certain listings of such words (*vocabulary*). These
five situations are end-results, however, not specialized functions at that
time, and there was no guarantee that any one of them would become long-
term expressions in any future language or even in Latin. Additionally, it is
worth recalling that even today sharp-edged distinctions do not exist in practice between the terms 'dictionary', 'lexicon' and 'thesaurus'. The term
'dictionary' in particular, since its first recorded appearance as *dictionarius* in
1225 (in the title of a work by the English poet and grammarian John
Garland), has tended to be a coverall term for all sorts of presentations of
information about 'words', however conceived. In 1340, the French compiler and friend of Petrarch, Pierre Bersuire, used *dictionarium* as more or less
meaning 'phrase-book' in the title of a commentary on Saint Jerome's Bible.
What he compiled was in fact an alphabetic list of more than 3,000 words used
in the Bible, accompanied by moral expositions. Both Garland and Bersuire
had close associations with the University of Paris, where the Latin term may
well have been popular as a convenient title for anything remotely dealing
with words.[7]

It was much later that the term entered English and French. In 1538, Sir
Thomas Elyot chose to call his alphabetic wordbook a *Dictionary* of Latin and
English, and about 1553 John Withals used the same term for his thematic
wordbook, the *Shorte Dictionarie for Yonge Begynners* (in Latin). In 1539, in
Paris, Robert Estienne brought out his thematic *Dictionnaire français–latin*. It
is also, interestingly, around the same time that the German scholar, Paul
Scalich, published in Basel his *Encyclopaedia: seu orbis disciplinarum, tam
sacrarum quam profanum epistemon* ('Encyclopedia: or an Understanding of the
World of Learning, both Sacred and Profane'). The title can be read as referring back to the *enkýklios paideía* and not as the generic title of a book, but it
nonetheless overtly brought together the odd medieval compound 'encyclopaedia' and the desire to cover the *omne scibile*. It served, therefore, to create
in the minds of others later the generic term that we are used to today.

By the end of the sixteenth century, therefore, in terms of printing practice and in the winnowing-out of generic names as well as in the clarification
of reference formats, we have arrived at a world that is recognizably modern,
whether or not anything was yet strictly functioning in the ways that we are
used to.

What we can also see is a fundamental dichotomy in terms of organization and format that is not always immediately obvious to us today because of the great success of alphabetization. This dichotomy is far-reaching, however, because it operates first at a real and practical level in terms of how works of reference are used and also at an ideal and theoretical level, because it relates to psychological attitudes and ideological stances with regard to how information is best presented and understood. In immediate terms it discusses convenience of presentation; in ultimate terms, it relates to how we as human beings have information organized inside our own heads. The dichotomy rests upon:

- the *thematic mode*, the older of the two procedures for handling such things as memorization, classification and the marshalling of information for reference purposes
- the *alphabetic mode*, the younger and currently dominant of the two procedures, most apparent in standard dictionaries and encyclopedias and taken by a majority of people today as definitive of the whole genre.

The pendulum has swung in 1,000 years from the thematic enthusiasms of the Scholastics to the alphabetic enthusiasms of our times. That up to the present there has been dominance of one over the other, however, does not mean that it need always be so, especially in the new technologies that are crowding upon us.

11

A blurring of languages: Latin and the vernaculars

In medieval times, as we have seen, the dominion of the Latin language was virtually absolute among the scribal élites of Western Europe. The bilingualism that it imposed upon all aspiring clerics ran for centuries in one direction only, but it was probably inevitable in the hodgepodge of empires, kingdoms and duchies that the tide would begin to turn.[1]

The vernaculars had long been regarded as no more than barbarous dialects, unsuitable for high, religious, literary and intellectual themes, and without anything resembling a canon of correctness. Languages that are clearcut and powerful today – French, Spanish, German, English – were not nearly such distinct entities then; more, they vied with others that were in those days just as significant, but which have dwindled in recent time into second-class status: Catalan, Occitan, Gaelic, Scots and a variety of others. Those forms that were used at royal courts in the heartlands of what are today nation-states had not yet become standards for others to emulate, but the process of standardization had begun, and influential people were writing both prose and verse in a variety of mother tongues: Chrétien de Troyes, Dante Alighieri, and Geoffrey Chaucer were only three among many. When printing was invented, works in the vernaculars began to roll off the presses as frequently as works in Latin, and in due course more frequently.[2]

This development was encouraged by the growth of the mercantile and artisan classes, who knew little or no Latin apart from snippets from church usage, but aspired to higher social positions and greater political power, especially in the increasingly important cities. Education seemed to them to be useful in the acquisition of such things, and printing in the vernaculars was important to them not only for this but also because it weakened the educational monopoly of the Church and its associate institutions.

The change that I am describing here was slow, spanning some five centuries, but it was ultimately potent both for society at large and the growth of alphabetic lexicography, a point which can be illustrated vividly from the history of wordbooks in France and England from 1400 onward.[3]

The Dominican friar known in Latin as Galfridus Grammaticus and in English as Geoffrey the Grammarian appears to have been the first compiler of wordbooks to attempt a switch-round in the presentation of languages in bilingual lists. Thus, he took an early Latin-to-English glossary, the *Medulla grammatica* ('Grammatical Kernel'), compiled around 1400 by an unknown scholar, and re-shaped it with the languages reversed. Known as the *Promptorium parvulorum sive clericorum* ('Storehouse for Little Ones or Clerics'), it appeared in 1440 and contained some 10,000 items in two lists, one for nouns and one for verbs (with various other parts of speech inserted wherever they seemed appropriate). The English words coming first may well have made life easier for learners than the time-hallowed practice of having the target language first (a practice which, as a matter of interest, certain scholarly Latin lexicons still maintain). It certainly suggests that students were accustomed to thinking in English, then looking for Latin equivalents, rather than knowing the Latin and then wondering what the English equivalent (if any) might be.

A printed version of Geoffrey's work appeared in 1499, and was apparently successful without, however, causing too great a stir or rush to emulate it in England. Whether because of an awareness of this novelty or a similar line of thinking, the Parisian lexicographer and publisher Robert Estienne brought out in 1539 his *Dictionnaire français–latin* (to which we have already referred) – and in it put the French first, where previously the Latin had been first or was so dominant as to make the French element unimportant.[4]

Lexicography as we understand it today began in the bilingualism of the late Middle Ages and Renaissance, and was fed in the sixteenth century by numerous bilingual wordbooks like those just discussed (although in most of them Latin still came first). Such widespread Latin-to-vernacular translation stimulated interest in the vernaculars themselves and in the possibility of doing the same kind of thing *sideways*, between vernaculars, rather than always *downwards* from the 'high' to the 'low'. As a result, the same century was also marked by a variety of interlingual works, such as William Salesbury's Welsh-to-English compilation in 1547 and John Florio's Italian-to-English in 1599.[5]

While this general interest increased, more and more attention was being paid (with mixed feelings) to an unanticipated effect of the high Latin language on the low vernacular vocabularies. Bilingual scholars the length and breadth of Western Christendom were no better than any other bilinguals anywhere in separating out the two language skills inside their heads. Both for convenience and in order to display their learning they constantly peppered their native languages with words and phrases from the high tongue: where some concept did not come easily in a vernacular it was conveyed through a Latin interpolation; indeed, the more one wanted to talk of higher things in the lower languages, the more one had to import the only material there was through which such 'higher' things could be tackled. It was, in effect, the Akkadian experience with Sumerian all over again.

Not indeed that the phenomenon is unusual in the world. The content of high classical, cultural and liturgical languages frequently flows 'downward' into vernacular, colonial, tribal or otherwise subordinated languages. While Europe was absorbing Latin, the inhabitants of Persia – conquered by the Arabs – were taking into their language a vast vocabulary of religion and philosophy from Arabic. For centuries in India elements of Sanskrit, the sacred language of the Vedas and the Upanishads, guarded by the god-like brahminical caste, have poured into the Dravidian languages of the south as well as into northern Indian languages that were already related to Sanskrit (whose very name means 'the perfected').[6]

More significantly still, for our purposes here, this process of 'classici-zation'[7] had already occurred inside Latin itself, with the influx of quantities of Greek from the first century BC onward. The Latin of the Scholastics (often known as 'Neo-Latin' to distinguish it from the classical tongue of Caesar and Cicero) was full of nativized Greek, which had entered in two streams: from the secular tradition of the philosophers, and from the Greek of the New Testament. On this point the lexicologist Hans Marchand observes of Neo-Latin that it 'has frequently extended Old Greek patterns so that they are more rightly Neo-Latin than Old Greek' (Marchand 1960:7).

The process was now repeating itself, and on a mammoth scale: the non-Romance languages of Western Europe were being more and more 'Latinized', while the Romance languages – already of Latin provenance – were being 're-Latinized'. The effects of these processes is particularly starkly evident in English, which had already experienced a limited inflow of Latin with the conversion to Christianity of the Anglo-Saxons, and then a massive infusion of Norman-French after the Norman Conquest.[8] The result has been a mongrel quality much commented on by historians and pedagogues. A flow-chart of the currents of Greek, Latin and French as they have moved towards English shows how curious and complex the whole process has been (see figure 4).

Nowadays, Latin is generally described as a 'dead' language, a metaphorical expression whose precise meaning is seldom considered. If we agree that it is indeed 'dead' because no one has it as a mother tongue, then in dying it gave several other languages a most vital transfusion of its blood. That colossal transfer served over a number of centuries so to strengthen

Fig. 4 A flow-chart of Greek, Latin and French into English

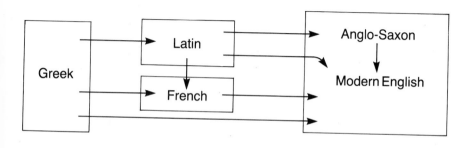

certain of the vernaculars that they became capable in their turn of serving as 'aristocrats' of communication; in recent centuries they have been themselves the high tongues of empire, commerce, religion and science.

The transfer, however, has not been painless and free from controversy. Quite the contrary, in fact, because a fierce dispute has waged since the Renaissance as to the rightness or wrongness of absorbing the old high language into the very bodies of the new and rising vernaculars. Essentially, this has been the controversy of innovator and importer against purist and defender[9] – a quarrel out of which emerged, among other things, the unilingual dictionary.

The importers saw no harm whatever in transferring the words they needed from Latin, while the purists in their more extreme moments contended that even Neo-Latin was a corruption of the original and beautiful language of Virgil and Varro. Sir Thomas Elyot was a confirmed Latinist, but he also wrote with enthusiasm in English, and was on one occasion congratulated by Henry VIII because his work was not 'therby made derke or harde to be understande'. He saw his mother tongue as in need of supplementation, and supplemented it from the one obvious source. He was on the whole a moderate in this, whereas others went to extremes that were severely criticized and mocked. Shakespeare, for instance, provides us with a good example of the extremist in the comedy *Love's Labour's Lost* (c. 1590). There, especially in Act IV, Scene II, the pedantic schoolmaster Holofernes struts his stuff, and has in the process become a kind of archetype for absurd excess in language.

Nowadays, when Britons are impressed or irritated by people who use long and abstruse Latinisms, they say that so-and-so 'has swallowed a dictionary'. This folk remark carries some historical weight, because it was the makers of English dictionaries who particularly abetted the Latinizing process. It came about in the following way.

The battle-lines were drawn well before the end of the sixteenth century. On the one side, in his *Arte of Rhetorique* in 1553, Thomas Wilson could state, cuttingly, that 'some seeke so farre for outlandish English, that thei forget altogether their mothers tongue'. On the other side, George Pettie could reply in 1586, as regards the 'aureate diction' of the supposed inkpot pedants: 'If they be all counted inkpot tearmes I know not how we should speak anie thing without blacking our mouths with ink.'[10]

Educators in particular were exercised about how to handle and teach the vocabulary of English, whether it was deemed 'natural or incorporate', and began to want to see it all laid out in *one* dictionary. Such a comprehensive effort was a long time coming, but small moves towards it began to be made by the turn of the century. The first truly English–English alphabetic glossary was appended to William Tyndale's translation of the Pentateuch in 1530 and was called 'a table expoundinge certeyne wordes'. Its potential was not developed, however, until a momentous little octavo volume appeared in 1604, the *Table Alphabeticall of hard usuall English wordes*, by the schoolmaster Robert Cawdrey. This 3,000-entry work was epochal in that it was unilingual

A
Table Alphabeticall, con-
teyning and teaching the true
vvriting, and vnderſtanding of hard
vſuall Engliſh wordes, borrowed from
the Hebrew, Greeke, Latine,
or French. &c.

With the interpretation thereof by
plaine Engliſh words, gathered for the benefit &
helpe of Ladies,Gentlewomen, or any other
vnskilfull perſons.

Whereby they may the more eaſilie
and better vnderſtand many hard Engliſh
wordes, vvhich they ſhall heare or read in
Scriptures, Sermons, or elſwhere, and alſo
be made able to vſe the ſame aptly
themſelues.

Legere, et non intelligere , neglegere eſt.
As good not read, as not to vnderſtand.

AT LONDON,
Printed by I. R. for Edmund Wea-
uer, & are to be ſold at his ſhop at the great
North doore of Paules Church.
1 6 0 4.

Robert Cawdrey's Table Alphabeticall *of 1604, the first English dictionary to explain the exotic to the 'unskilfull'.*

A

§ A Bandon, caſt away, oʒ yǽlde bp, to leaue, oʒ foʒſake.

Abaſh, bluſh.

abba, father.

§ abbeſſe, abbateſſe, Miſtris of a Nunnerie, comfoʒters of others.

§ abbettors, counſelloʒs.

aberration, a going a ſtray, oʒ wandering.

abbreuiat, ⎱ to ſhoʒten, oʒ make
§ abbridge, ⎰ ſhoʒt.

§ abbut, to lie bnto, oʒ boʒder bpon, as one lands end mǽts with another.

abecédarie, the oʒder of the Letters, oʒ hee that bſeth them.

aberration, a going aſtray, oʒ wandering.

The first entries in the Table Alphabeticall

English and yet *still* functionally *bi*lingual. It was directed at the educationally insecure in the upper levels of society – 'gathered for the benefit and helpe of Ladies, Gentlewomen, or any other unskilfull persons' – and essentially tried to let them in on the secrets of Latinization. In his table, the new inkpotisms were on the left and some homelier synonyms on the right, thus:

abrogate	take away, disanull, disallow
acquisition	getting, purchasing
aggravate	making more grievous, and more heavie
magnitude	greatness
manuring	dunging, tilling
paucitie	fewness or smale number
prompt	ready, quicke
ruinous	ready to fall
ruminate	to chew over againe, to studie earnestlie uppon

Cawdrey's table was followed in 1616 by John Bullokar's *The English Expositour*, in 1623 by Henry Cockeram's *The English Dictionarie or, an Interpreter of hard English Words*, in 1656 by Thomas Blount's *Glossographia*, and in 1658 by Edward Phillips's *The New World of English Words*. The popularity of these works has been marvelled at by later generations of commentators. Like the true bilingual dictionaries that preceded them, they were commercial successes, through to the thirteenth edition of Bullokar in Dublin in 1726. Their general history, however, is less relevant here than their lexicographic method, which was largely a process of definition by synonym that derived from bilingual translation. The investigators Starnes and Noyes in 1946 have clearly demonstrated the creative plagiarism in which these compilers engaged, by juxtaposing examples from earlier Latin-to-English works and the corresponding parts of the 'hard word' dictionaries (see tables 2 and 3, p88).

It is clear from this that the compilers of the hard-word dictionaries were not recorders of usage, as lexicographers are nowadays largely assumed to be. Instead, they were themselves partisan – active participators in the process of transferring the word-store of Latin wholesale into their own language. The later charges of plagiarism and corruption levelled at them would not have made a lot of sense to them, nor the parallel charges that some of their coinages or transfers were pretentious and unnecessary.

They knew precisely what they were doing, and were commercial successes in doing it. For them, the vocabulary of Neo-Latin and of the refined, elegant and academic level developing in English was the *same* vocabulary, the *same* resource, a conversion of international currency to local use by means of a few well-tried rules.[11] These men possessed, it would appear, one consistent trait: they sought (in the spirit of both Renaissance and Reformation) to broaden the base of the educated Elect. Their works were for the non-scholarly, for the wives of the gentry and the bourgeoisie, for merchants and artisans and other aspirants to elegance, education and power. They offered access to the new high English to many who felt discontented with the old low variety. Indeed, Bullokar is quite explicit about this educational role in his preface to the 'courteous reader':[12]

> And herein I hope such learned (professors) will deeme no wrong offered to themselves or dishonour to Learning, in that I open the signification of such words, to the capacitie of the ignorant, whereby they may conceive and use them as well as those which have bestowed long study in the languages, for considering it is familiar among best writers to usurp strange words . . . I suppose withall their desire is that they should be understood.

Whether the Latinization of English would have proceeded so well if these compilers had refrained from their creative plagiarism will never be known. It is unarguable, however, that they placed their mark upon the language, for good or for ill.

Some would argue that there was a fair degree of ill, because the educational intent of men like Cawdrey and Bullokar was not properly extended. As a result, the clash between the High Latinate and the low vernacular has never, in their view, been resolved. In *The Language Bar*, published in 1950, Victor Grove claimed that social and educational limitations still impede the development of many native users of English. Such individuals, all moderately literate, cannot however move on to exploit the resources of their own

The deliberate Latinization of English in the seventeenth century

Table 2

Thomas Thomas's *Dictionarium linguae latinae et anglicanae*, 1606 edition (1588, an adaptation of the work of Thomas Cooper that was already an adaptation of Elyot)	John Bullokar's *The English Expositour*, 1616
Alacritas . . . Cheerefulnes, livelinesse, courage, readines	*Alacritie*. Cheerfulness; courage, quicknesse
Catalogus . . . a rehearsall in wordes, or table in writing of the number of things, a roll, a bill, a scroll, a catalogue: also a register of proper names	*Catalogue*. A roll, a bill, a register of names or other things
Rumino . . . To chew the cudde as neate doe; also to call to remembrance and to consider with ones selfe, to study and thinke upon matters	*Ruminate*. To chew over againe as beasts doe, that chew the cud: where-fore it is often taken to studie and thinke much of a matter

Table 3

Some of the 'vulgar' English in Henry Cockeram's *Dictionarie* 1623	Equivalents in the Rider–Holyoke Latin–English dictionary (1617)	Cockeram's equivalent 'hard words' of English
to burden	onero	onerate
burdenous	onerosus	onerous
to charme, enchaunt	incanto	incantate
a charme, enchauntment	incantatio	incantation
cheapnes	vilitas	vility
to chide or rebuke	iurgo, obiurgo	objurgate
childishness	pueritia, puerilitas	puerility

Starnes and Noyes comment:

> It is obvious that Cockeram found most, if not all, of his so-called 'vulgar' words in the English–Latin section of the Rider–Holyoke dictionary; and the 'more refined and elegant' terms represent Cockeram's attempts to Anglicize Rider's Latin equivalents of the English. This process is significant in thus introducing a great many Latin words into the English vocabulary. Some of these were already current; others were not.

language successfully because they are intimidated by a 'high-brow' stratum in whose use they have never been properly schooled. The Latinate and technical remain a linguistic lump that they are unable to digest (Grove 1950).

Others, however, point – often with fascinated pride – to the enrichment that they see in this process of blurring Latin into English (and Greek with it). In 1964, for example, Lancelot Hogben sought not only to provide an aid to those whom Grove saw as excluded and disadvantaged; in his *The Mother Tongue* he also extolled the versatility of 'our hybrid heritage'. His book is a monument to how, with a little effort, people can indeed come to terms with that heritage.[13]

Among linguistic analysts few have considered the matter either positively or negatively, but in 1973 two German observers of English, Thomas Finkenstaedt and Dieter Wolff, made a historical and statistical study of English vocabulary that came to a conclusion that is significant to this review. They observed, with regard to the Latinization of English from the sixteenth century onwards, that 'apparently the Elizabethans discovered the possibilities of etymological dissociation in language: *amatory* and *love, audition* and *hearing, hearty welcome* and *cordial reception*: these quasisynonyms offer new opportunities for semantic differentiation. Two terms for the same denotatum: new connotations can arise, stylistic, poetic possibilities are offered when the new word is liberated from the restricted use in the language of science' (Finkenstaedt & Wolff 1973:64).

Be the arguments what they may, however, the facts are beyond dispute. The purists lost the battle, and in the process – by blending languages and adapting bilingual lexicography into unilingual lexicography – the English language at least got its first autonomous alphabetic wordbooks.

The modern world

If the lexicons of ancient tongues, not immutably fixed, and comprised in a few volumes, be yet, after the toil of successive ages, inadequate and delusive; if the aggregated knowledge, and co-operating diligence of the Italian academicians, did not secure them from the censure of Beni, if the embodied criticks of France, when fifty years had been spent upon their work, were obliged to change its oeconomy, and give their second edition another form, I may surely be contented without the praise of perfection, which, if I could obtain, in this gloom of solitude, what would it avail me?

SAMUEL JOHNSON, *Preface to the Dictionary*, 1755★

DI′CTATURE. *n. s.* [*dictatura*, Lat.] The office of a dictator; dictatorship. *Dict.*

DI′CTION. *n. s.* [*diction*, Fr. *dictio*, Lat.] Style; language; expression.

There appears in every part of his *diction*, or expression, a kind of noble and bold purity.

Dryden.

DI′CTIONARY. *n. s.* [*dictionarium*, Lat.] A book containing the words of any language in alphabetical order, with explanations of their meaning; a lexicon; a vocabulary; a word-book.

Some have delivered the polity of spirits, and left an account that they stand in awe of charms, spells, and conjurations; that they are afraid of letters and characters, notes, and dashes, which, set together, do signify nothing; and not only in the *dictionary* of man, but in the subtler vocabulary of Satan. *Brown, Vulg. Err.*

Is it such a fault to translate *simulacra* images? I see what a good thing it is to have a good ca-

Samuel Johnson and what his Dictionary of 1755 says about dictators, diction and dictionaries.

12

The legislative urge: authoritative wordbooks

The schoolmasters and other 'bibliophiles' who created the hard-word dictionaries of seventeenth-century England were individualists who laboured for both love and money. They owed no duty to any organization, and no organization felt any responsibility for them.

In this they epitomize an important element in the history and psychology of reference materials: the passionate individuals with a peculiar taste for the hard labour of sifting, citing, listing and defining. In such people the taxonomic urge verges on the obsessive. Thus, the wife of the Elizabethan lexicographer Thomas Cooper grew to fear that too much compiling would kill her husband. To prevent this, she took and burned the entire manuscript upon which he was working. Somehow, Cooper absorbed the loss – and simply sat down and started all over again.[1] (As a practising lexicographer, I understand Cooper's response to his wife's drastic methods. I am equally sure that my wife sympathizes with Mistress Cooper's frustration and anxiety.)

Such dedicated loners were not, however, the sole vehicle for the expansion of lexicography from the Renaissance onward.[2] Just as medieval Scholasticism had provided the impetus for the universities, so now the Renaissance was inspiring the development of a second range of public institutions. These new institutions were, however, of a much more secular and regionalistic nature than the early universities. The first of them sprang up in Italy, modelling themselves – as citadels of culture – on Plato's Academy in ancient Athens. They were therefore also known as 'academies', and ranged as time passed from specialized schools to regional and national institutions for the promotion of the arts and sciences. The Renaissance was a time when modern nation-states were taking shape, and certain of the new academies were therefore useful in helping to crystallize what it meant to be 'Italian', 'French' or 'Spanish'.[3]

Language was, inevitably, a foremost element in defining a sense of nationality and culture, so that a new national academy naturally took an interest in the state of the developing national language (which, in most cases, was simply one 'dialect' among a cluster of dialects). A national literature and a national standard helped to define a state and enable it to stand up to the international pressures of emperors and popes. The first of the great academies was the Accademia della Crusca, founded in Florence in 1582, giving a sense of 'Italianness' even where 'Italy' as such did not exist as a unified polity. In 1612, this academy published in Venice its *Vocabolario della Crusca*, a study of contemporary Italian that extensively cited usages from works of literature.

The academy that had the most influence on ideas of language, literature and lexicography, however, was founded in Paris in 1634 at the behest of Armand, Cardinal Richelieu.[4] This influence is due in particular to the first organizer of the Académie Française, the amateur grammarian Claude Favre de Vaugelas. He directed the work of the academicians from the mid-1630s till his death in 1653, and in the process made a lasting impression upon French language, thought and culture. In 1647, he published his *Remarques sur la langue française*, in which he elevated 'usage' as the proper legislator of a language and not any individual person, however talented. It is clear from his argument that for Vaugelas 'usage' was a kind of social consensus, the expression of the collective linguistic intent, skill and taste of a relatively homogeneous group. It is equally clear, however, that his group did not include all the members of the French nation. In fact, it specifically excluded the vast majority in that nation, in that Vaugelas took seriously only the 'good usage' of the 'fittest' persons at the royal court and the 'best' established writers.

In thus seeking to regulate the French language in terms of aristocratic good taste Vaugelas was not simply being a snob. He was seeking if not to establish then at least to delineate the new High Mode that would permit French to serve as a social, cultural and scientific successor to Latin. Anything that was not in the High Mode inevitably smacked of past centuries and the crude inferiority of the vernaculars. All the clamorous low modes of the provinces, the ports, the streets and the marketplaces were irrelevant to his and the nation's goals, which were a new classical age. Everything was present in the attitude of Vaugelas and his peers to feed the class hatreds that arose a century later, but it is not therefore necessary to suppose that it was a desire to grind the workers and peasants down that animated such academicians. Rather, they were high-mindedly concerned with raising the French language *up*. And such a newly confident vernacular tongue could not in their view be truly strong and autonomous until it had a proper national wordbook to demonstrate its worth.

The influence of Vaugelas is still strong in the French-using world. Maurice Grevisse, for example, the Belgian compiler of the present-day *Bon Usage* (eleventh edition, 1980) has freely acknowledged that his work descends in an unbroken line from the canons of Vaugelas, and still largely follows those canons.[5] This is in sharp contrast to the world of English, where no Academic legislature ever developed. It is highly unlikely, for example, that a grammarian or lexicographer working in English today would pay much attention to the strictures of a seventeenth-century predecessor; indeed, even the nineteenth century would be suspect.

The Académie launched its dictionary project in 1635 and spent the next 59 years intermittently and with much argument and incrimination bringing it to a conclusion. By the time the *Dictionnaire de la langue française* finally came out its early plan had changed completely and some of the academicians doubted that it reflected any honour at all on their institution. Certainly, in retrospect modern commentators like Georges Matoré and Allen Walker Read have noted that the massive work was not as scholarly or as functional as others brought out in the meantime by rugged individualists like Pierre Richelet in 1680 and Antoine Furetière in 1690.

Nevertheless, whatever the controversies and mishaps that attended its long gestation, the Académie's dictionary had the advantage of the Académie's prestige. It was a truly national work and showed that the French language was something to be reckoned with. Not only did other countries like Spain and Russia in due course follow the example of Italy and France, but even England, which had no academy, exhibited envy and a desire to do at least as well.

The nearest thing in England to a language-legislating institution was the Royal Society of London for the Improvement of Natural Knowledge, incorporated in 1662. Even this, however, was not very near, and was more interested in science than aesthetics and elegance. Its members were aware, however, that English did not yet match Latin 'for philosophic purposes', and formed a short-lived committee to consider how the language could be appropriately improved. Although nothing directly important emerged from the committee's deliberations, it remains significant for two reasons: it was part of an on-going debate that did eventually produce results, and it encouraged interest in the idea of a universal logical language, an artificial construct designed strictly for scientific purposes, that has had a variety of interesting repercussions (as we shall see in due course).

The success of the French in providing themselves with a genuinely national dictionary, however, continued to unsettle the literati of England. Such writers and social commentators as John Dryden, Joseph Addison, Jonathan Swift and Alexander Pope were all as eager as Vaugelas to see a proper High Mode developed and sustained in *their* newly confident mother tongue.[6] Latin was in full retreat now as the language of culture and learning, and they wanted English to be as strong a successor as possible (fearing, however, that French might take up the mantle of international language). Additionally, despite their own efforts to sustain a new classical or 'Augustan' age, they saw all around them barbarisms and corruption, and wished intently for some way to 'fix' the language of refinement against all comers. In this, despite their confidence and success in letters, they resembled the embattled monks of the Dark Ages more than they resembled Varro and Virgil in the Rome of Augustus Caesar.

In the meantime, however, the quietly obsessed individual compilers soldiered on in England as they had soldiered on in France while the national dictionary matured. Always idiosyncratic and often pastmasters of plagiarism, such compilers as John Kersey and Nathaniel Bailey[7] moved their craft forward from simple lists of hard Latinisms to a new vogue for 'universal' and 'technical' wordbooks, while showing more and more interest in such matters as etymology, orthography, stress patterns, syllabication and pronunciation as well as the use of illustrations (both woodcut and copperplate). They were not, however, 'academic'. Throughout, their aims were populist and commercial, uninfluenced by any desire to outdo the Frenchies and save the national honour. All the more ironic, therefore, that they provided the model for England's answer to Vaugelas and the Académie.

Works like Kersey's and Bailey's were well established when, in the late 1740s, a group of London booksellers decided to produce the great national dictionary (without benefit, as it were, of any guiding organization). They approached a possible compiler, the writer and critic Samuel Johnson, and offered to support him in the work of compilation for a period of three years. (Neither Johnson nor the publishers seem to have been perturbed that the French had striven for almost 60 years before producing their opus.) Johnson took on the task, and with his six clerks laboured for something over seven years in Gough Square, passing into the mythology of English just as the original Forty Immortals of the Académie have passed into the mythology of French.

During the period of compilation, Johnson presided over an interleaved copy of Bailey's folio *Dictionarium Britannicum* (1736 edition), using it as his base. As he worked he read a great number of books, which he annotated for usages and citations, passing the annotated copies to his assistants, so that the marked passages could be turned into hand-written slips that could be pasted as needed onto the pages of the new work, under the master's definitions.

Later commentators have generally praised Johnson's work as the crucible in which modern lexicography was formed, especially, of course, for the English language.[8] James Murray observed in 1900 that Johnson 'raised English lexicography altogether to a higher level', while in 1946 Starnes and Noyes stated that he 'invested the calling (of lexicographer) with lasting dignity'. In 1976, Roberts and Clifford have added that the new work 'surpassed all earlier dictionaries not in bulk but in precision of definition and in literary illustrations. Its 40,000 words were, in fact, rather less than those in the work of his predecessor, Nathaniel Bailey; but what distinguished Johnson's work was the range of reading by which he exemplified the different shades of meaning of a particular word'.

Comment, of course, has not been all favourable. In their history of the English language, for example, Baugh and Cable (1957 and 1978) generally admire Johnson's achievement but add the rider that by modern standards 'it was painfully inadequate', marred by 'ludicrous' etymologies and here and there 'by prejudice and caprice'. They note that 'its definitions, generally sound and often discriminating, are at times truly Johnsonian . . . (*Cough*: A convulsion of the lungs, vellicated by some sharp seriosity) . . . It includes a host of words with a very questionable right to be regarded as belonging to the language.' Despite the new rigour, therefore, we can see that (no doubt inevitably) Johnson was still affected by the aims, interests and style of the dilettante Latinizers of the previous century.

Most of the commentary on Johnson has touched on the form of his work, but in 1970 D.J. Greene extended his remarks away from the actual compilation towards certain wider geopolitical issues that are relevant here: 'Johnson's Dictionary is a very great and serious achievement in the history of the study of the English language. It is not merely the curious whim of a quaint eccentric, but a most important landmark in the development of English, from a set of unimportant dialects spoken by a small group of islanders on the fringe of civilization, to a great world language.' (It is significant that Greene's study of Johnson was published in New York.)

The comment is valid, but it is unlikely that Johnson (or his imitators, who were legion) appreciated the global role that was emerging for their language through the expansion of the British Empire in the eighteenth century (often at the expense of the French). Imperial adventures lay at the very edge of their lexicographic vision, in that Samuel Johnson, Thomas Sheridan, John Walker, William Perry and the others were very much concerned with consolidating the hold of a standardized 'High' English on the British Isles alone, where it still in places competed with several Celtic languages as well as a plethora of 'low' Cockney, Scots, Irish and other forms. Rather, they were concerned with stopping the general rot, about which however Johnson was largely pessimistic. Indeed, Johnson's pessimism grew with his realism as he worked.

In his *Plan for a Dictionary of the English Language* in 1747, he presented his aim quite simply as 'fixing' the language once and for all, in the quasi-Stoic belief that 'all change is of itself evil' and 'ought not to be hazarded but for evident advantage'. His view was echoed and enlarged by his sometime patron Lord Chesterfield who, in claiming to surrender his independence as a 'free-born British subject' to the new arbiter of English, observed (see note 6):

> I cannot help but think it a sort of disgrace to our nation, that hitherto we have had no such standard of our language (as the French); our dictionaries at present being more properly what our neighbours the Dutch and the Germans call theirs, WORD-BOOKS, than dictionaries in the superior sense of that title. All words, good and bad, are there jumbled indiscriminately together, insomuch that the injudicious reader may speak, and write as inelegantly, improperly, and vulgarly as he pleases, by and with the authority of one or other of our WORD-BOOKS . . . . The time for discrimination is now come. Toleration, adoption and naturalization have run their lengths. Good order and authority are now necessary.

By the time the dictionary appeared in 1755, however, Johnson himself had moved on to a different position. In his Preface, he sees his earlier ideas of 'fixing' the language as a futile effort as 'embalming' it, while 'to enchain syllables, and to lash the wind, are equally the undertakings of pride'. He altered his stance from the absolutism of halting perceived deterioration to simply stalling for time: 'If the changes that we fear be thus irresistible, what remains but to acquiesce with silence, as in the other insurmountable distresses of humanity? It remains that we retard what we cannot repel, that we palliate what we cannot cure.'

His pessimism contrasts sharply with the implicit optimism of the hard-word compilers, who believed they were doing their fellow-citizens a service by actively intervening in the enlargement of their mother tongue. It is typical of our attitudes to works of reference, however, that just as the variously deficient first dictionary of the Académie Française was nonetheless hailed as a monument to French culture, so Johnson's *Dictionary* – regardless of his own testimony – has been seen by many as having largely succeeded in 'fixing' the language. Greene notes, for example, that Johnson 'thinks stability in language is desirable, and of course he is perfectly right . . . Indeed, since the time of the publication of Johnson's Dictionary, the rate of linguistic change in written English, at least, has been notably retarded; and with modern methods of communication . . . the tendency of the language has been to standardization'.

This may or may not be so, depending upon what we mean by 'English'. If we mean the vast network of dialects and sociolects across the modern world, then clearly the language has long since escaped Johnson's net if it was ever in it. Nor is there any evidence that 'stability' in such a complex of natural instability is either desirable or possible. If, however, as Greene appears to imply, we mean the High Mode of English (using my terminology), then there may be truth in what he says. Certainly, the written standard is a relatively stable thing, and the spoken standards of the various élites of the English-using world today harmonize remarkably well. It should be clear, however, that when we talk about Standard English or *le bon français* we are not talking about 'low-level' widely-distributed things. What we are talking about, whether we discuss them in social or in educational terms, are artifacts of civilization designed in the seventeenth and eighteenth centuries through the slow consensus of the dominant classes for the purpose of inheriting the role of Neo-Latin. Inevitably, as a prominent element in that consensus, Johnson achieved part of his goal of 'retarding' the slide back to low modes of English.

English was, however, expanding across barriers that in the days of the Scholastics had been unknown and inconceivable. Trade and colonization were creating communities of English-users (and French- and Spanish-users, and so on) separated by thousands of miles from their homelands, living in enormously different environments and slowly creating distinct social systems. Such new communities could hardly keep their common language undifferentiated – and if they went to war with the mother country could hardly be expected to want to. As far as English was concerned, the mother country would fall as freely into the disdainful use of terms like 'Americanism' as it had been using 'Scotticism' and 'Irishism', while the colonials in their turn would staunchly assert that their usage was every bit as good as the dictatorial homeland's, if not indeed much better.

The seeds of counter-superiority (to cover any real or imagined slight) were planted early, in the case of the English language. Just before the outbreak of the American War of Independence, in the January 1774 issue of the *Royal American Magazine*, a writer signing himself 'an American' stated that 'the English language has been greatly improved in Britain within a century, but its highest perfection, with every other branch of human knowledge, is

DICTA'TOR, *n.* [L.] One who dictates; one who prescribes rules and maxims for the direction of others.
2. One invested with absolute authority. In ancient Rome, a magistrate, created in times of exigence and distress, and invested with unlimited power. He remained in office six months.
DICTATO'RIAL, *a.* Pertaining to a dictator; absolute; unlimited; uncontrollable.
2. Imperious; dogmatical; overbearing; as, the officer assumed a *dictatorial* tone.
DICTA'TORSHIP, *n.* The office of a dictator; the term of a dictator's office.
2. Authority; imperiousness; dogmatism.
Dryden.
DIC'TATORY, *a.* Overbearing; dogmatical. *Milton.*
DIC'TATURE, *n.* The office of a dictator; dictatorship.
2. Absolute authority; the power that dictates. *Tooke.*
DIC'TION, *n.* [L. *dictio,* from *dico,* to speak. Class Dg.]
Expression of ideas by words; style; manner of expression. *Dryden.*
DIC'TIONARY, *n.* [Fr. *dictionnaire*; It. *dizionario*; Sp. *diccionario*; from L. *dictio,* a word, or a speaking.]
A book containing the words of a language arranged in alphabetical order, with explanations of their meanings; a lexicon. *Johnson.*

Noah Webster, his aims, and what his Dictionary of 1828 says about dictators, diction and dictionaries.

Of his final lexicographical work Noah Webster observed:

> This Dictionary, like all others of the kind, must be left, in some degree, imperfect; for what individual is competent to trace to their source, and define in all their various applications, popular, scientific and technical, *sixty* or *seventy thousand words!* It satisfies my mind that I have done all that my health, my talents and my pecuniary means would enable me to accomplish. I present it to my fellow citizens, not with frigid indifference, but with my ardent wishes for their improvement and their happiness; and for the continued increase of the wealth, the learning, the moral and religious elevation of character, and the glory of my country.

perhaps reserved for this land of light and reason'.[9] He suggested that an American academy be set up to supervise this amelioration of English on transatlantic soil, but as in the mother country no such institution emerged, and it was left to yet another rugged individualist to become that institution.

Noah Webster (1758–1843) was a native of the state of Connecticut in New England.[10] He was not the first compiler of North American wordbooks, but he was certainly the first serious innovator in the United States, and like Sam Johnson has taken his place in the mythological pantheon of the English language. His long life spanned the formative years of the new republic and his attitude to language was at least as nationalistic as that of Vaugelas or Pope. A schoolmaster by profession, he began his publishing career with a little spelling book in 1783, the year the War of Independence ended, and a time when textbooks from the homeland were in short supply. He went on to produce a grammar and a reader, and for purposes of citation and exemplification drew upon American rather than British texts. His first dictionary appeared in 1806, but it was the wordbook that he brought out in 1828 at the age of 70 that has made him a household name in the United States. This was the radical *American Dictionary of the English Language.*

Webster disdained both British influence in general and Johnsonian influence in particular. In this he had his admirers, but he was not entirely popular in his lifetime with his fellow Americans, and hardly popular in Britain. In attacking what he saw as Johnson-worship he argued vehemently that 'by a minute examination of this subject' he could 'affirm that not a single page of Johnson's Dictionary is correct', and castigated Johnson on seven counts: that he incorporated certain Latin-derived 'barbarisms' from the old hard-word compilers, that he injudiciously quoted the inkpot terms of writers like Sir Thomas Browne, that at the other end of the scale he let in all sorts of 'low' and 'vulgar' words, that he did not adequately discriminate senses within words, that he failed to distinguish near-synonyms properly, that his quotations did not necessarily clarify the meanings of the words on whose behalf they were quoted, and that his etymologies were appallingly inaccurate.[11]

His objections of course reflect what many people firmly believed at the time and still believe: that there is some kind of True Way of compiling a dictionary, an ideal Platonic model against which faltering mortal efforts can be judged. Lexicographers and others who make such judgements, however, can often in due course be most humiliatingly hoisted with their own petard. Webster himself was hardly free of the sins that, in his nationalist enthusiasm, he attributed to the rival 'institution' across the waters.

Webster was in fact markedly similar in most ways to Johnson. He was concerned with clear definition, citations from 'good' writers, and very particularly with a consistent orthography. This last has been his most outstanding success, in that his spelling changes serve vividly to mark off American written and printed usage from traditional British.[12] Thus, he favoured 'magic' over 'magick' and has imposed his preference on the entire English-using world. In preferring 'color' to 'colour' he went back to the Latin norm, and in preferring 'theater' to 'theatre' he has gone by some kind of phonetic criterion that moves English away from French. Elsewhere, the Websterian approach has simplified the Latin inheritance by preferring 'fetus' to 'foetus' and 'medieval' to 'mediaeval' (spellings which may well one day become the international norm). Apart from these items of orthography, which are relatively few in terms of the mass of the language, the main thrust of his lexicographical declaration of independence was to propose 'good' American written sources as equal to 'good' British ones. In this, he marked a significant further stage in the evolution that we have traced from Latin as the High Language to the High Modes of the languages of the post-Renaissance nation-states.[13] Where, up till then, the emerging High Modes were *mono*centric, one per language community and linked with one capital city, one social class, one royal court and one set of writers, Webster made it clear that they could just as easily be *poly*centric. There could very well be two or more High Modes, with two or more capital cities, social élites and sets of writers vying for primacy if possible but certainly *equality*. It is a state of affairs which the old European nation-states have found hard to accept. They have been unwilling to concede their centrality, just as they are only now beginning to notice the consequences of there being more people using their languages (especially in the cases of English and Spanish) *outside* the metropolitan state than within its borders.

Two other points, however, remain to be noted in the career and aftermath of Noah Webster. First, he was catering to the needs of a new kind of territory, rapidly expanding and hungry for educational guidance. His dictionary was not just a word-bible for the new frontier; it was also the repository of other equally valuable information in appendices like chronologies, weights and measures, currencies and a list of all the post offices in the Union. In this practice, he fostered the now venerable encyclopedic element in American lexicography and encouraged the international practice of cramming all sorts of extra little lists in back of the master list that justified the book in the first place.

Secondly, simply by living, doing his work and bequeathing it as a commercial inheritance to the 300,000,000 people that he confidently foresaw as one day living in the United States, Webster helped create a rival to the academies: the publishing house as arbiter of language.

The 'Webster' dictionaries of G. and C. Merriam inherited his mantle where no company or institution inherited the mantle of Johnson. Although other dictionary publishers sprang up in the United States to challenge the pride of place of Merriam–Webster of Springfield, Massachusetts, they have only scratched its prestige slightly. Their books will sell, because the United States is a land designed by history to buy dictionaries and other such works, but the centrality of Springfield is as secure in the 1980s as ever it was. In this, the promise of the print revolution of the fifteenth century has been fulfilled: it has indeed been possible for the developers of an industrial and commercial process, that is not dependent on church, university or national academy but is rather dedicated to the idea of popular education, to stand squarely alongside such prestige-laden names as Oxford and the Académie Française.

13

Reference and revolution: the encyclopedia proper

As we have now seen, the development of High Modes in the leading languages of Western Europe related to certain kinds of social and educational élites and helped to create such powerful concepts and trends as the standardization of languages, the deification of 'good usage' and 'good taste', and the promulgation of ideas of 'correct' normative grammar.

These are all, effectively, aspects of social engineering; the people who promoted such social tools were conscious and deliberate in what they did and, as well as concerning themselves with elegance and culture, were aware that the nation-states to which they belonged were in fierce competition for such spoils as overseas territories, monopoly markets for their goods, and – ultimately – imperial positions reminiscent of Rome. One other element should, however, be added to the picture, and that is the growth of rational humanism, out of which an increasingly well-defined concept of 'scientific method' was developing thoughout the seventeenth and eighteenth centuries. Although we cannot forget the other factors just listed, it is this new humanistic-cum-scientific rationalism that began to move centre-stage as far as works of reference were concerned.

Throughout the decades around the turn of the sixteenth into the seventeenth century a wide range of 'universal' and 'technical' compilations were produced in Western Europe.[1] These were published both by secular individuals and groups and by religious organizations such as the Jesuits of Trévoux, and tended to swing between what today we would call a 'dictionary' on the one hand and an 'encyclopedia' on the other.[2] In effect, it was extremely difficult for compilers at that time to make a clearcut distinction between the two genres. Some modern scholars, such as Starnes and Noyes in their criticisms of Nathaniel Bailey, have looked back at those times and asserted that the distinction *should* have been made, but this is little more than hindsight and, I would suggest, a failure to note that in fact we have still not succeeded in distinguishing sharply between the two. Indeed, it may not be possible to do so. On this point, Allen Walker Read observes (1976:713f):

> The distinction between a dictionary and an encyclopaedia is easy to state but difficult to carry out in a practical way: a dictionary explains words, whereas an encyclopaedia explains things. Because words achieve their usefulness by referring to things, however, it is difficult to construct a dictionary without considerable attention to the objects and abstractions designated.

Many people nowadays do, nonetheless, seek to keep the two genres distinct. In their minds, presumably, there is something like the simple hyponymic model in figure 5. When the term 'encyclopedia' came into common use, however, in the period under discussion, this was far from the common assumption. Thus, Ephraim Chambers produced in 1728 a *Cyclopaedia, or Universal Dictionary of Arts and Sciences*, and when Denis Diderot, following the model of Chambers, published his own epoch-making compilation just after the mid-point of the eighteenth century he called it *L'Encyclopédie, ou dictionnaire raisonné des sciences, des arts et des métiers* ('The Encyclopedia, or Rational Dictionary of the Sciences, the Arts and the Professions'). These were both the first books to use the word 'encyclopedia' (or some variant of it) to describe a specific work of reference rather than a general education system, and also the first to organize their information in a format that we today would accept as 'truly' encyclopedic. In *their* minds, however, there must have been something like the simple hyponymic model in figure 6, which clashes sharply with the preceding one.

Fig. 5 Modelling works of reference (first version)

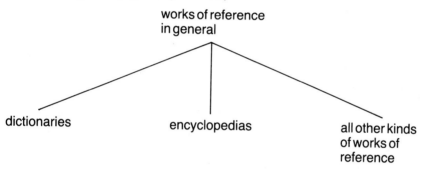

Fig. 6 Modelling works of reference (second version)

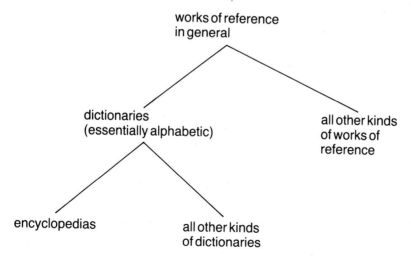

There are probably many people today who subscribe to both models simultaneously (without giving the matter much thought): we agree that dictionaries and encyclopedias are different things (model 1), but at the same time we may accept unreflectingly that an encyclopedia is also a kind of dictionary (model 2). We therefore also accept without too much distress that a 'strictly' encyclopedic book may be called, say, a Dictionary of Music or even that a book about a language could be called, say, an Encyclopedia of English. The probability that these two models co-occur in many minds is an interesting example of the semantic blur that affects much of vocabulary (and that a lexicographer has to contend with all the time in the effort to define precisely).

The simplest way of resolving the tension seems to be to accept the way in which the early encyclopedists handled the matter. Chambers, for example, saw his work as 'containing an explication of *the terms*, and an account of *the things* signified therein' (my italics); that is, he knew that he was legitimately concerned with both words and what words refer to (although the two should not be confused). Bailey was equally aware that he had to define words, but also that from time to time he had to reach out into the world in order to show what words do. It is a perennial dilemma, however, in lexicography that limits have to be established so as *not* to turn every dictionary into an open-ended review of the universe and its contents (and so let it become a medieval *summa* or *speculum*). In this dilemma we in fact work along a continuum rather than within strictly separate containers, where one extreme is words and words alone, and the other is referents and referents alone, as in figure 7.

Fig. 7 A cline from the dictionary to the encyclopedia

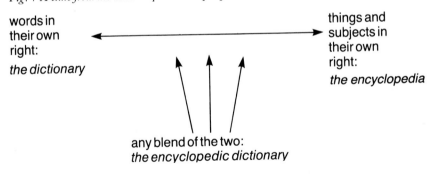

Be that as it may, Ephraim Chambers in 1728 elected to call his 'universal dictionary' a 'cyclopaedia', no doubt because the *enkýklios paideía*, like the *universitas*, has always implied totality. Like his predecessor Scalich in Basel in the sixteenth century, he may not have intended to establish a new generic term, but in effect he did. His work was both commercially successful and educationally influential. In 1749 the French publisher André le Breton was sufficiently impressed to want to make a translation of it, and to this end approached the writer Denis Diderot, much as some British booksellers were approaching Johnson at about the same time to undertake the definitive English national dictionary. Diderot found the idea interesting and enlisted tha aid of a friend, the mathematician Jean d'Alembert, but there is no sense in which what they finally produced could be called a translation of the *Cyclopaedia*. Le Breton must often have been disturbed by what began to emerge from his original proposition because, in the words of Robert Niklaus, it became 'an important organ of radical and revolutionary opinion' which would 'strike a resounding blow against reactionary forces in church and state' (Nicklaus 1976:723; see also Collison 1964:Ch. 4). It did indeed cause an upheaval, and was attacked by the Jesuits and for a time suppressed by the king. As a consequence, the *Encyclopédie* must be listed as one of the major intellectual forces that impelled France towards its Revolution in 1789, and therefore as one of the most politically significant reference books in human history.

In its final form, the *Encyclopédie* consisted of 35 folio volumes published between 1751 and 1780, the first 28 under the editorial care of Diderot himself. It featured articles by leading radical thinkers and reflected its chief editor's own revolutionary enthusiasms. Its incendiary qualities, however, co-existed with a creative and almost prophetic genius, in that a century before Louis Braille and Charles Darwin Diderot was speculating about teaching the blind through their sense of touch and about the possibility of biological evolution.

Matoré points out, as he did with the dictionary of the Académie, that Diderot's *Encyclopédie*, however seminal, was still enormously difficult to produce and replete with errors of fact, repetitions, plagiarisms and articles that did not knit together properly. In effect, the various strong-minded contributors tended to do their own thing to such an extent that the ensemble lost the shape originally planned for it. Nonetheless, as Matoré also points out, the *Encyclopédie* marked a special turning point in the history of works of reference. Certainly its editors and contributors were as period- and culture-bound as any compiler before or after them, but they gave to this kind of work a new direction and an emphasis which had no real precedent. Whereas earlier compilations had on the whole been backward-looking and conservationist, animated by a classical worldview and inclined to treat all knowledge as within an already delineated circle, Diderot's work was future-directed and innovative (indeed, aggressively so), animated by the idea of social progress and the desirability of change. Its worldview placed no necessary limits upon human knowledge, and whereas most earlier works are pervaded by an assumption of a divinely sanctioned order, this new work was sustained by a radical humanism not unlike that of the philosophers of ancient Greece, imbued however with ideas of social equality and the perfectibility of both society and the individual that would probably have intrigued the ancients.

It is no surprise that the Jesuits found the *Encyclopédie* alarming, for it challenged the fundamentals of their belief system and offered the world a free-thinker's alternative to heaven-and-hell salvationism. As a consequence, the *Encyclopédie* belongs with such other eighteenth-century trail-blazers of radical humanism as the American Declaration of Independence in 1776 and Thomas Paine's *The Rights of Man* in 1791. It did not simply inform; it incited.

In Collison's view (1964: 4f), Diderot was profiting from and extending an odd tendency that is built into both official and individual responses to major works of reference:

> Encyclopaedias have in truth long been convenient vehicles for unpopular or advanced opinions and ideas, and have long been the bugbear of censorship. While a monograph advocating seditious or irreligious or treasonable ideas might easily be seized before it left the press, the discovery of similar thoughts slipped in to various articles in an encyclopaedia might very well be delayed until copies had been distributed too numerously for their withdrawal ever to be achieved – a point of which Diderot took full advantage. Even when discovered, the offending encyclopaedia always appears to have enjoyed a privilege of comparative immunity that no individual author would have gained.

He suggests that in effect both Church and state have from time to time, happily or unhappily, 'winked at' the revolutionary implications in encyclopedias, and attributes this peculiar response to a kind of 'mystique' possessed by such works. Following the argument developed in earlier chapters, I would suggest that such unexpectedly tender-hearted treatment may arise, if it has indeed arisen regularly, because of the reverence that developed in the early Middle Ages, when such works had a quasi-scriptural or classical quality about them, together with the twilight position that works of reference have had between textbooks on the one hand and pamphlets and newspapers on the other.

Lexicographers and encyclopedists are not however generally disturbers of the peace and inciters to mutiny, and the next development after Diderot was much less inflammatory in its tone. Sponsored by a self-styled 'Society of Gentlemen' in Scotland, it was the work of a team or editorial board rather than of a single inspired *philosophe*. In the 1760s in the city of Edinburgh, Andrew Bell, an engraver, Collin Macfarquhar, a printer, and William Smellie, a printer and scholar, began work on a project that was to establish the word 'encyclopedia' solidly from then on as a generic term in its own right. The result of their collaboration, a three-volume work that came out between 1768 and 1771, was entitled the *Encyclopaedia Britannica, or a Dictionary of Arts and Sciences, compiled upon a New Plan.* Smellie, a friend of the poet Robert Burns, took the by now well-established procedures of Chambers and Diderot and shaped them into a work of rational humanism consisting of 75 long treatises interspersed with numerous shorter entries, many of them cross-referred to the larger articles. Some of the long items covered more than a 100 pages each, while some of the shorter ran to only a line. Collison argues that 'the key' to the success of the *Britannica* was 'the retention of the single alphabetical sequence' (Collison 1976:790). This is quite likely, but by adhering firmly to this sequence successive editors of the encyclopedia were forced to juxtapose the long and the detailed with the short and incomplete in an unevenness that has haunted such works into very recent times indeed.

In retrospect, the first *Britannica* has a crude and quaint look about it. Like Pliny, it mixed fact and fancy, science and supposition. Its practicality is demonstrated by a 39-page article on the farrier's art, the curing of the diseases of horses; its radicalism is shown by an illustrated article on midwifery so honest and direct that many saw it as a public scandal; its traditionalism, however, appears in a detailed discussion of the nature and contents of Noah's Ark, and its quirkiness in the assertion that the use of tobacco would dry the brain up into a little black lump. Smellie worked under considerable pressure to bring it out quickly and admitted plagiarism – 'With pastepot and scissors I composed it!', he is said to have announced in his cups (Kogan 1958:14).

Without knowing it, however, the Society of Gentlemen in Scotland launched one of the abiding institutions of the English language. Its history has been complex and controversial, and has drifted from total commercial independence in the hands of publishers like Archibald Constable and Adam Black in the nineteenth century to links with the universities of Cambridge and then Chicago in the twentieth. Since 1771 it has gone through 15 distinct revisions (often transformations) of varying quality, and in 1943 completed a slow drift since around 1900 from being a strictly British to becoming an internationalized American publication with its headquarters in Chicago. Praised for its humanism, relevance and comprehensiveness, condemned for its commercialism, its failures to keep abreast of the times, and its inaccuracies, it has in the course of its many editions received contributions from many of the great names of the modern world: John Stuart Mill, Walter Scott, T.H. Huxley, Peter Mark Roget, Matthew Arnold, Leon Trotsky, Henry Ford, H.L. Mencken, G.B. Shaw, Sigmund Freud, Harry Houdini, Marie Curie, Niels Bohr, Ralph Bunche, Linus Pauling, Jacob Bronowski, and many others.[3]

Himself a contributor to the radically revised 15th Edition in the 1970s, Robert Collison observes about the invitation to write for a work of this kind (1964:227):

> There is something in the very nature of an encyclopaedia that calls forth, on many occasions, something bigger than the man – be he writer or editor. The request to write an article for an encyclopaedia becomes a challenge for all but the worst hack-writers. There is something in the discipline imposed that confronts the specialist with an interesting problem. Is it possible to condense the salient points of his subject in readable fashion in only a few hundred words?

The *Encyclopaedia Britannica* reflects not only its inheritance from earlier encyclopedias but also a particularly Scottish enthusiasm for self-improvement that goes back at least to the Reformation and is linked with the advent of the printing press and the decline of monolithic religious authority. It is the 'home university kit' par excellence, whether or not it is hawked from door to door, tied in with the sale of newspapers, comes out all at once or in weekly parts, is bought in one payment or by instalment. The first edition lacked the fire of Diderot's *Encyclopédie*, but in the long run the *Britannica* has been just as revolutionary, and even more successful in making some kind of *enkýklios paideía* open to all, either through personal ownership or in a kind of social conspiracy with the public library systems of many modern nation-states.

The Chambers–Diderot–Bell line may be regarded as the strongest encyclopedic tradition in modern times, but it is by no means the only one and has powerful competition. Out of the variety of arts-and-sciences reference books in Western Europe at the turn of the seventeenth and eighteenth centuries there developed a parallel tradition of 'lexikons' in the German states that culminated at the start of the nineteenth century in the *Konversationslexikon* of Renatus Löbel (where *konversation* implies what one needs to do well in the polite drawing-room society of the new German middle classes).

In 1808, the unfinished work of the bankrupt Löbel was taken over by an industrious and innovative publisher called Friedrich Arnold Brockhaus (1772–1823), who in effect with this one work founded a family dynasty of encyclopedias that is still prospering. The Löbel–Brockhaus encyclopedia is typically both extensive and intensive, its information organized as compactly as possible and its vast range of entries interwoven by means of a network of cross-references. As an example of its style, the 1928–35 *Der Grosse Brockhaus*, for example, had some 200,000 articles contributed by over 1,000 authors, and rather like the Oxford dictionaries there has been a whole family of books: *Der Grosse Brockhaus, Volks-Brockhaus, Sprach-Brockhaus, Neue-Brockhaus*, and so forth. Of this tradition, Collison notes that 'whereas the *Britannica* model has prevailed throughout the English-speaking world, *Brockhaus* has been the model for most of the encyclopaedias prepared in countries in which English is not widely spoken.'[4]

It is clear from the foregoing that throughout the eighteenth century truly 'modern' works of reference were coming into existence. This is not to say, however, that even at this 'late' date the old uncertainties were banished. Right into the nineteenth century it was still by no means definite that an encyclopedia must be alphabetic (and it still is not definite today). Diderot's volumes were alphabetic, but in the period between 1782 and 1832 – a time of great turbulence in France – a second version known as the *Encyclopédie méthodique* was brought out, which was thematic. Additionally, in England at much the same time the *littérateur* Samuel Taylor Coleridge was involved in planning an *Encyclopaedia Metropolitana* to compete with the success of the Scots, and this also was conceived thematically. It failed, however, to establish itself.[5]

The bulk of such reference books was, however, by now alphabetic, and it is tempting to wonder, as Matoré seems to suggest in his study of French lexicography, whether the growing vitality of alphabetization owed something to the spirit of *égalité* that was in the air. He quotes Ernst Cassirer as pointing out that in using the alphabet one avoids hierarchies, superordination and subordination. In a climate of class tensions, this may have seemed an eminently sensible idea: all letters from A to Z are equal and yet still orderly. The *philosophes* and their friends had no more taste for higher and lower in taxonomy than they had for higher and lower in the estates of France. To the lamp-post with all élites.[6]

The development of styles of compilation in the Western world is a unity, but within that unity national tastes have clearly differed. As a consequence, it is unusual in the chronicles of English lexicography to find much space devoted to encyclopedias and how they are made, while in French studies encyclopedias and dictionaries are treated as intimately related. At the same time, neither of these mainline traditions has developed a clearcut generic term to cover the compilation of all such works of reference, and as a result I have been left without such a term throughout this book so far – as well as with the need to talk about 'works of reference' in order to cover all the formats that interest me. It is no doubt clear when I do this that I have not consciously been including the history of such things as warehouse inventories, street and telephone directories, military manuals, ship and railway timetables and so on within my schema. Nor, however, have I been consciously excluding them, for they too are significant artifacts, much of what I have been saying relates to them, and it would indeed be salutary if we had some terms that could cover them too. We do *not*, however, and my central interest remains works that can be classified as in some sense 'lexicographic'.

But the problem remains. No matter how I organize this review, certain encyclopedists will insist that their work is not in any proper sense lexicography, while certain lexicographers will argue that their generic term ought not to be extended to cover something which is not centrally concerned with lexis. I sympathize with both points of view, but it is nevertheless patently clear that the two great genres of educational reference have been intertwined throughout their histories, and that in countries like France and the United States such hybrids as encyclopedic dictionaries have been produced for years and will go on being produced. It is also a relevant fact that many of the publishing houses that produce one type of book also produce the other (or have done so at some time in their pasts).

From all of this, therefore, I would conclude that the term 'lexicography' *can* legitimately be stretched to cover both ends of the continuum that I discussed at the start of this chapter, in a similar way to the extension of the word 'politics' from the power-plays of nations to such areas as 'university politics' or 'hospital politics'. Consequently, I would like to propose a pair of terms (on the analogy of macro-economics and micro-economics, etc.) that could be useful in studying the world of reference materials:

1 *micro-lexicography*, which deals with the world of words and the wordbook proper (which in most instances is an alphabetic dictionary)
2 *macro-lexicography*, which shades out into the world of things and subjects, and centres on compendia of knowledge (which in most instances are encyclopedias, which in most instances nowadays are also alphabetic)

If one wanted to be truly scandalous, one could even propose that, on certain occasions, indexers, compilers of certain kinds of usage books and grammars, framers of the various directories and catalogues we use and of certain kinds of timetables and schedules have a 'macro-lexicographic' aspect to their work (whether or not one would want to call them 'lexicographers' and offer them membership in a very élite guild indeed).

14

Thematic lexicography:
word order and world order

Some historians regard Francis Bacon (1561–1626) as the first outstanding exponent of the scientific method, while others see him as the last great Renaissance thinker. It is probably safe, therefore, to think of this lawyer, courtier, statesman, essayist, rationalist and experimenter as a key transitional figure in human history. Certainly from the angle of vision of this study he was crucial, for he wanted to re-organize all of human knowledge.[1]

Bacon appears to have wanted to give mankind back what it had lost through the fall of Adam, and to this end proposed an *Instauratio Magna* or 'great renewal'. This was not conceived as a *summa* of all truth or as a *speculum* reflecting the absolute, but rather as a fallible human attempt to see shape in nature. In essence, therefore, it is what we today would call an exercise in model-making. His plan was for a 130-part hierarchical study that would first divide into three main areas (external nature, man, and man's action upon external nature), then into ranges of sub-areas and sub-sub-areas until everything was adequately covered. It is in effect prototypical of the great branching taxonomies of botany, zoology and other sciences that in due course began to shape our way of seeing nature. Following Collison, we can lay out his general schema as figure 8.[2]

The schema is new, in a rational humanist way, but is also old in that the influence of the liberal arts and Pliny can be detected in it. Bacon was unfortunately never able to take his plan much beyond the drawing-board, due to a charge of bribery while in the king's service, a period imprisoned in the Tower of London and various other tribulations. Of everything that he had hoped to accomplish we are left with only three treatises on the scientific method written between 1605 and 1623, the most famous and influential of which was the *Novum organum* of 1620. Of his views, Richard Gregory observes (1981: 235):

> Bacon saw science as an instrument giving power to men. Immensely ambitious . . . he rejected Greek philosophy as 'the talk of idle old men to raw young fellows'. His principal objection was that, as he saw it, the Greeks made few useful discoveries. Bacon stressed the potential usefulness of science, for medicine, for navigation, for all kinds of industry. He might even be said to be a martyr to his practical science, for he died of a chill caught on Hampstead Heath, after experimentally refrigerating a chicken with snow. He did not see science as important only for applications to industry but saw methodical experiment as the principal and perhaps the only way to discover the nature of things.

Fig. 8 Francis Bacon's taxonomy of knowledge

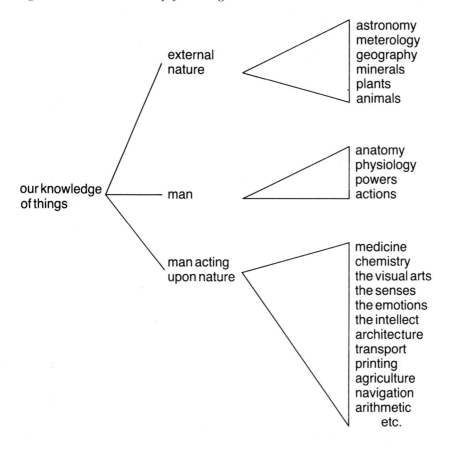

Of his actual taxonomic activities, Collison (1976: 781), in his review of encyclopedias, notes that Bacon

> had ensured that the encyclopaedists would have a comprehensive outline of the scope of human knowledge that would operate as a checklist and prevent their omitting whole fields of human thought and endeavour. Bacon had so profoundly altered the editorial policy of encyclopaedists that even 130 years later Diderot gratefully acknowledged his debt in the prospectus (1750) of *L'Encyclopédie*. Because every later encyclopaedia was influenced by Diderot's work, the guidance of Bacon still plays its part today.

There is something intriguing about Collison's use of the word 'checklist' in praising the contribution of Bacon to encyclopedism. Clearly, Collison does not see the Baconian schema as a *primary* way of organizing knowledge, because it is alphabetic ordering that centrally interests him. Bacon, on the other hand, could never have conceived alphabetic order as the means by which the *enkýklios paideía* could be handled. Like the Scholastics, he would have found it far too fragmentative. Collison, however, sees Bacon's schema as inherently *secondary* to the alphabetic mode: you check your work against it to see that you have got everything in, and so, in a sense, Bacon is concealed behind the alphabet. It is a curious situation that we shall encounter again.

Bacon was a theorist and philosopher, not a pedagogue with practical classroom needs and certainly not a teacher of languages. His work is therefore somewhat removed from the *vocabularia* of the Middle Ages and the *vulgaria* of the Renaissance that, thematically ordered, served to help students learn their Latin words.[3] In an intriguing way, however, the two streams were to flow together and become educationally useful only a few years after Bacon's untimely death.

'A 'vulgary' (sadly, the word never caught on in English) was essentially a Renaissance forerunner to the kinds of bilingual phrasebooks that travellers are encouraged to take with them and consult when they move in foreign parts. Thus, the 1520 *Vulgaria* of Robert Wittinton had a list of themes, and Latin and English sentences that translated each other running side by side within those themes, reminiscent of the tablets of ancient Akkad. Such aids, not quite wordbooks and not quite grammars, flourished variously in Western Europe and led in 1611 to a Latin-to-Spanish manual compiled by William Bathe, an Irish Jesuit working in Spain.[4]

Bathe's book was entitled the *Ianua linguarum* ('The Gate of Tongues'), of which a Latin-to-English version appeared in London in 1615. The work consisted of some 5,000 items arranged in 12 themes within which the words were further fitted into 1,200 illustrative sentences which also served – typically of the tradition – to inculcate certain elements of Christian morality. Bathe's creation was a commercial success, continuing through nine editions to 1645, but had of course no link with anything Bacon and Europe's early scientists might have been doing.

The link, however, was made by the great Moravian educator Johann Amos Komensky, often known as Comenius (1592–1670), who spent much of his life in exile because of the persecution of his sect, the Bohemian Brethren, within the Holy Roman Empire.[5] While studying in Heidelberg, Comenius read the works of Francis Bacon, and in the words of John Sadler, 'returned home convinced that the millennium could be attained with the aid of science'. Both clergyman and teacher, Comenius believed that universal education was the key to peace and even the creation of a confederation of the world's nations. He advocated that all children should receive schooling both in their native languages and in Latin as the international medium of culture, but had serious reservations about the rigid traditions inherited from the Schoolmen.[6] He proposed instead that pedagogy should 'follow the footsteps of nature', taking careful note of how children's minds work rather than insisting upon such things as the rote learning of grammar; Latin could be better studied, he argued, through the things around the learner than through conjugations and declensions. To this end he built on Bathe's foundation and Bacon's inspiration and in 1631 brought out a book wryly entitled the *Ianua linguarum reserata* ('The Gate of Tongues Unlocked'). This work appeared first in Latin and German, then later in the same year in London in Latin,

Francis Bacon

Although he saw himself as the herald of a new age of reason and experimentation, Francis Bacon could be most traditional in suggesting that the best was behind rather than ahead of the human race, and in quoting ancients to justify his own arguments:

And as for Virgil's verses, though it pleased him to brave the world in taking to the Romans the art of empire, and leaving to others the arts of subjects; yet so much is manifest, that the Romans never ascended to that height of empire till the time they had ascended to the height of other arts; for in the time of the two first Caesars, which had the art of government in greatest perfection, there lived the best poet, Virgilius Maro; the best historiographer, Titus Livius; the best antiquary, Marcus Varro; and the best, or second best orator, Marcus Cicero, that to the memory of man are known . . .

This only will I add, that learned men forgotten in states are like the images of Cassius and Brutus in the funeral of Junia; of which not being represented, as many others were, Tacitus saith, *Eo ipso praefulgebant, quod non visebantur* [they had the preeminence over all – in being left out].

(from *Of the Advancement of Learning*, Book I, 1605)

French and English all together. In the course of a few years it spread with improvements and variations throughout Western and Central Europe, contributing to the fame of its compiler and exerting considerable influence on the course of language teaching.

The content and method remained basically the same as Bathe's, with such minor but interesting changes as the gradation of sentences according to difficulty. The new *Ianua* had 100 chapters and just over 1,000 illustrative sentences. The numbering of the following thematic list does not follow Comenius precisely, but will serve to show that 20 main topics underlay his 100 original divisions:

1 the origin of the world
2 the elements, the firmament, fire and meteors
3 waters, earths, stones, metals
4 trees, fruits, herbs, shrubs
5 animals
6 man and his body
7 the qualities or accidents of the body
8 diseases, ulcers and wounds
9 the senses (external and internal)
10 mind, the will and the affections (emotions)
11 the mechanical arts
12 the house and its parts
13 marriage and the family
14 civic and state economy
15 grammar, dialectic, rhetoric
16 arithmetic and geometry
17 ethics
18 games
19 death and burial
20 Providence, God and the angels

The resemblance to Bacon's schema is striking, while their common debt to the ancient classical compilers is also easily discerned. The work was a success, but Comenius was not himself satisfied with it, and in 1657 supplemented it with a rather different book, the *Orbis sensualium pictus* ('The Illustrated World of Things we can Feel'), a compilation that is ancestor to a whole host of pictorial textbooks, workbooks, encyclopedias and dictionaries that depend heavily on illustration. Comenius considered that clearly delineated sense impressions lay at the heart of all sound learning and as a consequence emphasized the value of visual help. In a serious sense, therefore, he was the precursor of all later techniques of incorporating artistic illustration, photography, slide presentations, films and television documentaries into education.[7]

The *Orbis* had 151 chapters, ranging from the Creation to the Last Judgement. Its especial innovation lay in the way that an illustration – a composite cut or an engraving – served as the focus of each chapter, with each

JOH. AMOS COMENII
ORBIS SEN-
SUALIUM PICTUS.

Hoc est,

Omnium fundamentalium in mundo rerum, & in
vitâ actionum ;

Pictura & Nomenclatura.

Editio auctior & emendatior ; cum Titulorum juxtà atq;
Vocabulorum Indice.

Die sichtbare Welt.

Das ist :

Aller vornehmsten Welt-Dinge / und Lebens-
Verrichtungen /

Vorbildung und Benamung.

Aufs neue aufgelegt/ und an viel Orten verbessert ; neben einem
Titel- und Wörter-Register.

Cum Gratia & Privil. Sac. Cæs. Majestatis, & Sereniss.
Electoris Saxonici.

NORIBERGÆ,
Sumtibus MICHAELIS & JOANNIS FRIDERICI ENDTERI,
ANNO Salutis cIↄ Iↄc LXIV.

The frontispiece of the Orbis sensualium pictus *of John Amos Comenius, first published in*
1657.

The Study, *in the* Orbis sensualium pictus, *with Latin on the left, German on the right, and numbers relating picture to text.*

major item in the picture numbered. The sentences in the chapter in their turn had numbers, which correlated precisely with those in the picture. Thus, a picture of a study with its numbered parts corresponded to the sentence: 'The Study, 1, is a place where a Student, 2, apart from Men, sitteth alone, addicted to his Studies, whilst he readeth Books, 3, . . .'

Comenius here applied the correlational power of numbers as effectively as the medieval glossarists had learned to apply the ordering power of the alphabet. This innovation where numbers-placed-in-pictures are matched with numbers-placed-in-lists has been systematically exploited from the time of Comenius onward, in all manner of books – but is particularly strong in the German tradition of the Duden *Bildwörterbücher*. Owing much to the Bathe–Comenius tradition, the Duden books go into immense referential detail about such things as atomic reactors, navigation, offset printing, department stores, birds, art, gliding and fencing. In looking at a modern Duden book (in this instance, for convenience, the 1960 *English Duden, a Pictorial Dictionary*) we can see how surprisingly little the themes have changed over the centuries. This particular Duden list has 15 major topics (enormously subdivided in a style that Bacon would have approved) as follows:[8]

1 atom, universe, earth	9 office, bank and stock exchange
2 man and home	10 state and city
3 horticulture, agriculture, forestry	11 travel and recreation
4 hunting and fishing	12 sport
5 crafts and trade	13 entertainment and music
6 industry	14 science, religion and art
7 printing and allied trades	15 animals and plants
8 transport and communications	

God and His angels have been displaced in favour of more directly observable data, and the topics are somewhat reordered and adapted to modern concerns, but the structuring in essence is much the same as before, beginning with the universe in which *Homo sapiens* finds himself embedded, and then branching out into what he has done about it. Are such cosmic orderings all so similar because they reflect a universal way of responding to what is 'out there' and what we do about it 'in here', or are they the result of later compilers (wittingly or otherwise) copying and adapting what went before them? Would a Pawnee or a Martian do it all very differently, as the linguistic-cum-anthropological researches of Edward Sapir and Benjamin Lee Whorf have suggested?[9] It is a point worth bearing in mind as we proceed, and one to which we can return in due course.

Of the double achievement of Comenius, Starnes observes (Starnes and Noyes 1946: 208) that

> there were current before Comenius all the elements that are found in his *Ianua* and *Orbis* – the tested topics under which the words were grouped, the wide range, implying universality, the use of sentences to give coherence to word lists, and the arrangement in parallel columns with the vernacular first. But no other book, as far as I know, exhibited the particular combination of these elements that is found in the manuals of the Moravian bishop and educator.

At much the same time as Comenius was producing his books, another bishop was engaged on a thematic project that has also echoed down the centuries. This was John Wilkins, a founder member of the Royal Society of London, who in 1668 produced a detailed and abstruse work entitled *An Essay Towards a Real Character and a Philosophical Language*.[10] Wilkins, like many of his colleagues, was interested in improving English as a medium for science, but in his *Essay* went much further. Here he proposed the ultimate avoidance – even transcendence – of natural language in favour of a kind of intellectual shorthand. He advocated a kind of Platonic list of universal concepts that could be expressed in a 'real character' or actual script that related to 'things' in the world. He conceived of 'things' as sufficiently discrete as to be listable in an ideography of their own, and was convinced that such an ideo-graphy, when properly devised, would be superior to all natural languages and their current writing systems, of which he despaired: 'It cannot be denied, but that the variety of Letters is an appendix to the Curse of Babel, namely, the multitude and variety of language.'

In the *Essay*, Wilkins discusses such concepts as 'universal philosophy' and 'philosophical grammar', demonstrating a community of interest with such contemporary abstract theorists as René Descartes, John Locke and Wilhelm Leibniz as well as with a considerable list of later thinkers: Etienne de Condillac, George Boole, Gottlob Frege, Bertrand Russell, Ludwig Wittgenstein, Rudolf Carnap and Noam Chomsky, all of whom have variously been interested in systems of symbolic logic, or atoms of logic, or otherwise supposed that a calculus of language does (or ought to) exist. Wilkins, therefore, belongs not only in a twilight zone of lexicography but also in a powerful tradition of logic and philosophy in his own right.

In order to arrive at an ultimate list of basic concepts, Wilkins created a taxonomy that is strikingly similar to those that we have been discussing, so much so that one must suppose him to have been familiar not only with Bacon but also with Bathe and Comenius. His categories of nature, in a somewhat simplified and up-dated form, are as follows:

 1 God
 2 the elements, meteors, stones, metals
 3 planets, herbs, flowers, shrubs, trees
 4 animals, fishes, birds, beasts
 5 parts of bodies
 6 quantity, magnitude, space, measure
 7 quality (of natural power, habit, manners, the senses, diseases)
 8 action (spiritual, corporeal, in motion, in operations)
 9 relations (in the family, regarding possessions, and provisions)
10 public relationships (civil, judiciary, naval, military, ecclesiastical)

My simplifications and translations into modern idiom have been for the sake of convenience of presentation. Thus, where Wilkins has used the term 'oeconomical' I have used 'family', since his term meant at that time 'domestic' or 'pertaining to the home' rather than what we today understand by 'economical' or 'economic'. His cosmic scheme has an index, which is an interesting innovation in itself, and in this index certain basic devices are used to send the reader to the right category in Wilkins's system. The index entry for 'planet', for example, carries the code W.II.3, which means that the inquirer should go for information about 'planet' to W for 'world', part II, sub-part 3, in order to get it. Similarly, 'posterity' is coded as RO.I.I.0, which is the appropriate place for 'Relations Oeconomical'.

The scheme is complex but logical. Though expressed in English, it was intended ultimately to be organized in Real Character, a very alien-looking system of ideograms. The sheer abstruseness of the work militated against its success and general dissemination, but despite its apparent eccentricity and impracticality it has not been without influence, especially in the further development of thematic lexicography.

This development, however, has not been even and has to a great extent been eclipsed by the increasing success of the alphabetic mode. We have seen that various encyclopedic compilations were proposed or actually completed in the thematic mode, and from time to time small 'synonymies'[11] and other works on principles of word association came out in the succeeding years but in general terms the alternative to alphabetization was in the doldrums until the middle of the nineteenth century, when a momentous development occurred – indeed, one which for most people is the only serious example of a thematic wordbook. This was Peter Mark Roget's *Thesaurus of English Words and Phrases,* which was published by Longman in 1852.[12] Roget acknowledges few serious precedents to his work, but prominent among these was the *Essay* of Bishop Wilkins.

It is not surprising that Roget should have both known about and appreciated the work of Wilkins, because for 22 years Roget was the secretary of the Royal Society. He regretted that the idea outlined in the *Essay* was 'too abstruse and recondite for practical application', and set out himself to do virtually the same as Wilkins. Certainly he shared the same dream, for in his own preface he says:[13]

> The probable result of the construction of such a language (as Wilkins proposed) would be its inevitable adoption by every civilized nation; thus realizing that splendid aspiration of the philanthropists – the establishment of a Universal Language. However utopian such a project may appear to the present generation, and however abortive may have been the former endeavours of Bishop Wilkins and others to realize it, its accomplishment is surely not beset with greater difficulties than have impeded the progress to many other beneficial objects.

Later users and commentators might recommend the *Thesaurus* for crossword puzzles and see it only as a casual word-finder, but Roget aimed originally at a different target: at scientists in general, at philologists, at translators, historians, lexicographers, writers, speakers and indeed all thoughtful humanists, in the explicit hope of contributing towards 'a golden age of union and harmony among the several nations and races of mankind'. The similarity of his hopes to those of Bacon, Comenius and Wilkins is both striking and thought-provoking. The thematic mode has not lacked its philosophical and philanthropic idealists.[14]

Trained in Edinburgh as a physician and working for most of his life in London, Roget had a breadth of interests and talents comparable to those of Bacon and Comenius. He was equally at home discussing ants, arsenic, words and library organization. He contributed to various encyclopedias, including the *Britannica* and the *Metropolitana* and was, like many other nineteenth-century scholars and scientists, fascinated by taxonomics, whether in the natural and life sciences or in the practical everyday problems of the libraries of the Royal Society and the Medical and Chirurgical Society. His interest in language was entirely utilitarian, as a means towards the clear expression of ideas; words served him in particular as vehicles for concepts. From the start of his professional career in 1805 he had been collecting lists of words, but it was not until his actual retirement, just before he was 70, that he seriously began to compile the *Thesaurus*.[15]

Nineteenth-century science was dominated by the botanical metaphor of the tree as a model for taxonomic organization. Roget frankly acknowledges his debt to it when he states in his Introduction:[16]

> The principle by which I have been guided in framing my verbal classification is the same as that which is employed in the various departments of Natural History. Thus the sectional divisions I have formed correspond to Natural Families in Botany and Zoology, and the filiation of words presents a network analogous to the natural filiation of plants and animals.

The parallelism can be shown as in figure 9.

Fig. 9 Peter Mark Roget's biological analogy

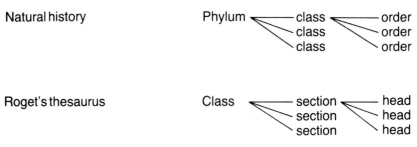

Fig. 10 Peter Mark Roget's taxonomy of ideas and words

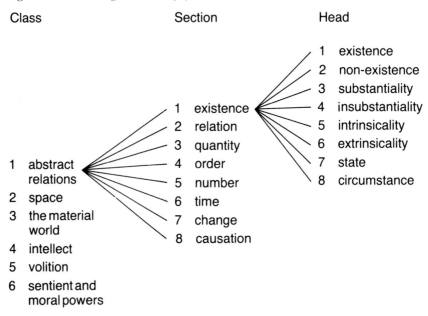

Roget did more, however, than simply adapt the taxonomy of biology; he fused it with the cosmic themes that he had inherited through Wilkins. His aim was to place a grid over reality, a kind of cartography of the mind, and label the appropriate nodes. He was aware, no doubt, that all such classifying is an exercise in putting continuums in containers, but went ahead with the work in the same spirit of optimism that animated natural history: because it was useful. The result was a truly Baconian artifact, part of which is reproduced in figure 10 (giving all six of his major classes).

Thus, *existence* is a head under the section *existence* in the class *abstract relations*. The general tone of the taxonomy is itself highly abstract and philosophical, with hard 'facts' like birds, beasts and animals vanishing almost from sight under headings like *volition* and *extrinsicality*. Roget's labelling is very much in the High Mode, using terms that the Schoolmen would have been at home with (though others might be forced to consult a hard-word dictionary). Roget, however, saw nothing cumbersome or daunting about such terms as *insalubrity* and *tergiversation*, insisting: 'I have . . . adopted such principles of arrangement as appeared to me the simplest and most natural, and which would not require, either for their comprehension or application, any disciplined acumen, or depth of metaphysical or antiquarian lore.' He saw Wilkins as abstruse and recondite, but did not feel that the same charge could be laid at his own door.

It is important to appreciate that the largely Latinate superstructure of the *Thesaurus* was intended by Roget to be the main way to his lists; the index that he provided was a brief afterthought. The experience of users, however, evidently prompted the realization that some kind of fuller alphabetic support was needed. A much more elaborate index was provided, therefore, by Roget's son John in the 1879 edition, and from then on has quite clearly been the principal way in for the vast majority of Roget-users. The *Thesaurus* was a commercial success from the start, but the detailed index added greatly to its usefulness, leading to sales in the millions since it first came out.

Roget saw his treasury of words as unique not just for English but for all languages. It was 'a desideratum hitherto unsupplied in any language; namely, a collection of the words it contains and of the idiomatic combinations peculiar to it, arranged, not in alphabetical order as they are in a dictionary, but according to the *ideas* which they express.'[17] Here the genre 'thesaurus' is for the first time held up as the converse of the genre 'dictionary': words are presented in terms of their meanings (the 'ideas' or 'concepts' behind them) rather than crudely in terms of their forms. It follows from this assertion that the taxonomic structure raised by Roget is not just a convenient tree with word labels at the nodes, but in some sense a structure modelling human thought (and just happening to use Latinate labels in the process). Like Wilkins, Roget wanted some kind of 'real character' as labels for something higher and more enduring. His 1962 reviser, Robert Dutch, in his own preface, defends Roget's position, arguing that as a result dictionary and thesaurus are complementary tools. In looking at node labels like *space* and *intrinsicality* we are invited to see them as the ideas they incarnate, not as words at all. Words may change (and have changed in the successive revisions of Roget), but in some absolute non-Whorfian way it is asserted that ideas do not – perhaps cannot – change. Thus, the idea relating to clothes, originally labelled *investment*, is in Dutch's edition *dressing*. Roget and Dutch ask that we suspend our knowledge that words are simply words, and treat some of them as other-than-words when they serve as node-labels (when, as modern linguists would say, they are part of a 'metalanguage'). Under such conditions they become the currency of the universal philosophical language to which Wilkins aspired.

That such labels are largely Latinate may have helped Roget – and may help us – to engage in such a neo-Platonic exercise. Elements of the old high language of Augustine and Aquinas may well be just right for the purpose. They serve equally well for such special terminologies as are used in chemistry and appear in botanical and zoological classifications: *sodium chloride, potassium cyanide, Homo sapiens, Rana vulgaris* and *Tyrannosaurus rex* being only a few in a vast register of specially coded scientific terms whose precise signification is seldom clear to the non-specialist.

Roget was interested in ideas and ideas belong in the mind. Inevitably, therefore, there is a psychological implication in Roget's work as regards what the mind is like and how *it* organizes its idea-and-word store. In 1962 Dutch made this implication explicit at two points in his own preface to Roget:[18]

– 'A thesaurus is operating on the same lines as a speaker or writer in the process of composition. It images in some measure the working of his (the user's) brain when, having his idea (corresponding to a thesaurus head), he mentally scans his stock of words (corresponding to the vocabulary of a thesaurus) for the right expression.'
– 'It is the counterpart of the thesaurus we all carry in our memories in which mentally we track down a word. Surely, this characteristic is implied in those criticisms which impugn the merits of all thesauruses: that it is the lazy man's book; that it saves him the trouble of thinking. It would not do this unless it were patterned on our process of thought and speech.'

In this claim the divide between the alphabetic and the thematic modes is at its widest and deepest (even though it was somewhat vitiated by the need in 1879 to develop that all-important index). If, however, the *Thesaurus* is indeed to be considered an analogue of the human mind (much as many people today are calling computers analogues of the mind), then it is a sketchy one, however large the book. Roget achieved a masterpiece of specialized cataloguing, but in the process left the following to the user:

1 providing the definitions (for the user must know the meanings of the words when he or she finds them)
2 making the necessary discriminations (for the user must know how the words differ and have the skill to use them appropriately)

3 adding the derivatives and compounds (for the user must know the principles of derivation and compounding in English and how far these can be
   pushed in coining new forms from established words).

These points did not trouble Roget; he had no intention of providing
definitions, etymologies, discriminations, citations, recommendations or
any other of the services that had developed in alphabetic lexicography by the
time he compiled his book. He settled for what he considered a unique
service: the making of the frames and the lists through which users could get
at words they were supposed already to know. In this, his compilation is a
kind of aide-memoire to the Elect.

There is, however, one important sense in which Dutch is right and the
Thesaurus is the converse of a dictionary and some kind of analogue of the
brain. Assuming that we cannot escape the tyranny of words and that Roget's
taxonomy is a hyponymic tree and no more than that, it is still a pioneering
attempt at semantic ordering, an arrangement of words in associative
catalogues that can be scanned for many purposes. The catalogues have been
compiled by a nineteenth-century man of science and carry the inevitable
mark of their time, but all in all they serve to remind us that whatever *does*
happen in our minds when we order and retrieve 'words' and 'ideas', it is *not*
done alphabetically.[19]

15

Alphabetic lexicography: the unendable dictionary

Right up to the end of the eighteenth century it was normal and quite unexceptional for language scholars to believe that all the world's languages descended from the Hebrew spoken by Adam and Eve in the Garden of Eden. This was, however, only one part of a larger Bibliocentric view of life that was steadily being weakened and supplanted by various newer and largely secular alternatives.[1] Although not everyone was aware of it, even the term 'Christendom' no longer properly applied to the Western World of Europe and North America. Religion was still a significant element in the collective experience, but with Darwin and Marx not far off in the future it is already possible to see the West at the time of the French Revolution as moving into a post-Christian style of life.

The circumstances that dealt the death-blow to the Hebrew-in-Eden view of language origins arose in part at least through European contacts with the ancient civilization of India, where investigators like the British orientalist Sir William Jones discovered that the classical Hindu language Sanskrit was a cousin of Greek, Latin, German and English, and not at all like Hebrew and Arabic. The interest that developed in this new 'comparative philology'[2] was pan-European, but was particularly intense in the Germanic countries, where it was also linked with the rise of Romantic nationalism. It was attractive, therefore, not only to sober scholars but also to poets, composers and political fantasists who would – much later – dream strange dreams about the Aryan Master Race.

Foremost among the scholars was Jakob Grimm (1785–1863) who was interested not only in philology and lexicography but also in mythology and folklore, and preserved, with the help of his brother Wilhelm (1786–1859), much of the oral tradition of the common German people by re-telling such now internationally known tales as Snow-white and the Seven Dwarves.[3]

Their monumental work, however, was lexicographic: the *Deutsches Wörterbuch*. This project was intended – somehow – to be both a work of proper scholarly reference and an everyman's guide to spoken and written German. Of it, Ludwig Denecke says: 'In the dictionary, all German words found in the literature of the three centuries "from Luther to Goethe" were given with their historical variants, their etymology, and their semantic development; their usage in specialized and everyday language was illustrated by quoting idioms and proverbs. Begun simply as a source of income in 1838 . . . the work required generations of successors to bring the gigantic task to an end *in our day'* (my italics). In fact, the work came to an end around 1960 – 142 years after it was begun. Jakob saw the work proceed to the letter F, but Wilhelm died before it had even progressed to D.

The Brothers Grimm had hardly appreciated what they had set out to do – a common failing in lexicography at large, and particularly common in those enterprises that have sought to embrace the entirety of national languages. There was a marked difference now, however, in the philological approach to recording a language and the approach that had animated the Académie Française or even Johnson and Webster. The desire to 'fix' the language had gone from the minds of the compilers (if not always from the minds of their readers), while at the same time a new enthusiasm for both historical accuracy and dialectal comprehensiveness had come in. Compilers were not so much concerned with delimiting the High Mode as with exhibiting the abundant riches of 'vernaculars' that no longer felt in the least vernacular. The long dominance of Latin had gone.

However, this did not mean that the classical languages had lost their significance or interest. Quite the reverse, in fact, for it was in the pioneering work of a German classicist that the basic principles of the new philological approach to lexicography were laid down. In 1812, Franz Passow published an essay which set forth his canons for historically respectable lexicography. This was the *Zweck, Anlage, und Erganzung griechischer Wörterbücher* ('The Aim, Construction and Completion of Greek Dictionaries'). He completed his own *Lexicon* according to these principles in 1819. His principal requirement was simple but radical: that the entries and definitions should be supported by citations from the available texts, and that these citations should be organized chronologically from the earliest to the most recent, thus objectively demonstrating change. Passow's influence was considerable, both on later classical lexicons and on the great dictionary projects that were about to burst, along with the project of the Grimms, upon Europe at large.

Not only did the new philological approach encourage new and ambitious undertakings; it also had a profound and sometimes dramatic effect on existing dictionaries. As we have already seen, Noah Webster's *American Dictionary* came out in 1828, just when the new movement was beginning to show what it could do. We have also noted that Webster criticized Johnson for the appalling inaccuracies in his etymological entries. Now, as Allen Walker Read has observed, 'it was Noah Webster's misfortune to be superseded in his philology in the very decade that his masterpiece came out. He had spent many years in compiling a laborious "Synopsis" of 20 languages, but he lacked an awareness of the systematic relationships in the Indo-European family of languages.' At a stroke, the new and increasingly powerful awareness of Indo-European and other language groups made the Websterian etymologies, and everything else like them, suddenly completely and hopelessly out of date.

The idea of the value of an orderly range of citations in illustrating the meaning of a word animated the work of an English lexicographer of the same period, who is now largely forgotten, by whose influence has lived on indirectly. This was Charles Richardson, who set out to organize his citations in such a way as to avoid the need for any kind of definition at all. He first used this procedure in a dictionary that appeared part by part in the grand but ill-fated *Encyclopaedia Metropolitana*, and when that enterprise failed, brought the work out in the mid-1830s as the *New Dictionary of the English Language*.

Allen Walker Read, as a historian of lexicography, is not impressed by Richardson's work, considering it 'largely a monument to misguided industry that met with the neglect it deserved'.[4] James Murray, however, discussing dictionaries in 1900, considered Richardson's approach sound in principle and interesting in practice (1900: 44): 'Quotations *will* tell the full meaning of a word, if one has enough of them; but it takes a great many to be enough, and it takes a reader a long time to read and weigh all the quotations, and to deduce from them the meanings which might be put before him in a line or two.'

Murray's opinion is significant here, as we shall see, because of Murray's own involvement in an enormous project that began in the mid-nineteenth century and has never really stopped. However, before passing on to that project, we should note that Richardson's bold and demanding exercise has a special value in the history of lexicology and semantics. He was pointing to a primary reality of which definition is only a secondary and often very unsatisfactory reflection: words gain their meanings in terms of the contexts in which they occur (whether immediately linguistic or situational and sociocultural). Words do not acquire meanings through definitions; definitions are little more than distillations from all the possible contexts in which a 'word' has occurred or might occur. In appreciating this and trying to avoid definition, Richardson was more than a century ahead of his time.

In 1842 the Philological Society was set up in London in order to investigate the structure, affinities and history of the English language, and shortly afterwards appointed a small 'unregistered words committee', a kind of temporary orphanage for the waifs and strays of the language that had not yet been assigned a home in any of the major dictionaries of the time. This committee had three members – Herbert Coleridge, Frederick Furnivall, and Richard Chenevix Trench – who in the course of their work came to the conclusion that the current dictionaries left out a great deal and suffered from a variety of other shortcomings. In 1857, therefore, Trench read two papers to the Society 'On Some Deficiencies in our English Dictionaries' and quite unaware of what would result from his observations drew his fellow members' attention to seven specific points which, in the committee's view, dictionaries failed to handle well (Sledd & Ebbitt 1962):

- obsolete words
- derivational families
- accurate and properly dated citations
- all the important senses of words

– the proper distinguishing of 'synonyms'
– sufficient coverage of the available literary sources
– elimination of redundant material.

For Trench a dictionary was an inventory of a language and not a tool for selecting only the 'good' words of that language (however judged); a lexicographer is properly a historian and not a moralist or critic. Trench maintained the literary and textual orientation of lexicography, but dismissed its legislative function: the door, as he saw it, should thenceforward be kept open for all the high and low, misshapen or handsome, useful or useless words in a language, and this quite simply because they had been or were being used somewhere by someone for some purpose. There should be a master list into which all such words could go, where they would be examined, classified and pronounced upon precisely as the botanist Linnaeus labelled his specimens. If there was to be an authority it would be that of comprehensiveness, of objective citation and definition, and not the arbitrary socioaesthetic inclinations of the compiler, or the social group to which the compiler belonged.

As a result of Trench's observations, the Philological Society decided that simply listing what Johnson and his successors had overlooked was not enough. In 1858 they passed resolutions calling for a new dictionary on proper historical principles (and in a format that both Passow and the Grimms would have approved): Every word which could be found in English from the year AD 1000 onward would be exhibited with its history, variant forms and spellings, and all uses and meanings, past and present, these last displayed by means of a representative selection of quotations from the whole range of English literature and records. Thousands of texts would have to be read in order to obtain these quotations, and a typically optimistic Victorian call for volunteers was issued in this regard. The response was gratifying: hundreds of readers not just from England itself but from all over the world hastened to send in material.

The project did not, however, grow in quite the way that the Society planned. Indeed, it is quite likely that if its members had foreseen the efforts, expense and enormous stretch of time that would be needed for the work they would not have started at all.[5] In the event, however, six men preeminently carried out the work from its close-to-amorphous start to its orderly 'conclusion' 70 years later. These men were: Herbert Coleridge, Frederick Furnivall, James Murray, Henry Bradley, William Craigie, and Charles Onions (four Englishmen and two Scots).

Herbert Coleridge, the first editor and Trench's colleague on the originating committee, supervised the work of two new ground-clearing committees from 1858 to his untimely death in 1861 at the age of 31. One committee dealt with the necessary historical and literary sources, while the other was concerned with etymology as understood in terms of the new comparative method. Coleridge also looked after the in-pouring of quotations from around the world, which was greatly facilitated by the recent development of an efficient international postal system.

 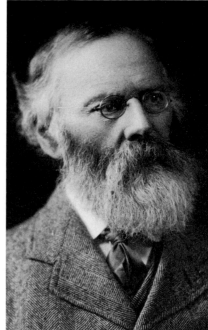

James A.H. Murray   *Henry Bradley*

On Coleridge's death, the editorship passed to Trench's third colleague, Frederick Furnivall, who realized that a satisfactory excerpting from the early texts could only be achieved if those texts were made both more accessible and more readable. Here the ancient scribal culture and modern print cultures were at odds, for the skills had been lost by the reading public at large through which hand-copied manuscripts could be easily read – and the manuscripts were neither readily available nor in a condition where they could be trusted out of the care of the libraries where they were held. The dictionary project consequently necessitated a whole new textual project that was educationally valuable in its own right. In 1864 Furnivall founded the Early English Text Society and in 1865 the Chaucer Society, organizations which duly provided accurate and readable printed texts not just for the purposes of the dictionary but for all interested scholars and students everywhere.

All this and other work remained, however, frustratingly *preparatory*. On the day when Furnivall handed the work over to *his* successor, one-and-three-quarter tons of submitted material had accumulated in his home – mainly in the form of slips providing quotations – in addition to the harvest of special full-length texts. This was the scholarly humus out of which a dictionary might grow, but not one line of such a dictionary had been written by 1879, all of 21 years after the first resolutions had been passed. It was not therefore even the work itself that seemed endless – the preparation for the work seemed simply to go on and on.

William Craigie   *C.T. Onions*

At this point, to replace Furnivall and to lend impetus to the project, the Society made two moves which changed everything: firstly, they engaged the services of the schoolmaster James Murray as the new editor, and then, together with Murray, entered into an agreement with the Delegates of the Clarendon Press, Oxford University, that the Press would publish the Society's *New English Dictionary on Historical Principles* and in the meantime finance its development. The work would be some 6,400 pages long, arranged in four volumes, and would be completed in 1889, a 10-year period that seemed more than generous. Murray was to be the part-time compiler, and to this end he built a special (and appropriately named) 'scriptorium' at his home to house his treasury of source material. He enlisted further volunteers from around the world, and began the actual compilation straight away. Five years later, however, working with meticulous care, he had completed only 352 pages and had moved from A to ANT. The experience of the Brothers Grimm was more than repeating itself.

The Delegates of the Press, in the words of a present-day editor for Oxford, Eugene Ehrlich, 'felt deep concern over the slow progress and made their concern known to Murray'. It was clear that the project could either be abandoned, or thoroughly reshaped and enlarged. It is to the credit of the Delegates that the second course was adopted. Additional editorial staff were appointed and the whole undertaking moved to Oxford, where the schoolmaster could serve, for the rest of his long life, as a full-time lexicographer. In this development we see the next stage in the slow transformation of the whole project from the plan of a committee appointed by a more or less national 'academic' organization into the thoroughly university-orientated work of an editorial team – all of this mediated by a printing and publishing house belonging to an ancient university. All four of the possible factors governing lexicography were in play by 1885: inspired individuals, an academy-type organization, a university, and a press with inevitable commercial connections. This coming together of such factors in such a powerful combination inevitably led to a new national and international institution and a landmark in the containerization of knowledge about any language – although the actors in this epic process could not at any point in its development have seen just where they were going.

The OED page that defines 'dictionary' (compact version, 1971).

In 1887 Henry Bradley was appointed as a second editor with his own staff, the end of B was reached in the same year, and everybody involved became content to let the wrestling with the English language take its course. In 1897 William Craigie joined the group and worked for four years directly under Murray before becoming a full editor with responsibility for the letter Q. In 1914, Charles Onions – better known as C.T. Onions – was promoted from assistant to full editor. His article on *super-* and its derivatives rivals Bradley's 23-page masterpiece on *set*, as two of the longest entries in the whole enormous opus.

James Murray died in harness in 1915, having just finished the section TRINK to TURNDOWN and only two years short of his 80th year. He also died well short of his friends' hope that he would 'live to see Zymotic', for the project did not get to the end of Z until the 1920s, when the entire work was published in 10 thick volumes in 1928. The *Oxford English Dictionary*, as it would henceforth be known, remains the natural home of superlatives and statistics: 70 years from idea to final volumes, 5 million quotations sent in by some 2,000 readers, almost 2 million of those quotations eventually used, 40 editorial days and 23 pages on the word *set* alone, and all in all 414,825 words defined in 15,487 pages.

Surely such an enterprise could merit the title 'authoritative'? Certainly, as Ehrlich notes, 'around the world each new installment was eagerly awaited by scholars and word lovers. The parts already issued (before the final form in 1928) were becoming the final authority on the English language in law courts, government bureaus, scholarly debates, newspaper offices, and publising houses' (Ehrlich et al. 1980: xi–xvi). This idea of finality and authority was important not just to the worldwide public that followed the work's progress but to the compiler-in-chief himself. Victorian optimism prevailed, and Murray permitted himself to observe in 1900 (1900:49):

> Be the speed (of compilation) what it may, . . . there is the consideration that the work thus done is done once for all; the structure now reared will have to be added to, continued and extended with time, but it will remain, it is believed, the great body of fact on which all future work will be built. It is never possible to forecast the needs and notions of those who will come after us; but with our present knowledge it is not easy to conceive what new feature can now be added to English lexicography. At any rate, it can be maintained that in the Oxford Dictionary, permeated as it is through and through with the scientific method of the century, Lexicography has for the present reached its supreme development.

The claim is put with care and some caution, but it is not a modest claim, any more than Roget's claim for his *Thesaurus* was modest. There is a clear suggestion that, if the *Oxford English Dictionary* was not the ultimate dictionary of English, then it was as near as we would be likely to get to the ultimate, and its lexicographic methodology was the acme of its kind. On a larger scale it is reminiscent of Webster's fate with regard to his etymologies, for the twentieth century has demonstratd quite conclusively – as I hope to show in the closing chapters of this review – that much indeed can be added to

Robert W. Burchfield,
editor of the four
Supplements to the OED.

Robert Burchfield commented as follows on ending the unendable in his 1982 preface to *A Supplement to the Oxford English Dictionary* (Vol. III O-Scz):

> In her *Personal Pleasures* (1935) Rose Macaulay notes that on a blank page at the beginning of her copy of the 1933 *Supplement to the OED* she recorded emendations, corrections, additions, and earlier uses of words.
>
> > 'To amend so great a work gives me pleasure; I feel myself one of its architects; I am Sir James Murray, Dr. Bradley, Sir William Craigie, Dr. Onions . . . If there is a drawback to this pure pleasure of doing good to a dictionary, I have not yet found it. Except that, naturally, it takes time.'
>
> With the publication of this volume we have now reached the three-quarter mark, proportionately about as far as the point reached by Dr Murray on the *OED* itself before he died in 1915. We are now preparing the fourth and last volume, and it should be ready for publication in 1985. It would not be prudent to start congratulating ourselves yet – no major lexicographical project has been brought to its last word without the final agonies of a marathon runner – but the glittering prize of completion now seems to be within sight at last.

lexicography at large as well as to English lexicography. It is always risky to foreclose on the future.

In addition, as they laboured, the compilers of Murray's Dictionary were moving through time alongside the language. Thus, when they reached S in 1910, they were 26 years away from the compilation of A, a period long enough to justify a major revision of any less epic wordbook. Furthermore, in Switzerland, Ferdinand de Saussure was already questioning some of the fundamental assumptions of 'the scientific method of the century' as regards the nature of language.[6] And finally, what no one could have imagined, men like Charles Babbage, Alexander Graham Bell, Thomas Edison and Herman Hollerith were already embarked upon technological innovations that will utterly transform the future of all works of reference everywhere, and are currently transforming the shape of the *OED* itself.

Fig. 11 The evolution of the unendable OED

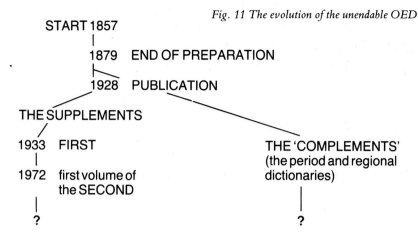

Murray could also hardly have imagined the explosion of lexis in the English language that would occur from around World War II onward. The dictionary may have been officially completed and bound in 1928, but in a serious sense it was not completed at all. Rather, a truce was established with the language. Already in 1919, William Craigie had proposed further schemes to the Philological Society, relating to special 'period' dictionaries to enlarge upon Old English, Middle English, and so forth. In addition, it was evident that regionalization was worth pursuing for American, Scottish and other possible kinds of English. Various universities have become involved in such spin-off projects – and are still engaged upon them in the 1980s.

Craigie and Onions in the meantime brought out the first *Supplement* to the *OED* in 1933, and the making of further supplements is now an institution-alized process in Oxford, until recently in the care of the New Zealand scholar Robert Burchfield, who became editor in 1957. The *first* volume of the *Second Supplement* appeared in 1972, the *fourth* in the mid-1980s. What likehood, however, of a supplement to the Supplements, the ultimate in a kind of lexicographic masochism (unless a whole new technological approach is developed)? In diagrammatic terms the unendable aspect of the *OED* looks something like figure 11.

It is all very sobering and thought-provoking – especially when we recall that English, though dominant as a world language today, is still only one among thousands of languages, most of which have not had anything like the lexicographic attention lavished on English.

The very nature of the world makes the *OED* imperfect, and already a historical document in its own right – but what an impressive piece of imper-fection it is! The superlatives that have been lavished upon it are in the main well deserved (and my own debt to it in the preparation of this book is not small). Ehrlich says that it 'was considered by many to be the greatest scholarly achievement of all time – and it still is'. This may be excessive praise, but it remains and shall remain one of the wonders of the worlds of reference.

16
Universal education: dictionaries for the people

In the year 1753, when Sam Johnson was still labouring in Gough Square, a small dictionary was published with the rather grandiloquent title *A Complete English Dictionary*, its author assuring potential users that it was quite the best there was. That author was John Wesley, the founder of the non-conformist Protestant movement that came to be known as Methodism, and his purpose in compiling the wordbook was a straightforward one: to raise the level of literacy in his largely working-class flock.[1]

In the mid-nineteenth century two brothers, William and Robert Chambers, established themselves in Edinburgh as educational publishers. They produced in the main dictionaries and an encyclopedia. *Chambers's Encyclopaedia* (no relation whatever to Ephraim Chambers and his *Cyclopaedia*) was a marked success and flourished until very recently, while the flagship of their company's present-day dictionaries, the *Chambers Twentieth Century*, is one of the most comprehensive yet compact single-volume wordbooks in the English-using world. When they set up in business, the brothers called themselves 'publishers for the people', expressing through this slogan a particularly Scottish and Presbyterian desire to spread learning to all men and women.[2]

In France at about the same time the son of a blacksmith started his own publishing house and created a national tradition in his own right. Pierre Larousse issued in fortnightly parts between 1866 and 1876 a 15-volume *Grand dictionnaire universel du XIXe siecle*. This work was permeated by the spirit of scientific progressivism and the example of Denis Diderot. Larousse was animated by a desire to facilitate universal education, to encapsulate the world so that everybody would understand it better.[3]

In 1894 there came out in New York a *Standard Dictionary* that was innovative in two ways: it put etymology in square brackets after all the rest of the definitions in an entry, and also reversed the chronological ordering of definitions that had been so typical of the philologists. It did both these things because the moving spirit of the dictionary, the Lutheran minister Isaac Kaufmann Funk, reckoned that the average user wanted contemporary information first and archaic information last of all. He co-founded the publishing house of Funk and Wagnall because he wanted to provide his flock with both books and tracts and the means to understand them better.[4]

These are four examples among many others that might have been mentioned that highlight the place of lexicography in the vast social and educational movement, stemming from the revolutions in the United States and France, that aimed at the emancipation, both physical and mental, of the bulk of the human race (whether conceived as a circumscribed middle class at odds with the clergy and the aristocracy, an oppressed proletariat, or those enslaved or otherwise victimized by commerce and imperialism).

As the examples suggest, there was a strong current of evangelism as well as secular humanism in this tide of reform. Companies that printed and sold dictionaries often printed and sold bibles too, and the two kinds of book were often offered for sale in similar solemn bindings. These popular dictionaries were lineal descendants not only of the monastery copyists of the so-called Dark Ages, but also of the printers and reformers who sought in the sixteenth century to give everyman's conscience into his own keeping. Such publishing houses as Chambers, Collins, Larousse and Funk and Wagnall have offered their customers a kind of secular salvation through literacy and an awareness of the power of words and organized information. They were not as radical and incendiary as Karl Marx and Friedrich Engels, but they played a comparable role in the transformation of society. Where Marx and Engels preached historical determinism and the last great revolution, these puritanical capitalists put in every bookstore better works of reference than had been available in the past to princes and prelates – and at manageable prices. They were to the mind what piped water, cheap soap and good public transport were to the body.

The work that they engaged in allows us now to grade macro-lexicography along the two axes of size and focus. Thus, as regards size, we can talk now about the continuum that ranges from the 'unabridged' through the 'college' and the 'desk' to the 'concise', the 'essential', the 'pocket' to the 'micro' and 'mini'. In terms of focus, such reference materials can be essentially encyclopedic or lexical, can be thesauruses or dictionaries, can be uni-, bi- or multi-lingual, can be general or specialized, can be standard or dialect or deal in jargon and slang, they can be literary or technical, musical or medical, historical or contemporary. Indeed, there are very few things in the world today that are beyond the reach of the lexicographer's art. And while such books were thriving, comparable genres like directories and gazetteers, indexes and concordances, manuals and textbooks, guidebooks and cookbooks, digests and condensed books, *ad* virtually *infinitum*, were also being produced – and selling well.

The growth of populism in such areas meant, inevitably, an alteration in the nature of the educated élite of the world. Most obvious is the increase in the size of that élite over the last 200 years, but sheer size is not the only factor. Today we take for granted the idea of upward social mobility, forgetting that in the tightly hierarchical societies of the past (and also today in certain parts of the world) this kind of mobility has been severely limited. In the course of such social mobility and the general democratization of knowledge, however, the old and fairly simple distinction between the knowledgeable and the ignorant was shattered; today, we live in complex societies of the *variably* knowledgeable and ignorant to a far greater extent than our ancestors, and the professions and levels of expertise today are far more graded and diffuse. Once, all priests knew much the same thing (with a few specially learned 'doctors'); today, the possible permutations of ignorance and knowledge are infinite, and it is very hard indeed to say just what 'a good general knowledge' is. It is unlikely, however, that the great populist educators and compilers who looked forward to the kind of 'universal education' we sort-of-have today foresaw the diversity and the new problems of inequality that would go with their egalitarian ambitions.

The populist educational movement has had startling effects upon the old citadels of learning as well as upon the mass of the people. The name of Oxford, for example, was once distinctly élitist. It is still for most people redolent with the idea of gowned Schoolmen and dreaming spires, but it is also today – in straight commercial terms – a name that its publicity people want to make synonymous with dictionaries. As we have seen, the link with *one* great scholarly dictionary goes back just under 100 years, to the agreement between the Delegates of the Press and the Philological Society. Supporting the vast lexicographic project taken over from the Society, however, was expensive and it is not surprising that Oxford University Press should have decided to diversify and at the same time benefit from the connection in financial terms.

To that end they commissioned Henry Fowler to compile a popular wordbook, a compact single-volume dictionary that would benefit from the cachet of the Great Project while serving as a handy desk companion. The result, the now world-famous *Concise Oxford Dictionary*, was published in 1911. Fowler had no experience of lexicography when he started and evidently received little guidance in how to produce the scaled-down version of Murray's Dictionary. As he noted in the preface, 'When we began the work, . . . we were plunging into a sea of lexicography without having first been taught how to swim.' He was able to draw on Murray's work for the letters A to R, but thereafter he was on his own. In the struggle that followed Fowler evolved five basic principles which have shaped all the subsequent editions of the *Concise* and set the tone for many later dictionaries published in England[5]. These were:

- not to be encyclopedic
- to give adequate space to common words and their idioms
- to supplement the definitions with illustrative phrases only when really necessary to clarify the meaning
- to order the senses of words according to casual logic and present-day appropriateness (not unlike Funk's decision)
- to have a layout involving 'the severest economy of expression – amounting to telegraphese – that readers can be expected to put up with'

Fowler was well aware that the line between lexis and general knowledge is 'a fluctuating and dubious one', but the *COD* in all its subsequent manifestations has largely kept to his promise to be neither encyclopedic nor obscure. Its basic policy contrasts quite sharply with what Harold Whitehall in 1958 saw as the typically American product, a compact but distinctly encyclopedic volume governed by the following principles (Whitehall 1958:161–2):

- American spelling and pronunciation
- strictly limited etymologies
- numbered senses
- pictorial or diagrammatic illustration wherever needed
- selective treatment of synonyms and antonyms
- scientific, technical, geographical and biographical information, both scattered through the main list and added in special appendices

Although these two lists do not match each other point for point they do serve to highlight the distinctly different emphases that have developed in the United States and England. The public in each country has come to expect its compact dictionaries to conform to these national styles (even if they have never thought much about them or had an opportunity to compare one style with another, or to compare these two styles with those in any other country with a distinct lexicographic tradition of its own, such as France or Scotland).

Many special factors contribute to the nature of populist lexicography today and it is not possible to go into detail about them all here. Thus, the existence of rival publishing houses had encouraged what the Americans have called 'the wars of the dictionaries', and such wars have in their turn encouraged the plagiarism that is virtually inherent in lexicography as well as a spirit of minor innovation and revision, so that one house can regularly claim that it has finally up-staged its main rival. Additionally, the interplay and tension between ivory-tower academic lexicography and clearcut commercial lexicography (as for example in Oxford) has tended to sustain a kind of scholarly suspicion of the commercial, whether in terms of dictionaries or encyclopedias. Something that might be sold in a dimestore or hawked from door to door did not necessarily appeal to the cultural aesthetics of university men. Although such men might be capitalists, they did not want to be seen as hucksters, and often their academic susceptibilities and principles were at odds with the marketplace interests of the publishers who more and more went to them for advice and information. Although commercial works of reference have inevitably benefited in terms of quality from their academic connections, and although academics have also benefited financially from their commercial connections, a certain (sometimes incompletely stated) resentment is still detectable on the part of scholars, in that they seem to wish they did not have to sully themselves in this way. Finally, it is worth noting that it is only because of the populist movement that women have been able to move into the world of reference books (and this quite recently) and become more than simply clerks. Nowadays, it is quite common to find the name of a woman as the editor-in-chief of a major reference work, where previously – as must by now have been patently clear – the preserve was 99.9% male.[5]

In terms of knowledge and attitudes to knowledge, however, the rise of populism in macro-lexicography has been most significant in the area of the authoritative versus the merely advisory, the prescriptive versus the descriptive, an aspect which is worth some comment here. In 1972, for example, in a paper entitled *Dollars and Dictionaries*, James Sledd deplored present-day general dependence, especially in the United States, on commercial publishers (Weinbrot 1972). Very particularly, he objected to the exaggerated claims and counterclaims of the marketplace while accepting that this very competitiveness could often produce healthy improvements in format, presentation and coverage.

Sledd suggested that dictionary-making might be better off in the hands of academics sponsored by governments, which was an interesting 'socialist' approach to suggest in the US, that greatest of all free-enterprise societies. He praised the decades-long effort of scholars, societies and universities around the world to produce the great national wordbooks, and seemed to feel that these were in many ways more worthy undertakings than the everyman dictionaries as currently organized. For Sledd, the dictionary that came nearest to the ideal blend of scholarly comprehensiveness and everyday utility was Webster's *Second New International Dictionary* of 1934, an American work that sought, however, to handle all English adequately. It was certainly generally highly valued in the United States, to such an extent that when its own publisher, Merriam, revised it as the *Third New International Dictionary* in the early 1960s a public battle ensued from coast to coast of the USA. Sledd and a colleague, Wilma Ebbitt, brought out a casebook relating to this remarkable controversy in 1962 which graphically portrays the dichotomy among dictionary users and producers, and serves here to sum up most effectively many of the points that I have hoped to make in this study.[6]

The New York Times (12 October 1961) led the assault on the new edition by charging that Merriam–Webster had 'surrendered to the permissive school' and thereby re-inforced the degenerate notion that good English is whatever is popular. This comment referred in particular to the decision of the editor-in-chief, Philip Gove, to take into consideration the descriptivism of modern linguistics as well as the new usages in an English that was exploding and changing as profoundly as at any time in its past. As *The Chicago Daily News* added (20 October), what now was the point of a writer trying to compose clear and graceful prose 'in that magnificent instrument, the English language, if that peerless authority, Webster's Unabridged, surrenders abjectly to the permissive school of speech?' It was all a symptom of the general decay of the times, a view that Sam Johnson would probably have heartily endorsed.

Other assaults followed, accusing Springfield of dealing English 'a serious blow', of dereliction of duty like a sentry forsaking his post, of abdicating the trust they had inherited from Noah Webster, assaults which curiously echo the ancient controversy of purist and innovator in sixteenth-century Europe.

However, Merriam and Gove were also defended. On the 22 October 1961, Mario Pei, writing in *The New York Times Book Review*, asserted that the extent and range of a language's vocabulary reflect the state of civilization of its speakers . . . Far from viewing with alarm our astounding language growth within the last 130-odd years, we should rejoice over this index of material and intellectual progress. At the most, we may wonder how many 2,720-page volumes will be required for the Merriam–Webster Unabridged of the year 2000.

Bergen Evans added, in *The Atlantic* of May 1962:

As written English is used by increasing millions and for more reasons than ever before, the language has become more utilitarian and more informal. Every publication in America today includes pages that would appear, to the purist of forty years ago, unbuttoned gibberish. Not that they are; they simply show that you can't hold the language of one generation up as a model for the next. It's not that you mustn't. You can't.

The two sides were powerfully entrenched in this lexical civil war. One by-product of their battle was the spirited prose employed by both sides, for the contestants clearly enjoyed their use of the language to defend their positions. Not just conservatism and radicalism were on display here, however, but the kind of sincere concern for the true and righteous that has always animated the discussion and production of dictionaries and encyclopedias. Dwight Macdonald was on target when, in *The New Yorker* of 10 March 1962, he referred to his postbag after a classic attack on the new wordbook: the letters were, he asserted, 98% against the new policy and the new book, and *twice* the postbag when he had attacked the most recent revised translation of the Bible. A telling comparison.

What exactly was being attacked, however? What had Gove and Merriam–Webster perpetrated upon an unsuspecting American public? In the 1961 preface to the *Third International*, the statistics that Gove presents in describing the new product seem to be a triumph of New World enterprise. The *Third International* was being offered to the English-using world as 'a prime linguistic aid to interpreting the culture and civilization of today', which is no small claim for a dictionary. It cost over $3.5 million to produce, with a staff that included a resident mathematician, physicist, chemist, philosopher, political scientist, comparative religionist, classicist, historian and librarian as well as many outside consultants. The definitions and the master list were based on systematic reading programmes since 1936, and had a 'citation background' of over 10 million items. Surrealistically, the work 'absorbed 757 editor-years' and not without some hubris Gove asserted that, with its vocabulary of over 450,000 words, the 'new Merriam–Webster unabridged is *the* record of this language as it is written and spoken' today, and able to supply '*in full measure* that information on the general language which is required for accurate, clear and comprehensive understanding of the vocabulary of today's society' (my italics).[7] Gove added, in the October 1961 issue of *Word Study*, that modern lexicography 'should have no traffic with guesswork, prejudice, or bias or with artificial notions of correctness and superiority', a declaration that traditionalists could very well take as an assault upon their worldview.

However, what Gove said in his answer to the attack of *The New York Times* (printed on 5 November 1961) should perhaps have given later assailants pause, if they had read it. The major objection made by that newspaper was to the presence of items like 'double-dome' and 'yakking' in the dictionary (with the tacit impression that these items were treated as standard). Gove assured the editors, and other American periodicals, that with regard to such words all he and his staff had done was record *their own usage*. He pointed out that the *Third International* cited *The Times* on some 700 separate occasions as evidence of such usage, and 'we plan to continue reading and marking *The Times* as the number one exhibit of good standard contemporary cultivated English' (a neat concession both to authoritarianism and descriptive linguistics).

Ethel Strainchamps of the *St. Louis Post Despatch* (17 December 1961) may have reached the heart of the matter when she noted:

> The critical reaction to Webster's Third New International Dictionary has revealed a cultural lag in unexpected places. The Merriam–Webster editors must have known that most people are linguistically more conservative in theory than in practice. But modern writers, who are more free-wheeling with their language than any of their predecessors since Shakespeare, might have been expected to accept the consequences. The comment in the press on the first new unabridged since 1934 indicates, however, that our writers are more modern in what they do than in what they think. They don't, in short, approve of their own uninhibited practice.

On the other hand, Wilson Follett in 'Sabotage in Springfield' (*The Atlantic*, January 1962) would not release Gove and his minions from their social responsibilities, for the lexicographer 'may think of himself as a detached scientist reporting the facts of language . . . but the myriad consultants of the work are not going to see him so'. The dictionary, like it or no, comes to the mass of its users as the definitive report of a 'synod' (the word is worth noting) of trustworthy experts: 'The fact that the compilers disclaim authority and piously refrain from judgments is meaningless: the work itself, by virtue of its inclusions and exclusions, its mere existence, is a whole universe of judgments, received by millions as the Word from on High.'

The great irony of the debate, however, was the position of the publishers themselves, who – like many publishers – wanted to be all things to all customers. While the new edition with its new 'objective' and 'linguistic' policy was being put together, the company brought out in 1947 a booklet entitled 'Noah's Ark', which celebrated a century of publication and sounded a fanfare for the authoritative use of its major product throughout the United States of America. Dwight Macdonald duly quoted from this booklet in his attack, and with justification, because it stated unequivocally: 'Clear through indeed to the everyday American's most trivial and jocose of doings, Webster is the unquestioned authority.'

Thus we live with our cultural schizophrenia. The publisher was right, of course, as Norma Isaacs of *The Louisville Times* (October 1961) pointed out: 'The net is that we have a new dictionary and it will become the accepted authority, despite all the literary hassles that will ensue.'

What, however, can we say about such ambivalences as this fascinating episode reveals? Both positions, prescriptivist and descriptivist, were sincerely held, and with all their disparities between attitude and actual use of language are the outcome of the historical processes that I have been trying to describe, especially with regard to the tensions between populist and élitist, academic and commercial, authoritarian and libertarian, conservative and radical, subjective and objective. The processes at work appear to go something as follows.

Someone may be reading and finds a word or phrase that is unclear or new. He or she might then ask someone nearby for a quick gloss, and then scribble the explanation in the margin. In this careless but useful act such a person recapitulates the very beginnings of lexicography in the scribal culture of the Middle Ages. The matter may not, however, be so easy. The material being read might be foreign and a reader might want the equivalent in his or her own language. This time, help might be sought in a bilingual dictionary, a work whose origins date back to the late Middle Ages (if not indeed to the scribal schools of ancient Mesopotamia). Such a reader would usually accept the equivalent given in such a dictionary as right beyond question. Why, indeed, should it be wrong? Translation has been going on for a long time.

Readers, however, will also want from time to time detailed help or reassurance with a difficult, opaque kind of word in their own language, something that disturbs their linguistic peace of mind. When they went to a dictionary this time, they would be looking for its 'hard-word' aspect, its capacity to handle the exotic, the classical, the technical, the aberrant. This in its turn recapitulates the seventeenth century, when the vocabulary of Neo-Latin and other languages was flowing liberally into the vernaculars of Western Europe. Again, however, a word might be known, but raise doubts. Readers this time might seek another kind of reassurance, that it was all right to use a word in a certain way (as regards spelling or pronunciation, grammar or usage). For this they would go to a 'good' dictionary for what it had to say with authority on 'correct' language, and here they would be reflecting attitudes that were dominant in the seventeenth and eighteenth centuries.

Lastly, readers may go to dictionaries and other such books for comprehensiveness, accuracy and objectivity (for some research purpose or specialized professional need). This time well-marshalled evidence could be invaluable as showing all the nuances of a word. This time they would go to one or other of the 'unabridged' works, and in so doing would reflect the profound desire of the nineteenth- and twentieth-century scholars to apply scientific rigour to the description of vocabulary.

All these needs are legitimate, though sometimes they may clash, and any reasonably educated person in any society influenced by Western European traditions will have such needs (and confusion among such needs) from time to time. It would be utopian, however, to hope that any *one* dictionary as we understand such tools at the present time could fulfil *all* of our pressing, varied and ambivalent needs. We can only rejoice that over the centuries the regiment of Johnson's 'harmless drudges' has put such a variety of tools in our hands.

17

Semantic fields and conceptual universes:
the unshapeable lexis

James Murray reckoned, in all honesty, that his dictionary was close to the ultimate in what lexicography could do, but was wise enough to add that no one can predict where future generations will go. Even at the time when he made these comments, however, at the turn of the nineteenth and twentieth centuries, sociolinguistic investigators were already moving in a direction which would one day open entirely new vistas to the recorder of words.

We have seen that the nineteenth century was a time of classification through form: of atoms and molecules, of animals and plants, and of words in lists. The dominant metaphor in philological language studies was botanical, in terms of roots, stems, branches and trees, or zoological, in terms of families, mother-and-daughter languages, and languages that were 'living' or 'dead'. The great success of philology was the minute comparison of forms across a variety of languages, allowing scholars for the first time to catalogue the histories of word-forms and draw in the outlines of whole cognate groups of languages. This, in effect, was what made Noah Webster's etymologies useless and James Murray's dictionary possible.

The very success of the historical linguists, however, led to new questions and approaches to language. One of these was the structural and synchronic linguistics of Ferdinand de Saussure that in due course influenced Philip Gove and Webster's *Third New International Dictionary*. Another, however, was the work of the French linguist Michel Bréal who published his *Essai de sémantique*[1] in 1897.

Bréal was interested in correcting the overly form-related work of, in particular, the German philologists towards a greater concern for systems of relationships among items of language. Such systems of relationships were to be approached from an entirely different angle – not morphologically, but semantically, in terms of meaning and function. Semantics today is an enormously varied subject that can be approached from the historical point of view, as Bréal did, from the synchronic or static contemporary point of view, as John Lyons largely does, or variously from the standpoints of logic, philosophy, psychotherapy, sociology and anthropology. The results can be conflicting, but this does not mean that the Pandora's box that Bréal chose to open should have been left closed. The meaning of 'meaning' has to be examined, if for no better reason than to see whether, in Lyons's words, 'what we refer to, in English, with the word "meaning" has some kind of existence or reality' (1981a,b:137–8).

Lyons notes that even in near-neighbouring languages like French and German terms like *signification* and *Bedeutung* do not have quite the same area of reference as 'meaning', with the consequence that a theory of semantics framed in the lexis of one language could be different from one framed in the lexis of another language. If this is so, and it probably *is* so, then a properly universal theory of semantics is going to be hard to come by.

Anthropologists have already become uncomfortably aware of this problem. Their discipline hopes for a secure set of universals of description through which all the cultures that interest them can be studied; their discipline has suffered however, perhaps inevitably, from its understanding of non-Western cultures being filtered through a Western lens. Despite their innumerable small differences, such languages as French, German and English belong in the same general sociocultural matrix; the more one studies languages and cultures far removed historically and culturally from that matrix, the more one becomes aware of the hold that this matrix has on the minds and attitudes of the investigators.

There is now a strong tradition within anthropology of researchers who have been aware of the relativity of cultures and the differences among the grids that such cultures place upon 'reality'. This tradition includes Franz Boas, Edward Sapir, Claude Lévi-Strauss and Benjamin Lee Whorf, and from the 1960s onwards has been strengthened by the work of various 'cognitive' anthropologists and cross-cultural researchers in the United States.[2] For this tradition, distinct communities each possess an interacting complex of language(s), general behaviour, particular ritual and belief, body language and mindset that makes all such communities unique interpreters of the cosmos. 'Getting inside another culture' or 'seeing ourselves as others see us' are therefore difficult matters because, initially at least, we do not even know what to look for in another culture that distinguishes it significantly from our own; at first, we can only look for what our own culture has conditioned us to see. As John Fieg puts it (see Smith and Luce 1979:32):

> Neither the typical Thai nor the average American is aware, of course, of certain advantages and disadvantages inherent in both patterns of behavior. For each accepts his own way – both in the social and the business sphere – as the norm; he sees no real alternative to the pattern which has evolved in his own society. It is only when the two societies are compared that the more efficient American approach to tasks and problems and the more empathic Thai approach to interpersonal relations come into sharper focus. This certainly does not mean that there are no efficient Thais or empathic Americans. It simply highlights a different cultural tendency in the two countries and shows how such terms as 'individualistic' and 'group-oriented' can be misleading unless they are related to specific areas of behavior within a particular society.

Cultures as disparate as those of Thailand and the United States are called 'anisomorphic' (that is, they do not, and cannot be made to, fit neatly into or onto or under or over one another). Unfortunately for our peace of mind, however, this anisomorphism can be pushed even further: if no language, religion or set of social behaviours is isomorphic with any other, then *inside* specific cultures no dialect, sect or set of individual behaviours is isomorphic with any other. Nothing ever quite fits in a world of approximations.

Acutely aware of this problem, various anthropologists have tried to find analytical procedures that might offer safer assessments of what goes on in a culture and its means of expression and communication. For this, they have tried such techniques as semantic analysis, componential analysis and ethnosemantics. The first of these focuses on the general problem of meaning, of how people organize their world and talk (and write) usefully about it, and possibly why societies and individuals do not always understand each other very well. The second is a concern for the actual components or 'atoms' of meaning, with the aim of setting up a kind of universal inventory of such components common to all of us (and in this strikingly reminiscent of the aspirations of Bishop Wilkins and Peter Mark Roget). The third re-emphasizes that the centre of interest is a people-cum-culture rather than a language for its own sake: language is a means of getting at worldviews, and a part-shaper of those worldviews. Cognitively orientated anthropologists try to ask questions, but are more interested in uncovering the questions that a society has asked itself than in simply getting answers to questions that the worldview of the West conditions us to ask (Tyler 1969).

And in the process of this kind of investigation, these anthropologists have come hard up against the problem of lexicography. In 1969, Harold Conklin observed: 'While extant dictionaries and vocabularies do provide glosses and definitional material, many of the non-trivial, and often essential, semantic and contextual relationships obtaining among lexical items are often neglected or handled in an imprecise and unsystematic way.' This, for Conklin, is as true for English as for his special interest, the Hanunóo language of the Philippines. Thus, if a dictionary lists a Hanunóo plant name simply as 'a kind of plant', then the syntactic aspect may have been covered but no useful semantic-cum-cultural analysis has been done, because we do not know how and where that plant fits into the local view of plants. Conklin adds that he could, in his analysis of Hanunóo terms, have ended up with some 2,000 such lexical items, all identically labelled but systematically unresolved. Instead, he tried to build up an internally consistent framework of what the various items meant within Hanunóo society. Finally, Conklin suggests that the problem is just as real in reverse, if a Hanunóo wants to learn about English plant terms from an English dictionary, and concludes that an ethnosemantic approach might also therefore be of interest 'even to lexicographers who work only in relatively familiar cultural surroundings'.[3]

Cognitive anthropology and structural semantics together offer some interesting ideas to lexicography, among them a description of 'vocabulary' that does without the overly familiar concept 'word'. I talked in broad terms about 'words' at the start of this study as one of the currencies of the mind in dealing with the world. The earlier observation can now be amended somewhat by saying that 'words' as such are difficult things to manipulate in terms of language universality; that is, what one culture understands by a 'word' may be – and usually is – very different from what another culture understands. Our own concept of 'words' is massively influenced by how we see them on paper – with white space before and after them in lines, asserting their 'wordness'. However, even a cursory examination of two or three languages shows that words are not isomorphic any more than anything else: the 'word' *reguntur* in Latin, for example, is translated by the three 'words' *they/are/ruled* in English. How we define the concept 'word' in Latin is therefore very different from how we must define it in English.

Morphological studies of language have never been entirely efficient in coming to terms with this fact, whereas semantic studies have achieved some success by proposing three distinct layers of lexical organization. These are:[4]

- the *lexeme* – an elementary unit of 'content' meaning that may or may not be regarded as a distinct 'word' in a language. Thus, 'rule' in English is both a lexeme and a free word, while its rough equivalent *reg-* in Latin is a lexeme and a bound base on which proper Latin words are formed. Lexemes, in this view of language, are organized into longer stretches of speech and writing by means of various processes that are morphemic (that is, concerned with formation). In English, lexemes are what we generally class as nouns, verbs and adjectives.
- the *lexical set* – which consists of all the lexemes that relate to, but contrast with, each other in a particular way (whether in terms of synonymy, antonymy, hyponymy or any other specific and apparently universal semantic relationship). Sets, of course, can contain subsets, as for example when the set of all plants in English subdivides into the set of all trees on the one hand and grasses on the other.
- the *lexical domain* or *semantic field* – which is the major area or range within which a lexical set or sets operate, such as 'living things', or 'military terms', or 'religion'.

Such an analytical procedure as the above does not solve all our taxonomic problems overnight, but it does offer a formal system which makes thinking about those problems easier. Additionally, in dealing with such areas as kinship terms and plant taxonomies, cognitive anthropologists like Conklin have developed tentative structures for expressing them in, as it were, a graphic shorthand. Three such structures are shown in figures 12, 13 and 14, adapted from the work of Stephen Tyler, also in 1969. They are a binary tree arrangement, a hyponymic tree arrangement, and a tabular paradigm.

Critics of the cognitive approach to anthropology, such as Robbins Burling, have found it salutary in principle but suffering in practice from a

Fig. 12 Stephen Tyler's binary tree

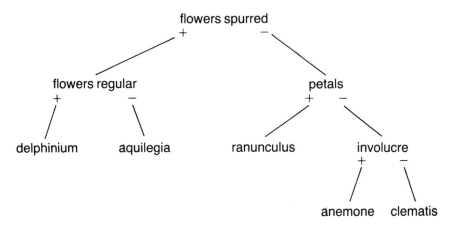

Fig. 13 A hyponymic tree arrangement

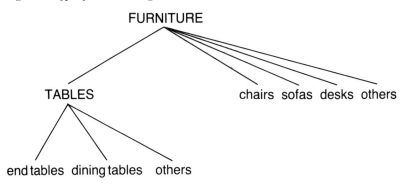

Fig. 14 A tabular paradigm

		Sex		
		male ♂	female ♀	neuter ∅
Maturity	adult M–1	stallion boar	mare sow	gelding barrow
	adolescent M–2		filly gilt	
	child M–3	colt shoat		
	baby M–4	foal piglet		

surfeit of programmatic articles and few detailed and integrated descriptions of a complete ethnosemantic system. Among his most telling criticism is the problem of indeterminacy, in that a multitude of orderings, all equally satisfactory, are possible for certain kinds of lexical material, and no method exists of deciding which ordering is the best. What he is saying, in effect, is what we have found in this review – that there are no absolute answers in the field of taxonomics, though there may be better or worse answers in particular instances. Dell Hymes welcomed Burling's criticism as a valuable corrective to over-enthusiasm, but felt that scepticism should be laced with humanity in any area where researchers are struggling to chart values, attitudes, beliefs and other notions relating to what goes on inside other people's heads. The implication is that we cannot go back simply because we fear to claim too much at any particular time (Tyler 1969: 419–31).

In lexicography, however, there is no need to look for absolute certainties; lexicographers learned long ago that the ultimate definition of any word or set of words is not humanly possible. What the makers of wordbooks can do, however, is note Conklin's pessimistic observation that 'despite encouraging signs, . . . most dictionaries will continue to be organized primarily as alphabetical indices' and so fail to come to terms with lexical systems as a whole. His remark is especially worthy of attention in terms of the present historical review, since we have seen that, however dominant alphabetic listing may be at present, there has always been an alternative tradition available for exploitation.

All in all, by about 1970, linguists and anthropologists were aware that a 'structural' and 'systemic' approach to lexis was possible at least in principle as an alternative to the alphabetic mode, and were beginning to see traditional lexicography (where they thought about it at all) as far too concerned with instances and far too little concerned with the overall picture and interplay of lexical items. The severest criticism of lexicography by a linguist that I have come across is Uriel Weinreich's, in 1964, when he referred to Webster's *Third International* as 'an anecdotal dictionary on a dinosauric scale'.[5] The infinitely varied thumbnail sketches that were so loved by the nineteenth-century classifiers were now no longer good enough. Lexicographers, said Weinreich, should cease to be indifferent to their own methodology.

In a report to the British publisher Longman in 1971, the linguist David Crystal summed up the general feeling by saying that 'we all know information about stylistics, semantic structure, and the like *ought* to be immediately usable (for new kinds of wordbooks), but none of us, in the present state of knowledge, can be sure'.[6] He proposed, therefore, that Longman, who had a long-term interest in lexicography, should undertake a project to see what could be done and, if the results of the project were viable, to publish them as a new kind of semantic wordbook.

I was the researcher who undertook this work in early 1972. It had, looking back at it now, something of the quality of the search for a heavier-than-air flying machine – people were either enthusiastic and supportive, or sceptical and unimpressed. The small and shaky project survived, however, and at the end of nine years' work the *Longman Lexicon of Contemporary English* was published in 1981. This work, it should be stressed, though 900 pages long, does not seek to present the whole of the English language in semantic terms, but presents a core of some 15,000 words in a format which is particularly geared for the advanced foreign learner of the language. It contains, however, all the elements necessary to show what could be done if one wanted to tackle the major part of the lexis of any language.

In effect, the *Lexicon* is a blend of two things: the kind of thematization we have seen over the centuries in the work of compilers like Pliny, Bacon,

Fig. 15 Tom McArthur's taxonomy of semantic fields

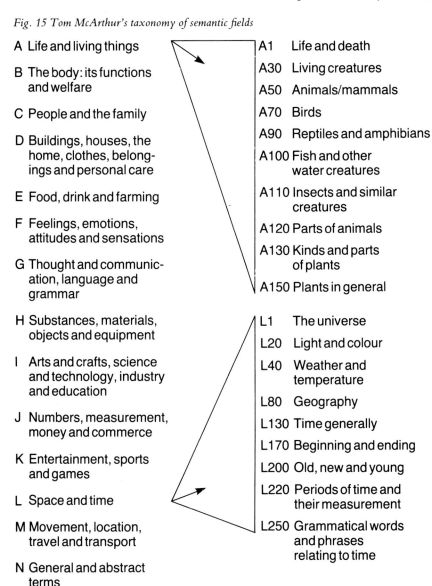

A Life and living things	A1 Life and death
B The body: its functions and welfare	A30 Living creatures
	A50 Animals/mammals
C People and the family	A70 Birds
D Buildings, houses, the home, clothes, belongings and personal care	A90 Reptiles and amphibians
	A100 Fish and other water creatures
E Food, drink and farming	A110 Insects and similar creatures
F Feelings, emotions, attitudes and sensations	A120 Parts of animals
	A130 Kinds and parts of plants
G Thought and communication, language and grammar	A150 Plants in general
H Substances, materials, objects and equipment	L1 The universe
	L20 Light and colour
I Arts and crafts, science and technology, industry and education	L40 Weather and temperature
	L80 Geography
J Numbers, measurement, money and commerce	L130 Time generally
	L170 Beginning and ending
K Entertainment, sports and games	L200 Old, new and young
	L220 Periods of time and their measurement
L Space and time	
M Movement, location, travel and transport	L250 Grammatical words and phrases relating to time
N General and abstract terms	

Comenius and Roget, and the kind of semantic structuring proposed by linguists like John Lyons and anthropologists like Stephen Tyler and Harold Conklin. As such, it belongs squarely in the thematic tradition, but does not quarrel with the utility of the alphabet, in that it has a conventional index like the one that was added to Roget's *Thesaurus*.

The organization of the Lexicon has a 'macrostructure'[7] and a 'micro-structure'. The macrostructure is the set of themes or major topics, similar to Bacon and Roget but without being too philosophical or Latinate. There are 14 such themes, identified by the letters A to N and containing a range of sub-themes or supersets, in that the organization goes down into a microstructure of lexical sets. The 14 themes, with two complete sub-themes displayed, are shown in figure 15.

It would be extremely space-consuming to exemplify the range and variety of the microstructure in the *Lexicon*. Figure 16a, b and c, however, is a representative sample that will serve to show how certain linguistic and anthropological ideas have been absorbed and re-shaped for the specific pur-poses of a *lexicon* or 'word-store' for (foreign) users of English.

A moment's reflection will make it clear that the framework I adopted for the *Lexicon* could have been different in innumerable ways; no two

A representative sample of the word sets in the Longman Lexicon of Contemporary English *(1981) (Figs. 16a-c below).*

Fig. 16a

A51 *nouns* : **the horse and similar animals** [C]

[⇨K199 HORSE RIDING, K200 HORSE RACING]

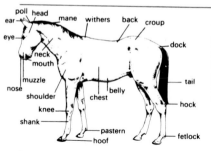

age ＼ sex	*male*	*female*
full-grown	stallion	mare
young	colt	filly
very young newborn	foal	

Names for the horse according to age and sex

horse

Other varieties and breeds of horses and similar animals

pony a horse of a small breed, esp as used by children: *The children enjoyed riding (on) the ponies. They enjoyed the pony rides.*
gelding a stallion which has been castrated [⇒ A18]

mustang a small wild horse of the North American plains
stud 1 *esp AmE* a male horse kept for breeding
2 a number of horses or other animals kept for breeding

donkey *or* ass   mule

zebra

donkey, ass (*fig*) a foolish person: *Don't be such an ass—It's a silly thing to do! He's a bit of a donkey; he does silly things.*
jackass 1 a male ass **2** (*fig*) a foolish person

mule a cross between a horse and a donkey: *The cart was pulled by two mules.*
zebra a striped animal from Africa, related to the horse

Fig. 16b

C13 nouns : names for one's father and mother [N; C]

father

dad	infml also with any much older man	Come on, Dad! The dads and mums were invited to see their children's work at the school
daddy	infml esp by & to children	Help me, Daddy! 'Is your daddy at home, dear?' he asked the little girl.
pa	infml esp AmE & BrE working class	Come on, Pa; time to go.
papa	old use esp by & to children, esp upper class	Papa, may we leave the room, please? Ask your papa about it, darling.
poppa	infml esp AmE	Come on, Poppa; let's go now. My poppa says I should work hard at school.
pop	infml esp AmE also with any much older man	Come on, Pop; let's have a drink.

Fig. 16c

C80 SOCIAL ORGANIZATION   100

C80 nouns : towns and cities, etc

general and smaller	town
larger	city
small	village
very small	hamlet

town 1 [C] a group of houses, buildings, etc where people live: *There are several little towns in this valley. London is a big town; it's usually called a city.* 2 [S] *affec* a city: *Dear old Glasgow/London town; it's nice to be back!* **townspeople** [P] the people in a town **townsfolk** [P] *infml* townspeople

city [C *often in names*] a (very) large town with a centre where business goes on and entertainments [⇨ K2] can be found: *New York is one of America's busiest cities. Mexico City is the capital of Mexico. The city police caught a lot of criminals last year.*

village 1 [C] a (small) group of houses: *It's quite a big village now with its own village school, but you couldn't call it a town. He walked down the village street to the village shop.* 2 [S *esp in names*] part of a city still regarded as a village: *She lives in Duddingston Village in Edinburgh. Tye Green Village is in the town of Harlow.* **villager** [C] a person living in a village

hamlet [C] a very small village; a few houses together: *He lives in a sleepy little hamlet beside the river.*

settlement [C] a place with some buildings where people have (fairly recently) started to live: *There are four settlements along the river. We hope to build a permanent settlement near the mines (= a settlement which will become a town).*

township [C] 1 a town (and the area around it) which has its own local government 2 a small town which serves as the business centre of an area 3 a settlement which is developing into a town

thematic lexicographers, left to themselves, need ever come up with the 'same' scheme. Another compiler, starting with the same basic material as I did (drawn from elementary word lists for the teaching of English) would have assembled a slightly different set of 15,000 items and would have presented them and defined them somewhat differently. A further moment's reflection, however, will make it equally clear that the same is true for alphabetic lexicographers: they start off with the same alphabet and some shared conventions of columnar listing and layout, but after that it is each compiler for him- or herself. Thematic lexicography is therefore no better or worse because it is so apparently subjective. Language being so diffuse and diverging a thing, however, it is highly unlikely that we will ever get a safe-and-sound God's-Truth way of handling it. This work, consequently, is McArthur's *Lexicon*; if it is not sufficient for its purposes, or for other purposes, then others can make *their* lexicons. I look forward to that possibility.

However, this said in the full awareness of imperfection and unfulfilled possibilities, a proponent of the thematic mode can take refuge in at least three significant factors:

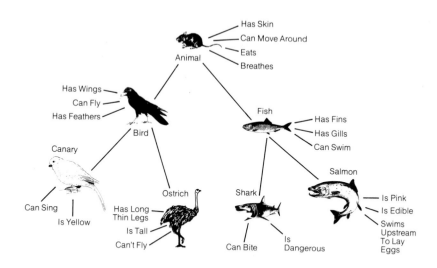

From Quillian's 'Language Comprehender' program, a hierarchical lexicon for birds.

- Any reasonably well-constructed conceptual framework is far closer to 'reality' and how our minds work than anything that is alphabetically ordered (however useful alphabetic ordering may be).
- There is, as we have noted, a considerable consensus down the centuries, in the Classical-to-Christian-to-Rationalist culture of the Western world, as to what the primary categories need to be in any ordering of the cosmos from a human point of view.
- None of the preceding matters too much, as long as by such means a user can gain an insight into the nature of a language (or whatever other target is involved), through entries being defined in sets whose members have well-displayed and graspable associations.

These three principles extend beyond normal lexicography, and may well in the near future be developed in interesting ways by computer specialists, psychologists and others. We have already noted, in discussing Roget's *Thesaurus*, that the thematic mode offers one possible analogue for how 'ideas' are organized in the mind. Robert Dutch pointed this out in 1962, and it need come as no surprise that since then various investigators have experimented with conceptual thematization.

A cast in point is the work reported by A.M. Collins, a psychologist, and M.R. Quillian, a computer programmer, in 1972.[8] Quillian devised a program called 'The Teachable Language Comprehender', a logic system which suggests certain things about how the mind/brain works (Collins going on to test these suggestions in various ways which are not immediately relevant to our concerns here). Of the Quillian program, Alan Baddeley says (1982:79):

> The heart of this program is a system for representing and accessing knowledge. Knowledge is stored in terms of a network of interrelated concepts; more specifically the relationship is hierarchical, with particular instances being linked together at a more abstract level . . . Take the concept *canary*; this is linked to the more abstract concept of *bird* which in turn is linked to the concept of a *living thing*. Attached to each concept is a series of attributes, hence *canary* is associated with its characteristic colour, *yellow*, the fact that it can sing and so on. This model has a further interesting feature, namely that it economizes on the amount of information directly stored by only storing at the level of *canary* information that is not characteristic of all birds, and only storing at the level of *birds* information that is not characteristic of all living things. In order to decide that a canary can fly, the program uses a process of inference, moving from the fact that a canary is a bird to the fact that birds can fly.

This is essentially the thesaurus/lexicon approach to handling information about language (tied in, as we have seen, with recent developments in anthropology and linguistics). There is every likelihood that it will be considerably extended as part of work both on natural and artificial intelligence.

Apart from such developments, other thematic compilations like the *Lexicon* have been, and no doubt are being, produced in the last third of the twentieth century. To look at a selection of reference books in a high street bookshop (or a main street bookstore), however, is to suppose that thematization is a very minor matter compared with alphabetic presentation. On the surface this is certainly true, and will probably continue to be true for the remainder of this century, but just below the surface in many instances something noteworthy is happening. It suggests that very little serious work is currently being done in the alphabetic mode without close attention being paid to the other tradition.

18

Tensions and trends:
overt alphabet, covert theme

Peter Mark Roget brought out his *Thesaurus*, as we have seen, to serve as a converse to the dictionary and to display associations among words in a format that approximated to the mind. It is both ironic, therefore, and indicative of the sheer gravitational pull of ABC ordering that a number of books calling themselves Roget's *Thesaurus* now exist in standard alphabetical arrangement.

The rationale of such works as *The New Roget's Thesaurus in Dictionary Form* and *The American Roget's College Thesaurus in Dictionary Form*[1] is the same as that behind the adding of an index to the basic format: People can handle alphabetization much more easily than thematization, because they are used to it. The alphabetized Roget spin-offs apparently make good commercial sense, however dubious they may be when they claim to preserve the essential Roget, and it is worth a little inquiry as to how they manage to provide the basic thematic service while utterly dismantling the original conceptual system.

What in effect happens with such books is that they create an entirely new style altogether, which was much more honestly displayed in a compilation published in 1902 by the American philologist Francis March and entitled *A Thesaurus Dictionary of the English Language*.[2] In all such syntheses, there is a basic alphabetic list of all the words to be covered, but some of the entries are more detailed than the others. What we end up with is one list but two tiers of entries combined in that list:

- the majority of minor entries which are simply followed by some kind of definition or list of synonyms, and then a specially signalled (usually capitalized) cross-reference to one or more key words which are among
- the minority of words which serve to head up detailed displays of synonyms (with further cross-references to antonyms)

The system works well, and the blend is entirely legitimate (especially as promoted by March), but it has nothing to do with what Peter Mark Roget originally set out to do. For our purposes here, however, it shows how themes can be used as a skeletal structure (the original Roget) in order to make alphabetic wordbooks that to some extent cover what the themes were already designed to do.

It is in France, however, that a bolder and more imaginative method of presenting synonyms and antonyms (etc.) within an alphabetic format developed. In 1950, the French commercial lexicographer Paul Robert[3] brought out his *Dictionnaire alphabétique et analogique de la langue française*, a work whose main innovative thrust was (in his own words, in translation) 'principally in the enriching of the alphabetic format by the interplay of the association of ideas'. In 1952, Robert founded his own publishing house, La Société du Nouveau Littré, whose general editor since 1959 has been Alain Rey. *Le Grand Robert*, as his master dictionary is now called, in contrast with its offspring *Le Petit Robert* and *Le Micro Robert*, is a six-volume work of 5,600 pages and some 120,000 entries. For convenience I shall concern myself here, however, with *Le Petit Robert*, a work of more immediately manageable proportions (one volume, 1,972 pages, around 50,000 entries), whose tripartite plan, according to Rey in 1972, seeks to cover three major aspects of the French language:

- the *descriptive aspect*, covering the contemporary language
- the *historical aspect*, providing information about earlier forms of the language
- the *analogical aspect*, enabling users to bring words together virtually despite the alphabetic order.

Of such matters, Rey notes (in translation):

Every dictionary is a list of words, organized in a certain order: that order, the alphabet, is used by the majority of works of reference. It is known by anyone who is not illiterate, but it is nonetheless completely arbitrary and does not respond in any way to the reality of spoken language. For example, synonyms and members of the same word family are kept apart from each other in alphabetic ordering by various quite unrelated words. Not only is *façon* very far from *manière* and *mode*, but it is separated from *façonner* by *faconde*, which has no connection whatever with it. These inconveniences are neutralized in the *Petit Robert* . . . Thanks to Paul Robert, language dictionaries have benefited from a new method that is at once practical and pedagogical, while still being based on a precise and deep appreciation of the phenomenon of language. The author calls this method 'analogy' in order to emphasize its comprehensive nature: both linguistic and conceptual. From word to word by means of relations among ideas, from idea to idea by means of words – that is the route that Robert's analogies invite us to take.

Where Johnson worked with words and Roget sought to work with ideas, Robert has sought to operate simultaneously with words and ideas. The method used to incorporate non-alphabetic elements into the standard dictionary format is a straightforward one not at all unlike the re-orderers of Roget: the use of the symbol *V* for *voir* (see) placed at appropriate points in an entry and followed by the cross-referred items in bold-face type. The procedure covers not only synonyms and antonyms but also words related to one another variously within certain 'semantic fields'.

For synonyms, if one looks up for example the word *facile* ('easy') on page 673, one finds as part of the general information in the entry the following cross-referencing in sets of associated words:

for sense 1 of *facile*:	*aisé, commode, élémentaire, enfantin, simple; faisable, possible*
for sense 2	*aisé, coulant*
for sense 3	*habile*
for sense 5	*accommodant, arrangeant, conciliant, doux, malleable, tolérant*

As regards coverage via semantic fields, one can find an abundance of cross-references on page 271 under *cheval* ('horse'), of which the following is only a selection:

mustang, tarpan	(for wild horses)
centaure, hippogriffe, licorne, pégase	(for fabulous horse-like beasts)
hippologie	(for the study of horses)
étalon	(for the male horse)
hongre	(for the castrated male)
jument	(for the female horse)
poulain, pouliche	(for colt and filly)
bardot, mule, mulet	(for hybrids with the ass)
hennissement	(for the sound made by a horse)
crottin, pissat	(for the excreta of a horse)

The field is rich, with well over 100 terms to go to, and covering anatomy, appearance, colours, breeds, activities, harness and equestrian equipment, personnel and so forth. The only drawback is that the inquirer would have to do all this cross-referring and presumably make notes or put markers in the various pages in order to fit together once again the scattered parts of a theme *that the Robert editors must have possessed in the first place in order to make the system work*. Despite the ingenuity, there seems to be a kind of mischief-mongering here: the very ingenuity of Robert's scheme is required as an antidote to the inadequacies of the alphabetic mode. The alphabet is *convenient*, however, every literate person knows it, therefore it must be used and the world fragmented if necessary so that its convenience can be benefited from.

It is not only the dictionary-makers who have laboured hard to handle themes (however raggedly) while making more and more ABC lists. The encyclopedists too have regularly come up against the frustration of never quite knowing how much to encapsulate in a particular entry, how much in another cognate entry half the alphabet away, and how much to cross-refer. What one sees in all the works of reference that have tried to cover both semantic–conceptual realities and in-depth information, as well as masses of small nuggets of information, is a model in which a long line develops blisters

Fig. 17 A 'line and blister' model of alphabetic reference books

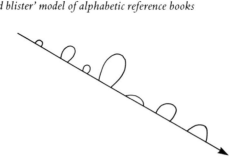

of various sizes, as in figure 17. Here, the line represents a, b, c, . . . z, and each of the blisters represents a special group of synonyms that are best explained together, or a semantic field that should be kept reasonably unified, or a special subject that ought to be covered in depth in one place – despite the alphabet. It is the problem that we saw already developing in the first edition of the *Encyclopaedia Britannica* in the late eighteenth century, and it is appropriate that we return to that problem and that particular encyclopedia now.

The general style of the *Britannica*, as we saw, won the day for encyclopedias at large in the English-using world: plenty of short entries, a number of lengthy entries, and enough cross-referencing to fit the two together. This was a tolerably efficient format which survived with little alteration for some 150 years. It is worth noting, however, that the format did face one last great challenge from the thematic mode, one that failed but whose influence has lingered on. This last challenge was from the *Encyclopaedia Metropolitana*, as planned by Samuel Taylor Coleridge, who is better remembered now as a poet and friend of William Wordsworth.[4]

Of the *Britannica*, Coleridge somewhat scornfully observed: 'To call a huge unconnected miscellany of the *omne scibile*, in an arrangement determined by the accident of initial letters, an encyclopaedia, is the impudent ignorance of your Presbyterian bookmakers.' He proposed instead a Baconian schema, and it is ironic not only that this plan failed, but that his own nephew Herbert Coleridge in the not too far distant future became the first editor of an even huger 'unconnected miscellany' (what is now the *Oxford English Dictionary*), a work that was also to be delivered into the hands of Presbyterian compilers.

Coleridge's plan for the *Metropolitana* covered the pure and applied sciences, thematically arranged, biographical and historical material chronologically arranged, and various lexicographical appendices (such as Charles Richardson's dictionary) that would be alphabetically arranged. Bacon and Wilkins would certainly have approved it, and Roget probably did, as a contributor, and may have kept the scheme in mind over the years till he could produce his own *Thesaurus*. The *Metropolitana* began to appear in 1818, but Coleridge immediately dissociated himself from it, because in his view the publisher made changes in the original plan without consultation or even warning. In due course, the project folded.

Of it, however, Collison notes that 'although the *Metropolitana* was an impressive failure, the ideas for it had a lasting influence. Even though nearly all encyclopaedias today are arranged alphabetically, the classifications of Bacon and Coleridge still enable editors to plan their work *with regard to an assumed hierarchy of the various branches of human knowledge*' (my italics).[5] It is Collison's 'checklist' approach once again, where a concealed thematic structure lurks behind the ABC surface of encyclopedists' work.

The evolution of the *Encyclopaedia Britannica*, in the 215 years of its existence, has been as uneven as the lengths of its original entries; through 13 revisions the line-and-blister model has dominated, or, as Warren Preece has put it, 'a combination of relatively long "systematic" articles supported by thousands of shorter and more specific entries'. Saturation point was reached, however, in 1929, when 'it had become clear to almost everyone that the system of numbered editions, revised in a major way only erratically and supplemented by new material only occasionally, could no longer meet the demands of a serious encyclopaedia and its users.' A new policy of continuous revision was therefore instituted that meant, for the 14th Edition, 'for more than 40 years no two editions of the *Britannica* were ever completely similar', a rather curious state of affairs for an internationally respected work, but one that did reflect the real flux of life. It also provoked, however, from 1947 onwards, a complete re-appraisal of what an encyclopedia should be doing, and this re-appraisal resulted in what may well be, to date, the largest and most adventurous piece of publishing in history.

The 15th Edition of the *Britannica* is essentially the achievement of three men: William Benton, its publisher, who most unfortunately died just before it was completed, Mortimer Adler, its planner, and Warren Preece, its chief editor. The vast undertaking took more than a decade of concentrated effort to produce, cost $32 million, involved around 5,000 people, and was offered to the public in 1974 at about $700 per set, a sum that may seem large but is a bagatelle when one considers that it buys more encapsulated knowledge in one language than was ever available before to any of our ancestors. Though assembled in the United States, the end-product is nonetheless cosmopolitan, in that fewer than half of the contributing specialists were American, and assistance of one kind or another came from 131 countries. It is a remarkable achievement, and one cannot help wondering what the original Society of Gentlemen in Edinburgh would have thought of it.

What makes the 15th Edition, or *Britannica 3* as it is sometimes called, remarkable is both its tripartite structure and the unique way in which it blends the alphabetic and thematic modes. The alphabet still dominates, but where in other modern works the themes are concealed as checklists in the 15th Edition they are revealed as the essential skeleton of the whole. The result is a synthesis of very new and very old. Indeed, as one commentator, Anthony Quinton,[7] observed in 1974, 'the movement in Chicago . . . has sought to restore unity to learning of a kind exemplified in the work of Aristotle and with a pronounced neo-Thomist inflection'.

The editors of *Britannica 3* solved the problems inherent in the line-and-blister model by quite simply separating the line from the blisters; they solved the alphabetic/thematic dilemma by having an alphabetic ordering for everybody and a thematic secondary arrangement for the *aficionados* who might want it. The core of their radical re-organization was to turn one encyclopedia into two, the first set of ten volumes being called the *Micropaedia*, and the second set of nineteen volumes being called the *Macropaedia*. The *Micropaedia* handles, alphabetically, a vast number of short general entries and serves as a quick-answer work of reference, while the *Macropaedia* provides just over 4,000 in-depth articles, also arranged alphabetically. The two sets are unidirectionally linked by means of detailed cross-references from the short entries to further reading across in the *Macropaedia*. In addition, the lone index volume that used to appear *at the end* of earlier editions was promoted *to the beginning* of the 15th Edition, and the old alphabetic index transformed into a conceptual scheme dwarfing anything Pliny, Aquinas, Bacon or Coleridge ever conceived. This set of themes and sub-themes makes up the bulk of the one-volume *Propaedia* that the user may consult or ignore, but which offers a rational reading plan for any range of subjects in the in-depth *Macropaedia* volumes. To give some idea of the size and complexity of the *Propaedia* system I cannot do better than quote Quinton once more:

> The first of the thirty volumes, the *Propaedia*, or 'Outline of Knowledge', or 'Guide to the *Britannica*', devotes nearly 800 of its 900-or-so pages to a massively detailed articulation of the whole, all-inclusive field of the encyclopaedia's concern under something like 15,000 headings, themselves arranged in seven levels of taxonomic stratification. Thus, forced labour in modern states . . . is item ii under servitude and slavery in the late nineteenth and twentieth centuries, itself item c under social immobility: slavery, servitude and forced labour. The latter is item 6 under social stratification and social mobility, which is part B of social status, itself the third ingredient of social organization and social change, which, finally, is division II of human society, Part Five of the whole system.

Mind-numbing as the thematic hierarchy is, it is built upon a relatively simple foundation of 10 grand themes of an evolutionary anthropocentric nature, up-dating the kind of cosmic ordering with which we are now familiar. These 10 grand themes are:

1 matter and energy
2 the earth
3 life on earth
4 human life
5 human society
6 art
7 technology
8 religion
9 the history of mankind
10 the branches of knowledge

Mortimer Adler, the architect of the Propaedic system, indicates in his introduction to the scheme that, although it is presented as a list or line, it should be perceived rather as a circle, indeed as *the* 'circle of learning' of the ancients that is intended in the word en-cyclo-paedia. The circle, he claims, has no particular beginning-point or end, and is not intended to impose any particular view of the world upon the user. It can, he says, be represented

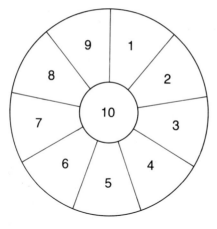

Fig. 18 Mortimer Adler's rotary 'circle of learning'

diagrammatically as follows, where the 10th grand theme, the branches of human knowledge, occupies a central and unifying position (see figure 18). It is an attractive model, especially when Adler converts it into a wheel that can 'rotate around its axis' so that 'any of the ten [*sic*] parts may be regarded as standing at the top'.[8]

Here at length the 'checklist' emerges almost openly from its shadowy place behind the alphabet. To forestall any possible criticism about the still obviously secondary role of the themes, Adler says: 'It may be asked why it was not thought better to abandon the alphabetical principle entirely and construct a purely topical encyclopaedia, in which all the articles would be assembled, volume after volume, according to some general schema for the organization of human knowledge.' In answer to such a question, he offers two reasons:

– A purely topical (thematic) organization 'cannot avoid the appearance of a certain tendentiousness or arbitrariness in the editorial commitment to one rather than another organizing schema or set of principles', provoking thereby awkward questions about whether the adopted schema is the One True Presentation.
– 'A purely topical encyclopaedia provides its readers with only one mode of access to its contents.' An alphabetic index might alleviate this, of course, but such an index 'does not provide a general and systematic mode of access to the contents'.

As we have already seen, there are serious issues at stake with regard to Adler's first reason for not making the themes primary and the alphabet secondary. As I did with the *Lexicon* themes, however, it would be perfectly possible to make whatever disclaimers one wished in the introduction, and then leave it to the user to judge how successfully the system worked. Adler, however, falls into his own trap, because *any* 'purely topical organization', whether primary or secondary, is faced with the problem of tendentiousness and arbitrariness; one does not escape such a problem by making the set of themes secondary (and therefore less visible to the general user). Additionally, as regards the second point, it is curious to fault thematic compilations for having 'only one mode of access' to their contents, since alphabetic compilations also have only one mode of access to *their* contents, but no one objects to *them* on those grounds. Finally, it is specious to suggest that indexes cannot be so organized as to provide a properly systematic access system, because all alphabetic compilations are simply indexes, no more and no less. If this last point were true, nothing alphabetically organized would ever be much use at all (and we know from the telephone directory that this is just not so).

We must look elsewhere, therefore, for the real reasons why Adler and his colleagues did not go the whole hog and make thematization primary. These reasons seem to me to be basically as follows:

- The public expects the *Britannica* to be alphabetic, and changing it suddenly to a thematic format would be too radical and therefore too great a commercial risk.
- Since alphabetized works of reference have used thematic structures as 'checklists' for a very long time, making such a checklist explicit would appear radical without necessarily really being so. Users accustomed to ABC ordering could ignore the *Propaedia* without feeling guilty, while the minority that might be interested in themes and the en-cyclo-paedia would enjoy the new secondary access system.
- One could then always watch how things went and consider further moves towards primary thematization or co-equal alphabet and theme in the 16th Edition, if and when it was decided to have one.

All of these reasons are entirely legitimate; if they were indeed in the forefront of the organizing team's minds as they developed *Britannica 3*, it would have been good to see them explicitly stated, rather than to be offered arguments which are not consistent either with logic or the general standard of the *Encyclopaedia Britannica* itself.[9]

Given that the *Britannica* has shifted so far in the direction of overt thematization, it is not surprising that another publisher should have completed the journey. In 1976, there came out in London a 10-volume work called the *Joy of Knowledge Library*, published by Mitchell–Beazley. Its producers claim for it that it 'employs the best of both thematic and alphabetic approaches in the construction of the encyclopaedia'. Their plan was just as simple as the *Britannica's*, but does everything that Adler avoided: the public is offered eight 'purely topical' volumes (each with its own index), plus two complementary volumes called 'fact indexes' that provide quick-answer reference in the normal alphabetic way. The general editor, James Mitchell, has in so organizing his work simply stood the *Britannica* principle on its head.

The result is a set of books which I see as an encyclopedic parallel to what I have attempted in the *Lexicon*: there is a seven-part thematic list with subdivisions in the Baconian style and within it a system of continuous numbering that allows for easy staging of information through the themes, thus:

(A)   the themes:
    1   science and the universe
    2   the physical earth
    3   the natural world
    4   man and society
    5   history and culture (two volumes: early/recent)
    6   man and machines
    7   the modern world (a gazetteer)

(B)   identification of elements within a theme-volume by means of numbers, say, from 1 to 300 (according to page), without any complex
system of coding, as follows:
    16   Introduction
        The growth of science
    20   Prehistoric and ancient science
    22   Asian and medieval science
    24   Alchemy and the Age of Reason
        Mathematics
    26   Mathematics and Civilization
    28   The grammar of numbers
        etc.

(C)   The use of a 'spread system', the basic unit for the thematic volumes,
where each entry is spread over two complete open pages and never
more, so that the whole unit can be studied as one piece (with integrated
art work that would have gladdened the heart of Comenius). Each
spread system is about one-third text and two-thirds integrated
graphics with captions.

(D)   The provision in each spread of a small square of 'connections', cross-
referring to related spreads elsewhere in the same volume. (Not forgetting that each such volume also has the fail-safe device of a conventional
index.)

    Mitchell's creation demonstrates what modern print technology can do
with the thematic tradition as far as providing what Mitchell–Beazley itself
calls 'a new "family bible" of knowledge' for 'a visually oriented age'. The
work is manifestly secular, and yet this figurative reference to the Bible links
it forcefully to a past of faith and dogma when such thematic formats were the
norm and not the exception.[10]
    Such a time is unlikely to return, either in terms of monolithic faith or
scribal technology, but there is every reason to suppose that as we progress
into the electronic age all sorts of permutations will be tried out as regards the
fundamental options available in the storing, accessing and display of information, so that no particular bias will be favoured simply because it has been
the dominant convention for a time. The options available to us are easy to
display now themselves, but we should not forget that it has taken over 5,000
years of continuous effort with the contingent and the universal elements in

Fig. 19 The options for storing, accessing and displaying information

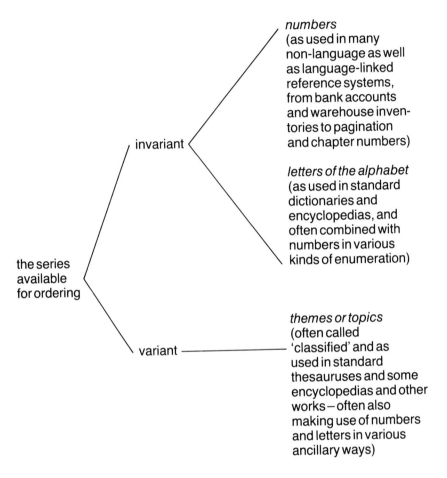

the series
available
for ordering

invariant

numbers
(as used in many
non-language as well
as language-linked
reference systems,
from bank accounts
and warehouse inven-
tories to pagination
and chapter numbers)

letters of the alphabet
(as used in standard
dictionaries and
encyclopedias, and
often combined with
numbers in various
kinds of enumeration)

variant

themes or topics
(often called
'classified' and as
used in standard
thesauruses and some
encyclopedias and other
works – often also
making use of numbers
and letters in various
ancillary ways)

the containerization of knowledge to get to where we are now. The basic
options are shown in figure 19.

These options are simple, but – as with atoms and molecules – the
permutations and combinations possible are indefinitely large. Given our
present situation, where all sorts of pressures exist for the encoding and
presentation of information, it is just as well that they are.

Tomorrow's world

After this I looked, and there before my eyes was a door opened in heaven; and a voice that I had first heard speaking to me like a trumpet said 'Come up here, and I will show you what must happen hereafter'.

JOHN, *Revelation*, 4★

Evolution and miniaturization: from Charles Babbage's analytical engine to a present-day desk-top computer.

19
Shaping things to come:
the priests of High Technology

In terms of both their etymology and their evolution, 'computers' are 'counters'. In the earlier stages of their development, back in the Dark Ages of the 1940s and 1950s, they were intended to perform certain basic calculating functions that their own specialists today rather disparagingly refer to as 'number-crunching'. The verbs 'compute' and 'count' both derive from the same Latin verb *computare*, which can be translated as either 'to add up' or 'to think out fully'. The primordial meaning allows, therefore, both for the business world's interest in better machines for calculating and displaying information, and the computer buff's desire to see smart machines put to work in an ever widening range of problem-solving.

The detailed history and description of computers are not central to this review and are amply covered in a variety of recent texts. It is worth noting here, however, that the historical processes that have given rise to computers are not at all far removed from those that have given rise to what I have been calling 'macro-lexicography'.[1] Thus, for example, the prehistory of both compilation and calculation lies in notched bones and other early tally systems, while the proto-computer, the abacus, was a parallel development to such artifacts as clay tablets, papyrus rolls and skin parchments. Additionally, both reference works and mathematics make use of the two sets of symbols – numbers and letters.

Logic in particular has always been a central area of interest, and we have seen how philosopher–scientists from the Renaissance onwards have been involved with both the organization of knowledge and the development of such systems as 'real character', calculus, symbolic logic and linguistic notations. Today, as an outcome, there exist several forms of 'mathematical linguistics', a discipline that might at one time have been considered a contradiction in terms. Students of language in the nineteenth century, with their enthusiasm for taxonomy, were not so very far removed from men like Charles Babbage, the inventor of the analytical engine, and Herman Hollerith, who created the tab-card sorter for use in counting election results. Their aims might have been different, but all were interested in orderly processes.

Today, the synthesis of those interested in compilation and language on the one hand and those interested in computation and mathematics on the other is quite remarkable. Philosophers, logicians, mathematicians, linguists and others share an interest in structures, systems, signs, signals and symbols that has led to a great deal of cross-reference and inter-fertilization, so much so indeed that it is sometimes hard to separate kinds of logic and programming from kinds of syntactic and semantic analysis.

As it stands today, however, the computer – like the printing press before it – is the end-product of a variety of theories and techniques that slowly converged over a long period of time. It does not work with the arithmetic of 10 fingers, but with an even more basic system, the night-and-day or yin-and-yang of binary numbers. The organization 'programs' that make it so versatile a tool derive from the world of textiles around the time of the French Revolution, when Joseph Marie Jacquard invented a kind of loom that was primed for complex pattern-making with a system of rods and punched cards. In recent decades, however the motive force of electricity and the technology of semiconductors have served to set the computer apart, not just from all previous reference and calculating technologies, but from all previous machines, in terms of its efficiency, economy and miniaturizability.

Basically, however, and despite its 'high' technological gloss, the universals of the computer are only four in number:[2]

- a *processor*, which is in effect the high-speed 'harmless drudge' that carries out the sequence of operations specified by the program governing the system at any time. (In the same way that automobile engines are measured in terms of 'horse-power', harking back to past analogies, so we might say that the activities of the processor can be assessed in terms of 'clerk-power'.)
- a *memory*, which is the storage component, and is in two parts, the primary or main store and a secondary or backing store. The main store holds both the general instructions and a certain amount of immediately important data, while the backing store is the essential reservoir for the great mass of data, which may be kept – depending on the type of computer – in such containers as drums, tapes, or discs. (The memory store is the precise equivalent of such things as traditional filing systems with cards or folders in cabinets, or books on shelves, or pages in books, or indexes in the backs of books, or alphabetic orderings in dictionaries, and so forth.)
- the *input*, which is what goes from the outside world into the main store, via such 'interface' devices as card-readers or terminal keyboards. (The input is the rough equivalent of consulting a clerk at a desk, or a catalogue, or cards in a cabinet, or filling in a form – or simply opening a reference book at the right page.)
- the *output*, which is what comes from the main store back to the outside world after the required operations have been performed by the processor, via further interface devices such as line-printers, typewriters, or visual display terminals. (The output is the rough equivalent of what the clerk, the catalogue or the reference book provides as a response to your specific act of inquiry.)

From this basic description it can be seen that, although the technology of the current generations of computers is arrestingly novel, the work done is the same work as has always been done (however much slower the pace or larger the scale of operations). Awareness of this point may help strip computers of something of their mystery, but equally that awareness should not obscure the curious aspect of computers: that what can be called a 'mechanism' or a 'machine' can equally well be called an 'organism', if we follow such a definition of 'organism' as is provided in Webster's *New Collegiate Dictionary* (1977, sense 1), which is:

> a complex structure of inter-dependent and subordinate elements whose relations and properties are largely determined by their function as a whole.

If, even after only a few decades, we can think of the computer as an organism, it is not at all surprising that comparisons fly thick and fast between computers and living creatures, and in particular between computers and one paramount organ of creatures like ourselves: the brain (which brings us right back to the container for the processing of knowledge that we considered briefly at the start of this review).

In the early days of computer technology, hardly 40 years ago when it was not even 'high', it was considered that a standard transistorized computer capable *in theory* of replicating the work of the human brain would need to be about the size of the Statue of Liberty (Evans 1979: 54–7). Many commentators, therefore, felt that comparisons between brains and computers were both sensation-mongering and just plain silly. Such observations, said Christopher Evans in 1979, make 'quaint reading' today. In the *Micro Millennium*, he demonstrates how, because of advances in miniaturization, estimates of the necessary size needed to match the brain are now nearer to typewriter-size than building-size – and this just between 1950 and 1980. Of course, truly brain-like computers do not exist and may never exist, but what such commentators as Barr and Feigenbaum call 'intelligent technology' already very nearly exists.[3]

As part of the fast development of computers, 'language' is moving into the mechanism-cum-organism. So-called 'low-level machine language' is not language at all in any conventional sense, but it does constitute the building blocks of what can more legitimately be called language. It is binary, a two-term on-and-off system for exploiting electrical signals and has already been organized into what are known as 'high-level computer languages'. These again are not quite language in the conventional sense, but coding systems (such as ALGOL, BASIC, FORTRAN, PASCAL) that lie at various points on a continuum between algebra-type notations and natural human expression as such. Because of this idea of a continuum, various researchers and developers consider that it is only a matter of time before – with the help of linguistics – quasi-human language will be computer-possible.

Some observers now consider it likely that the organizations of the neurons or communication cells of the brain (through which we construct all our mental systems, including language) are also basically binary codes. If this is so – and it probably *is* so – then when Ernest Kent, a psychologist and psychopharmacologist with a long-term interest in computers, publishes in 1981 a book called *The Brains of Men and Machines*, we have to pay some attention. Additionally, it is also arresting, especially in terms of this review, when in 1983 Benjamin Compaine can write:[4]

> Looking back over the 35 or so years since the development of modern computers, we can spot trends similar to the much slower advance of traditional literacy. At first, computers were strictly for a 'priestly' class that could read and write the *lingua electronica*. All computer users were dependent upon this group of plugged-in clergy. As computers became more widespread and their application more pervasive, however, they began to have a greater impact on business and social institutions. The language (COBOL, FORTRAN, BASIC, etc.) evolved into something closer to the vernacular, and more people were able to use them.

Compaine sees the possibility in the near future of all sorts of 'lay' people participating in computer literacy without, however, having to enter the guild of 'the electronic élite' – just as one does not have to be an automotive engineer in order to drive a car. The analogy with pre-modern times and the clergy is of course striking and seductive, but its attractiveness should not obscure the essential point, which is that the machines are being 'educated' even more than we are; step by step, they are acquiring systems that are more and more like organic nervous systems, and talents that are more and more like our talents – including the subtleties and frustrations of natural language. Computers are in fact moving much more towards us than we need to move towards them.

The electronic age is nevertheless forcing us to look at ourselves and our brains in novel ways. We have traditionally said that human beings study such things as human language in order to make such artifacts as dictionaries, and this of course is as legitimate a statement as it ever has been. Today, however, we can also say, with equal legitimacy and more than a touch of awe, that at its present point along the line of evolution the human brain is studying its own nature. It seeks , for the first time ever, consciously to understand – and in very precise terms indeed – what it has been doing for millennia in other-than-conscious ways (whether in terms of neurons, or language, or psychoanalysis). The brain is also now engaged in studying itself and its attributes with – among other things – a view to replicating its own carbon-based cellular processes in silicon. As the astronomer Frank Shu put it, in 1982:[5] 'Granted, computers are not now alive, but what is there to prevent them from attaining life in future? We believe biological life arose from nonliving matter by chemical evolution. What is there to prevent electronic life from arising fron nonliving matter by computer evolution?'

He also observes that 'once computers catch up with us intellectually, they will soon race ahead', a statement that appears in a standard textbook and not in a pulp sci-fi magazine. Evans adds to this: 'At what period will the average child own a portable personal teaching computer of great power, more knowledgeable and, in certain areas, more intelligent than any human

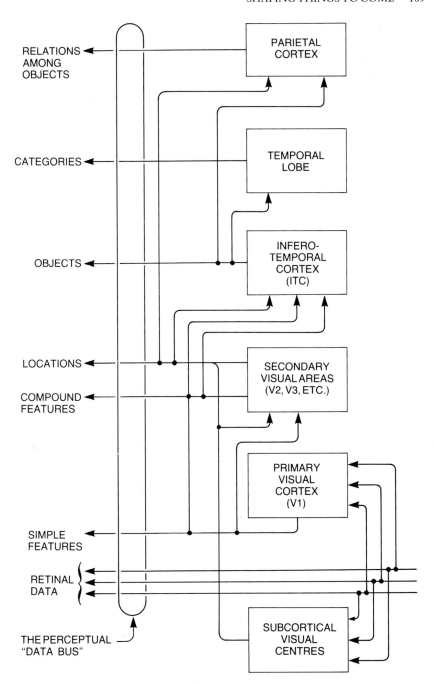

Full circle: Ernest Kent's hypothetical 'perceptual bus', which links thematic taxonomies of the world to appropriate parts of the hardware of the brain .

teacher? The seeds of these developments are firmly planted in today's technology' (Evans 1979:205). Anyone who wants to dismiss the remarks of commentators like Shu and Evans is of course free to do so: what they suggest is indeed bizarre by the standards of the past. In dismissing them, however, we should recall how in less than one century the heavier-than-air machine has gone from a gleam in the inventor's eye to our present space shuttles and satellite systems, and will go further yet.

Quite regardless of such matters, however, the computer and the compiler would seem to be natural allies – eventually. The same mentality animates lexicographers, encyclopedists and programmers, while the basic nature of computational systems disposes them to be helpful to compilation systems. Indeed, their potential in this area changes everything.

Out of six issues that macro-lexicographers must consider in the last decade of the twentieth century, five of those issues could not have been discussed at all before about 1930, four before about 1955, and three before about 1970 (which is thought-provoking when we consider how, in 1900, James Murray could not imagine any further peaks for lexicographers to scale). The six issues are:

The perennial issue	(1) How best to scan for, amass, file, retrieve, define, illustrate, display and distribute lexicographic and encyclopedic information.
Since about 1930	(2) How best to reconcile the lexicographer's 'anecdotal' and 'dinosauric' collecting style with linguistic science's desire for tidy generalization, rigour of presentation, and economy and elegance of theory as well as practice.
Since about 1955	(3) How best to use computer facilities in both academic and commercial compilation for such workhorse purposes as, say, scanning texts, excerpting citation data, and sorting it all out.
Since about 1970	(4) How best to integrate what one might call 'lexicomputers' and 'compupedias' with the work of human editors, analysts, definers and writers in handling basic organizational matters: that is, the machine not just as synthetic file clerk, but as co-compiler.
	(5) How best to integrate international telecommunications systems with varyingly astute local compusystems so as to reorganize the whole concept of macro-lexicography as book-based and of libraries as place-based.

(6) How best to integrate telecommunications, computer technology and photoreproduction facilities (etc.), so as to change quite dramatically the traditional relationship between compilers and publishers on the one side, and user–consumers on the other; in effect, inviting the user–consumer to share in the formulation of services and in the customizing of macro-lexicographic products.

For a variety of reasons, the publishers, editors and compilers of macro-lexicographic materials may not wish to explore such issues too far beyond, say, numbers 1 and 3, or may wish to approach them with caution. Whatever the responses, however, the issues involved may become compelling with the passage of less time than one might suppose.

Not, of course, that compilers have been ignoring the coming of the computer. Quite the contrary. From about 1960 onward the use of computers in linguistics, literary research, encyclopedia work, and lexicography has been on a rising curve. Everybody is either aware of their impact and potential, or is already locking horns with them. While the various early projects went ahead, scholars with backgrounds in literary humanism were variously sceptical, alarmed or cautiously enthusiastic about the arrival of this machine in their sanctuaries, and appear from time to time to have felt the need to reassure themselves that the human brain was still secure (much as the scribes and scholars of the late Middle Ages must have felt disturbed by the printing press). It is interesting in this regard to note the observations of two speakers at the 1972 conference on lexicography in English held under the auspices of the New York Academy of Sciences:[6]

> *Laurence Urdang*: By this time, everyone might be assumed to know what a computer is and what it is capable of. To summarize, however, we assume that the modern general-purpose computer is an idiot-box capable of performing only the simplest of routines. Let no one be deluded into believing that these routines are anything but simple just because advances in design have yielded devices capable of performing them at breakneck speeds, giving the illusion of thought.

> *Frederic Cassidy*: Do we have much hope that the computer will solve our problem? . . . Of course the computer is a very clever invention; and it's damned fast. I think I may claim the phrase for myself, 'The Electronic Drudge', the title of an article I published some years ago (1968) in *Leeds Studies in English*. The electronic drudge is what it is: a drudge. It has no brains. What we have to do is furnish the brains.

Neither speaker was a lexicographical Luddite, both had considerable experience of the computer and fully appreciated how useful it could be in the basic scanning, selecting and collating work so important to their craft, but there is a marked lack of oomph in their papers as regards their new synthetic clerk. Another presenter at the same conference, however, approached the matter rather differently. Urdang and Cassidy appear to have been thinking in terms of issue number 3 in my list, but the other speaker, the computer specialist Richard Venezky, was already moving on to issue number 4, the computer as co-compiler rather than as humble clerk, when he said:

> While computers are only now finding their way into commercial dictionary firms, we can already see a severely limited impact for this technology so long as it is restricted to data transfer and data matching. This is not to say that there are no advantages to be gained from automating such processes as sorting and typesetting – there clearly are; but it is to say that if computer technology is to have the same impact on lexicography as it has had on such fields as meteorology or demography, then uses beyond transfer and matching must be considered and the most promising beyond these two appears to be analysis.

Venezky's view of things is both positive and pragmatic: it is fine if a machine can be programmed to do quickly what 10 or 20 human clerks might only manage slowly, if at all, but the substitution of one fast drudge for umpteen slow ones is not the crucial issue, any more than the quality of the paper one uses for printing dictionaries is the crucial issue. What would be central is the use of a computer to improve the essential nature of lexicography, just as the printing press qualitatively altered it. There are many areas in which this qualitative improvement could take place, but for purposes of exemplification here I would like to discuss only the following four:

- manipulating data that is already available in a traditional format, in order to obtain something uniquely new and useful
- checking content and consistency in a new compilation in ways that human beings might not be able to do well or at all
- text-scanning for the purpose of excerpting material which can then be used for a specific project or as a permanent archive resource
- the creation of universal archives, to which various interested persons could refer in order to quarry out the information or materials that specifically interest them.

I will take these four areas one by one, in order to show how they might be variously realized.

An interesting early project in computer lexicography was undertaken in Switzerland and West Germany in the 1960s and published in 1970 as the *Chronological English Dictionary*.[7] To create this entirely new artifact, the organizers of the project, Thomas Finkenstaedt, Ernest Leisi and Dieter Wolff, first went to the *Shorter Oxford English Dictionary* (3rd Edition, 1964), in which chronological information is given, naturally, entry by entry. There is no way of getting from this dictionary without enormous labour such valuable information as the collated dates of the earliest occurrences of words, and yet the dictionary contains this information. The investigators felt that it was regrettable that one could go to words and get dates but could not go from dates to get words, in order to answer questions like 'Which words were modern when Shakespeare began to write?', or 'Which foreign languages were providing the most neologisms around 1650?'

By using a computer, however, Finkenstaedt and his colleagues completely altered the situation. They prepared and mechanically sorted 81,182 punched cards from alphabetical to chronological order. The information was then transferred to tape and a program written for processing the data and printing out the results, which are a veritable mine of new historical information about English. The work was still a labour of academic love, but it was much less a labour and was done much faster than it ever would have been by using human clerks. There are many things we would do in life if the effort involved in doing them was reduced, and many things that become possible because new labour-saving devices allow us to think in new ways. This dictionary is a good, practical example of just such a project.

To exemplify the second area of interest – computers used to check for internal consistency and completeness in a new compilation – we can look at the *Longman New Universal Dictionary*, published in 1982. In the preface the managing editor, John Ayto, refers to the difficulty of ensuring that 50,000 words are defined in a uniform and clearcut way, adding:[8]

> This is where technology of the computer comes to the aid of the art of lexicography. Longman have devised a unique processing system that has enabled us to perform a number of automated operations on the dictionary that previously could only have been done manually, with much labour and less than 100 per cent accuracy, or indeed might not have been attempted at all. Among the tasks the computer has performed for us has been the monitoring of every word we have used in definitions. This has involved, in the first place, a cross check against all the entries, to make sure that every word used in a definition is itself defined in the dictionary; and in the second place, a careful examination of all vocabulary items used in definitions in over 180 different subject areas, ensuring consistency of treatment and the elimination of words that would present too great difficulty to the non-expert.

This, Ayto adds, is 'technology in the service of art', a service that, if widely adopted for dictionaries in future (as I am sure it will be), could wonderfully tighten up all sorts of nuts and bolts in the general organization of entries and definitions.

To cover my third and fourth areas of interest – the excerption of data for archives and those archives themselves – I would like to review and develop some observations made in this regard by three lexicographers of note at the start of the 1970s: A.J. Aitken, who in 1971 opened the discussion, Richard Bailey who expanded it in 1973, and Clarence Barnhart who, in the same year, outlined a plan for such an archive. They are not the only people to have discussed these issues, but they cover the core areas.

Aitken, editor of the *Dictionary of the Older Scottish Tongue*, raises the issue of 'a computer-readable textual archive' in discussing how computers could help in the compilation of academic-historical dictionaries. Like Urdang and Cassidy, he sees computers as essentially dull-witted super-clerks, that could, however, 'be harnessed to more or less selective, if at the same time monumental, dictionary projects'. Better than one dictionary project, however, would be the creation of actual archives, data in a kind of pre-lexicographic state:

Unlike the fully worked out dictionary, the computer archive is potentially exhaustive: it offers access to all instances of given forms or groups of forms which occur within its corpus. Also unlike the dictionary, however, it must leave the detailed analysis or final arrangement of these to its users . . . Eventually, no doubt, both archive and dictionary will become available for general consultation at remote terminals so that dialogue communication with both, perhaps using a screen outlet, will become possible. As things are now, for a scholar whose needs transcend the information supplied in a conventional dictionary and who is prepared to work out his own analysis of the exhaustive material he can obtain from a computer archive, the dictionary may still be helpful in laying out the guidelines of his investigations.[9]

In this bold vision, Aitken is effectively saying:

- the background citation materials on which dictionaries are often based are not usually accessible even to a limited public, but could be made accessible quite widely in future as a resource that interested persons could study and edit in their own ways
- certain kinds of users are capable of doing certain kinds of customized lexicographic work for themselves, and could do this via a computer facility without the mediation of a strictly professional lexicographer (as in the past)
- technology could make it unnecessary for such a person to visit an archive physically
- traditional dictionary formats could still play a useful role as guides for such do-it-yourself lexicographers
- computer archives could help alter our whole conception of such stores of information as books and libraries.

Bailey widens the discussion by arguing that 'commercial dictionaries will shortly be obliged to enter into some such central arrangement' as an archive. This 'grand resource' would be a kind of electronic pot into which all sorts of source materials could be cast for basic editing, so that various interested parties (presumably subscribers to the service or fee-paying) could draw out what they needed at any time. In such a vision, books about language – and indeed knowledge of any kind – escape their bindings and the limitations of paper and print and explode into something quite new. The work of reference up till now has been a holdable, openable, consultable single product, but in future such an item need only be one of a number of possible end-products emerging from a properly maintained 'lexicentre' which is neither a book nor a library, but instead a network of information points.

Barnhart takes the idea of the archive one stage further, seeing it – in this instance for lexicographers of English – as a central pool for linguists, psychologists, social scientists and lexicographers to work with adequate samplings across the language worldwide, the information organized in lexical units that all specialists would agree on (a very useful development indeed!), an accessing system so that people could get what they wanted precisely when they wanted it, and a sufficient back-up of contextual information and sources so that users would know exactly what they were dealing with. The extension of such an idea to a super-encyclopedic archive is an easy one to make (McDavid and Duckert 1973: 296–7, 302–6).

At the time of writing Barnhart saw the central archive as a fixed place donated by one or more university-type organizations and not unlike some lexical centres already in existence in various parts of the world. Such an institution would set up a bibliographical and research centre, a depository for various files, and a planning group for the development of marking and coding practices (and presumably also for hardware and software problems, marketing, and other financial matters). Basically the conception is still sound 10 years or so later, but technology has moved on so fast that the necessity for a single super-Oxford or mega-Springfield is no longer so apparent. The network idea is now more feasible and more reassuring, where a number of safe depositories could be linked by satellite and other means around the world, as part of the electronic nervous system that we are now building, almost without contemplating the enormity of what we are doing, for the planet we inhabit.

By creating such a nervous system and the virtually instantaneous accessing that it implies, we may at last transcend the oldest distinction of all, with which I started this review: the separateness of reference place and reference object. The new technology will make such things fluid in a way that humankind could never have envisaged before.

20
Knowledge, knowledge everywhere: planetary network, global book

The expression 'high technology' has crept up on us almost unawares, and now we find it everywhere.[1] 'Hi tech' and 'hi-fi' are sister terms that can, semantically speaking, be tied in with such long established metaphors as High Church and Low Church (in the Anglican communion), and of course the 'high' and 'low' languages that have been considered in this review. 'High' is a social value judgement not unlike 'classic', and belongs within the taxonomic frames that we have been making since time immemorial: we don't just classify, we stratify, and all caste systems have their upper and lower echelons.

What the expression 'high technology' implies – although we do not often talk explicitly about it – is that around this new and shiny force are all sorts of 'low technologies'; indeed, in terms of time, the implication is that *all* our technologies up till now have been of the low kind, vernaculars of technology that did not quite measure up. Like vernaculars and barbarians and the heathen, these older technologies had a vaguely polluting, unrefined and dark satanic quality about them, and the metaphor of height suggests that we are now emerging into the uplands of a finer, cleaner way of doing things.[2]

There could well be truth in back of this image: electronic machines do not belch smoke and gobble fossil fuels the way earlier industrial processes have done, and they have a clinical and antiseptic look about them which distances us from the grime and gore of everyday past reality. Most importantly, however, especially from the angle of this review, High Tech belongs with and extends the values of an élite that stretches back to Egypt and Sumer: as Compaine suggests, the electronically literate are the inheritors and expanders of the tradition that began with the bards and genealogists, moved 'up' through the scribes and philosophers, and brought us to modern times with the printers, compositors, publishers, writers, and compilers that we have been looking at over the last 10 or so chapters.

They are changing the face of the planet Earth and the attitudes and mindsets of *Homo sapiens* far more completely than scribe and priest or printer and scientist did in the past (though the evolutionary–revolutionary process has been much the same on each occasion). The worldwide 'nervous system' that I touched upon at the end of the preceding chapter is already half-established, in terms of the radio, telephone and television systems that are already

A British Telecom satellite in orbit: The global nervous system is already half-established, in terms of radio, telephone and television.

at our disposal (if we can pay for their services). However, 100 years from now many of these 'early' telecommunicative systems will be museum pieces or archeological items like the Victorian canals and railway branch-lines that can be found all over the island of Britain, largely disused or transmuted into tourist and holiday facilities. Our present mass of semi-compatible international communication networks will evolve quite rapidly into a uniform whole (presumably founded on satellite relay systems) that may be expensive to use or as cheap as current television costs. And into it will be plugged a variety of personal and institutional computer gear that will give large numbers of people access to interactive information-retrieval services that will dwarf the 15th *Britannica* and Murray's *Dictionary*, just as they dwarfed Diderot and Johnson, and Diderot and Johnson dwarfed their predecessors all the way down the line to the cave painting and the tally bone.

How can one picture these developments in practical terms? There is no shortage of conventional literature being produced to tell us how conventional literature will shortly go the way of the dodo and the brontosaurus. One way of getting a handle on tomorrow's world is to look at some of the statements made by the various futurists. In *The Electronic Cottage*, for example, a survey that appeared in 1981, Joseph Deken looks at what he calls 'the retooling' of conventional media, and refers back – as I have done – to the days of the ancient Sumerians when information transfer was dependent on pressing symbols into wet clay, drying the clay, and then passing the resulting tablet around. He adds drily:[3]

> Try to conjure up for a moment the image of your *New York Times* being delivered to the doorstep, impressed on clay! You'd be lucky to find the door under it, much less the doorstep. When you stop and think about it, information is not much better suited to being pressed on paper than it is on clay, once you have large amounts of it to contend with.

Deken considers that we are now beginning to see the ebb of 'the paper wave', just as centuries ago clay, papyrus and parchment passed into limbo as regular mediums for writing. He notes that it is already possible to subscribe electronically to several major newspapers: 'No smudgy package of newsprint arrives daily at your door. Instead, you are given a phone number and a password. When you wish to see the day's news, you simply sit down in front of the television screen on your home computer, call up the number given, and are automatically linked up with the newspaper.'

The vision is tantalizing, but it is in its way just as much a one-sided vision as that of Urdang and Cassidy warning (or reminding) their fellow lexicographers that 'idiot-boxes', no matter how 'damned fast', cannot think, and will not replace *Homo lexicographicus*. Deken, as he hints at the prehistoric clumsiness of both clay and paper, is selling us a future, where we 'simply' sit at a video screen instead of having to handle 'smudgy' newsprint. When we reflect on such things, however, we know that nothing is ever as easy and clearcut as that. I have a teletext system tied in to my television set; it is interesting, cute and often useful, but equally often it cannot serve me as well as paper and print. Additionally, between us and the electronic millennium stand whole battalions of gadgets that will fail in the race to standardization and long-term efficiency in hardware and software. Good dependable equipment is on its way – just as it was on its way when Gutenberg took up printing – but it is not here yet and enthusiastic estimates of how soon it will be here should be taken with a pinch or two of salt.

Deken, of course, is aware of all this, just as a car salesman is aware of the deficiencies in the car he is selling (as well as its virtues). As he points out, there is no ultimate difference in a newssheet and a video display if all you have at the end of the day is the same page in a different medium: an electronic page-turner is simply a labour-saving device. More interesting for him, and for me, are the following possibilities.

Instead of going page by page through a tele-newspaper, or a tele-dictionary, or a telepedia, we might work from a menu and, via an alphabetic or thematic-and-numerical indexing system, operate according to our own system of priority. Teletext systems already offer this service to some degree, but once again it is little more than what most of us do already: in a paper or a reference book we turn to the bits that concern us most (virtually discarding the rest). One improvement on this would be to prime the computer in advance to read on our behalf and provide us with, as a kind of electronic clipping service, only what we wanted. This kind of pre-editing is already within our technological reach, if we program a machine to search for and retrieve material containing certain key words. Indeed, it is a reading and culling service similar to what has already been recommended for an international lexicographic archive.

The next stage, however, would be to blow open entirely such concepts as 'newspaper', 'magazine', 'book', 'dictionary' and 'encyclopedia'. Given the right kind of comprehensive storage and retrieval, we could dial for a whole range of current news items, background features and old news stories to flesh out current events, as well as support 'documents' from various other publications (including a specialized encyclopedic article and maybe even a customized glossary for the language involved – both in the sense of the technical or specialized terms in our own language, and relevant material from any foreign language linked with the subject matter). The mind, conditioned as it is by the limitations of our culture in the past, has difficulty coping with the abundance of information that such a possibility implies. Anyone who could pay for such a service would have at his or her disposal data beyond the dreams of avarice; we would be millionaires of information.

However, there is more. Ultimately, instead of waiting somewhat passively for the pre-digested stuff to come to us, we might want to use the home terminal as a search-and-find system that we consciously direct, by putting our own questions to human or silicate experts out there somewhere, foraging for data just as a feature journalist does today. In such a world, dialogue between informer and informee could blur the edges of the book–reader relationship most interestingly.

Such a dynamic reference technology would/will transcend limitations that we are conditioned to believe cannot be transcended. It once took ships years to circumnavigate the globe, yet now we talk glibly about the next-to-instantaneous availability of information on a round-the-world, round-the-clock basis. Even if this becomes real for only a minority of the human race, it will be a marked change in how we live and how we perceive ourselves. The interactive element makes such contacts far more interesting than any book, radio or television set. The relationship between the authority-cum-writer-cum-compiler-cum-presenter on the one hand and the disciple-cum-reader-cum-user-cum-consumer on the other hand would/will undergo a profound sea change. An author could receive more direct feedback faster than any past writer ever hungered for. Even lexicographers could develop fan clubs in a world like that.

The question here is: Would enough people want to bother in order to make it all economically viable? Is it not all a bit like video games, which catch on for a time but do not necessarily supply anything lastingly worthwhile?

The answer to these queries is, I suspect, nearer to what has happened with the personal telephone than to the video-game fad. Before Alexander Graham Bell invented the telephone nobody perceived how it would affect them. As we know, Bell did not perceive the effects initially either, because he was primarily interested in improving hearing for the deaf. When efficient telephone links were established, however, millions of people answered the call 'to reach out and touch somebody', and far more effectively and rapidly than even the international postal system would allow them to do. Given that an awareness of immediate-response machines like electric equipment is now part of our culture, given that the micro-chip exists and the telecommunications are in place, given that human beings have always responded in the end to labour-saving and efficiency-enhancing equipment, and given finally the commercial possibilities, it seems unlikely that we will hold back.

One example is probably enough to show that the potential market is there. In the early 1980s, in at least two places in North America, universities set up a 'grammar hotline'.[4] The first was Illinois State in the United States and the second the University of New Brunswick in Canada. The purpose of such a hotline was simple: a team of English teachers would be available at the end of a telephone line to anyone out there struggling for the right word or the right nuance of style in a letter or a report. As with other 'samaritan' services, the callers were guaranteed anonymity, and did actually call in considerably numbers. The English professor Murray Kinloch in Canada suspects that most of them were businessmen and civil servants – even journalists – and they displayed all the hang-ups traditionally associated with commercial lexicography and usage books: the need for help and reassurance as regards spelling, pronunciation, style, proper usage, and so forth. Such hotlines parallel in terms of the general public other computerized services that now exist, here and there, for specialists. One such is a dial-a-translation-equivalent service available in Quebec, Canada, for translators looking for the 'right' French equivalent for various English technical usages.[5]

People will use such services, and apparently will not worry unduly if the services are provided by silicate rather than human mediators. There is a virtually classic experiment undertaken in Glasgow which demonstrated that medical patients unburdened themselves of their alcohol problems more freely to mechanical analysts than to human beings; the sheer anonymity seems to work in favour of the computer here, in that people do not need to worry about the social issues of high and low, good and bad, censorious or sympathetic, that often beset them in dealing with such human mediators as the clergy, physicians and teachers. This anonymity has always been one of the advantages of the reference book, which is never directly judgemental.[6]

Given that the global network will exist and that computers and tele-links will alter our ways of doing things, does this however mean that good solid traditional human-to-human ways of doing things will be endangered, or superseded? Many people fear this, especially those with a humanist bent that enjoys 'real' as opposed to 'piped' music, or making pottery and engaging in calligraphy, or good conversation with people who have their knowledge at their fingertips (but not in terms of a computer console). As a thorough-going humanist of this ilk myself, I do not see any real basis for such worries, and can even suggest that the opposite may be true: far from swamping such pursuits, the new technology, well-used, may liberate us in a variety of ways to engage *more* successfully in them.

As I suggested at the beginning of this review, no later shift or jump in human capacity has supplanted the preceding activity or skill: while we speak we still breathe, while we read and write we can still listen and speak, while we use printed books we still write by hand. Similarly, while we engage in new electronic ploys, we will still have all the old ones nearby, and may have more time rather than less in which to enjoy them.

More importantly, however, and in strictly educational terms, there are ways open to us nowadays in which we can be extremely traditional in technological and social terms and still be as avant-garde as the space shuttle. The new High Technology need not make anyone disdain the variety of old 'low technologies'; rather, such technologies can be harnessed to help us all, but particularly our children, to understand ourselves better. In this, the skills of macro-lexicography can come out of the monastic cell and right into the streets. Here, I am not specifically thinking of getting kids to make and write on clay tablets (although I have seen this successfully done in a school in which I once worked). This is a perfectly reasonable thing to do, but I am considering something much more radically interesting: turning students on occasion into once-in-a-lifetime Sam Johnsons and Noah Websters.

At least one remarkable precedent exists for this idea: a project undertaken between 1978 and 1982 on the lower East Side of New York City which produced a 'Trictionary' without a single really-truly lexicographer being involved.

The *Trictionary* is a 400-page trilingual English/Spanish/Chinese wordbook, covering a base vocabulary of some 3,000 items per language.[7] Much of the basic cost was covered by a grant from the National Endowment for the Humanities, and the bulk of the work was done on the premises of the Chatham Square branch of the New York Public Library, on East Broadway. The librarian there, Virginia Swift, was glad to provide the accommodation, while the original idea was developed by Jane Shapiro, a teacher of English as a Second Language at Junior High School 65, helped through all the stages of the work by Mary Scherbatoskoy of ARTS (Art Resources for Teachers and Students). They organized the work, but they were not the compilers as such.

The compilation was done, as *The New Yorker* reports (10 May 1982) 'by the spare-time energy of some 150 young people from the neighborhood', aged between 10 and 15, two afternoons a week over three years. New York is the multilingual city par excellence, in which, as the report points out, 'some of its citizens live in a kind of linguistic isolation, islanded in their languages'. The *Trictionary* was an effort to do something about that kind of isolation and separateness. One method used in the project was getting together a group of youngsters variously skilled in English, Spanish and

Chinese and 'brainstorming' over, say, the word ANIMALS written on an otherwise empty blackboard. They would think of animals and considered how they were labelled in each language, putting their triples on the board and arguing about the legitimacy of particular terms. Another method was the review session, a more sophisticated activity where a stack of blue cards with English words on them was used to create equivalent stacks in pink for Spanish and yellow for Chinese. It was out of this kind of interactive effort that the *Trictionary* developed, until in its final form it had a blue section with English first, a second section that was yellow and Chinese, and a third section that was pink and Spanish. Each part had three columns per page, with each language appropriately presented. In all three sections, the material was punctuated here and there by line drawings done by the youngsters themselves.

Jane Shapiro told *The New Yorker* that when she first went to work in the area she had had no idea what the language situation was like. The neighbourhood is about 80% Chinese and 20% Spanish-speaking, and in class she had often found herself in the position of comparing all three languages. Out of that 'small United Nations' came the idea for the book, because she had often wished for such a book, but of course no right-minded publisher had ever thought of that particular combination as commercially viable or academically interesting. Additionally, and damningly, Shapiro felt that what dictionaries *were* available 'were either too stiff or out of date or written on a linguistic level far different from that of the students'. In other words, because formal lexicography had nothing to offer, grass-roots lexicography had to serve instead.

As with Vaugelas, neighbourhood usage was the authority, and as work progressed the women and their charges actually kept away from published dictionaries so as to be sure that the words came from the youngsters themselves. Reality also prevailed, in that there is a fair quantity of legal and medical terms in the book. These were included because the children often served as interpreters between their elders and lawyers and doctors. Motivation was high, despite a shifting population of helpers, evidently because the children could see the practical utility of what they were doing. One youngster engaged in the work was Iris Chu, born in Venezuela of Chinese parents and brought to New York about five years earlier. She told *The New Yorker* that she made a lot of friends while working on the *Trictionary* (the opposite to what often happens to lexicographers), adding: 'It's funny to see it as a book now – before, it was just something we *did* every week. I'm really sorry it's over. For us, it was a whole lot of fun.'

It was also a prototype for a whole new kind of educational lexicography (with or without the additional advantage, where available, of electronic and other aids). The ancient Sumerians and the medieval Scholastics would have understood the general idea of the *Trictionary* very well, and Comenius would certainly have approved of it. I approve of it wholeheartedly because it simply broke the mould of conventional thinking. Additionally, we can see in the brain-storming sessions and the use of the cards the two modes of lexicography creatively at work side by side: themes and word relationships on the one side, alphabetic order on the other. The women of the lower East Side certainly discovered a formula for getting the taxonomic urge working in ways that are just as spectacular as any instrument that beeps, blinks and hums.

I have barely scraped the surface here of what can be done and may yet be done in broadening the base of macro-lexicography and in democratizing the handling of information. What I hope I *have* done, however, is to indicate that conditions are in fact good in the worlds of reference. Our society is bursting open in terms of information, and the bombardment may be regarded as disruptive and mind-numbing, a kind of cultural nuclear bomb. Equally well, however, it can be regarded as a whole new shift in what it means to be human, radical certainly, but also a natural development from everything that has gone before.

It is in our nature to structure reality and to make containers, whether physical or mental, for what we learn about the continua of life. It is also in our nature to want to keep what we learn safe, to pass it around like wine in a bottle, and to leave it for future generations to add to, like wine in a cellar. It is also, for good or for ill, natural that we place the golden age or the millennium somewhere in the past or somewhere in the future, and to assume that 'it was better done then' or that 'it will be better done then'. It is all rather unlikely, however, as I have tried to show, that an obsession with either the remote past or the remote future can solve the problems of here and now. The Greeks, the Scholastics, the Académie Française and Sam Johnson stumbled as we stumble, and there is no guarantee that some twenty-second-century Webster's *Tenth International* will please all its users.

We do, however, have our record of the marvels of reference, glorious in their very imperfection, from the Altamira caves to the great present-day works of taxonomic scholarship. The record exists, falteringly kept, but it is there to add to, and to benefit from. What is more, nobody has a monopoly on it any more.

Envoi

*Many shall run to and fro
And knowledge shall be increased.*

DANIEL 12:4 (*King James Authorized Version*, 1611)

*Many will be at their wits' end,
and punishment will be heavy.*

DANIEL 12:4 (*New English Bible*, 1970)

Given the development of recording and reference over the last 5,000 years, I tend to prefer the King James version of the future to the later one. On all the evidence, it would appear that knowledge will indeed be increased, and we may not be at our wits' end. We often agonize over 'progress', wondering whether it was just a Victorian dream, but in the worlds of reference progress appears to be much more fact than fancy.

Other works, of course, deal in the steady upward climb of *Homo sapiens*, as for example *The Ascent of Man* (1973), a book that accompanied a successful television series. In it Jacob Bronowski discussed the evolution of head and hand, the imaginativeness of cave art, the agricultural revolution, and the slow development towards successful natural science; there is hardly a mention, however, of the major themes of this book. None of the key words that I have used here ('writing', 'printing', 'communication', 'education', 'reference', 'encyclopedia', 'dictionary') appears in Bronowski's index, and where 'language' and 'information' appear, they are closely tied to the natural sciences and mathematics. Such an arrangement would be entirely legitimate in a work that studied the worlds of science and mathematics, perhaps, but in one which purports to deal in all the successes of humankind, the absence of these themes is curious. Indeed, that absence serves as an indicator of how cavalierly we have tended to ignore recording and reference as prime elements in our sociocultural evolution.

In order to talk constructively about these neglected subjects, I have had to find a suitable frame of reference in which to operate, one that would give me the freedom I wanted without however being too alien to the reader. I chose finally the metaphor of 'worlds', and gave those worlds of reference such classic labels as 'ancient', 'medieval' and 'modern'. Such labels are familiar to anyone educated in the Westernized worldview, but there is nothing absolute about them. Indeed, they are just as much *post-facto* constructs as the arrangement of the Chinese classics, the Vedas, or the books of the Bible. We accept them as we accept the days of the week or the months of the year; they are comfortably *there*, we are used to them, and we hardly need to ask ourselves what they are meant to convey. But how 'right' is Monday, how true is 'June', how 'ancient' did the ancients feel, how 'dark' were the 'Dark Ages', and what exactly were the 'Middle Ages' in the 'middle' of?

These worlds are fictions; they have no existence whatever save in our minds, as the sociomental furniture of our civilization. They are currently quite useful, like BC and AD, and we may dispense with them all one day, proving them to be as contingent and transient as clay and cuneiform, Pliny's ordering of facts and fancies, or Ibn Qutayba's priorities of power, war and nobility. The universals of recording and reference lie elsewhere, in our understanding of the interplay of technology, taxonomy and culture.

However, my various worlds have served their purpose here, and might serve their purpose again elsewhere, some day: in a Museum of Reference and Information. It is an intriguing possibility. Future generations could go into the complex at one end, as they go today into Disneyland, and move from caverns, paintings and tally bones to the reconstructed scribal schools of Mesopotamia and Egypt, to the Schoolmen and their scriptoria, to Aquinas in his cell and Gutenberg in his print shop, stage by stage up to the most dazzlingly 'modern' video display terminals. Such a museum would tell the same story as this book but, as in an ancient Egyptian temple, one could walk around inside the story, *touching* and *smelling* the clay, the wax, the lampblack, the rolls and codices, *seeing* the progression and what it was like to be Cassiodorus dictating the contents of precious rolls to his copyists, or Sam Johnson at work in Gough Square.

It would have to be more than just a museum, of course. Actual calligraphers would have to work there, and researchers, people for whom the past still had vivid meaning. As we move from the third to the fourth great shift in the information skills, we shall need such things to help us keep our balance, to remember where we have come from, as well as how far we still have to go.

Notes, references and related reading

Many of the works cited in the notes that follow, in addition to their relevance as sources and as background, and in addition to the expertise of their authors, are also interesting as representatives of the various genres of reference book. Indeed, a number of them are discussed as such in the body of this review.

In general, these notes follow the usual composite pattern: they relate quotations to sources, list further works to which I owe a debt and/or to which I want to draw the reader's attention, and allow me to add some further thoughts here and there which are not, however, in the main line of the argument. This pattern of annotating scholarly works also has a history, which is an integral part of the subject I have been discussing, but which (like so many other aspects of that subject) I have been unable to enlarge upon here.

As regards my technical references, I have tried to be as true as possible to the sources of my inspiration and information. With the passage of time, however, one finds a blurring among the many books and articles one has read, and so a clear assignment of ideas to sources may not always have been possible. In some instances, I have been content to cite only the more significant and/or the most recent works that I have consulted while actually putting this book together. In doing so, where there has been a choice between the unyieldingly academic and the more populist (by which I mean a respectable work that is also a good transparent read), I have erred on the side of populism.

I am also, not surprisingly in a work of this kind, indebted to a variety of dictionaries and encyclopedias. Without their help on innumerable occasions, this book could not have been completed in a bearable time. I would like in particular to acknowledge:

> The *Encyclopaedia Britannica*, 15th Edition, 1976
> The *Oxford English Dictionary* (Compact Edition: 1971)
> The *Oxford Dictionary of English Etymology*, 1966
> Skeat's *Concise Etymological Dictionary of the English Language* (Oxford 1881, impression of 1965)
> Chambers *Twentieth Century Dictionary*, 1983 Edition
> *Le Petit Robert 1: Dictionnaire de la langue française*, 1972
> *Le Petit Robert 2: Dictionnaire universel des noms propres*, 1981
> Larousse *Etymologique*, 1971
> The Merriam–Webster *Third New International Dictionary*, 1966
> The Merriam–Webster *New Collegiate Dictionary*, 1977
> The *Chronological English Dictionary* 1970
> The Liddell and Scott *Greek Lexicon* (Oxford)
> The Lewis and Short *Latin Dictionary* (Oxford)

I would also like to commend two Time–Life series: the *Emergence of Man* and *Human Behavior*, and the Mitchell–Beazley *Joy of Knowledge Library*, both of which may be regarded conventionally as derivative from scholarship rather than works of scholarship in their own right (a point of view with which I would be in total disagreement, since works like these serve to bridge gaps among specialisms and help us to see things whole, in this way making their own serious contribution to knowledge).

Foreword and Forewarning

★ The quotation on life, knowledge and information is from T.S. Eliot, *Choruses from 'The Rock'*, Faber, London 1934, p. 107.

Mind, word and world

★ The quotation concerning Socrates and Ion is from *Great Dialogues of Plato*, translated by W.H.D. Rouse (Mentor, the New American Library, 1956, p.21).

1 Knowing, referring and recording

1 Sources that I have consulted with regard to human evolution and its time scale include:

> Darlington 1980 (general, but esp. Ch. 9: 'Human Evolution')
> Fisher 1982 (the evolution of human behaviour)
> Leakey 1981 (general human evolution)
> Leakey and Lewin 1978 (human origins)
> White and Brown 1973 (human origins)

2 Although I do not say much about the human brain in Ch. 1, I nevertheless regard it as fundamentally important in discussing the broader implications of information and reference, both as the directing organ in our lives and as a container for information in its own right. For a list of background sources, see Ch. 2, note 6.

3 Baddeley 1982 provides a comprehensive account of what we currently understand about memory and how it stores, retrieves and allows us to use information.

4 The quotation on mind and technology is from Gregory 1981, one of the seminal background sources to this review.

5 Most linguists have recognized the first and second shifts to which I refer as the basic mediums of the language (cf. McArthur 1983:16ff, and note 11, below). Ong 1982:26 implies the existence of shifts two, three and four when he talks of 'writing or print or electronic culture'. Eisenstein 1979:43ff specifically discusses the 'shift' from script to print. Smith 1980:324 refers to a major 'shift' in recent years from print, etc., under the influence of new technological developments.

6 Animal awareness is discussed in Griffin 1981, which presents the argument that humans tend to under-estimate the inner life of the non-human world.

7 Two recent general studies of the chimpanzee are Goodall 1971 and Tanner 1981. Goodall studies the chimpanzee in its natural state, while Tanner treats it as a model for understanding the ancestral pre-human population, while also reviewing recent studies of chimpanzee behaviour and communicative abilities,

including Goodall's pioneering work. Discussions of chimpanzees and communication can also be found in Griffin 1981 (Ch. 4: 'Animal Semantics'), and in Leakey & Lewin 1978 (Ch. 10: 'The Origin of Language').

8 Pattison 1982 provides a useful and provocative study of literacy and our attitudes to it, while Gudschinsky 1982 looks at literacy from the point of view of linguistic science. In addition to such sources, there have been in recent years many newspaper and magazine articles pointing to the high levels of 'functional illiteracy' in the Western world (an interesting state of affairs on the edge of the fourth great shift).

9 My reference to Toffler relates to both the 1970 and 1980 publications, synthesizing the main approaches to history in these works.

10 McLuhan 1964 discusses various issues relating to the communication media, while Fiske 1982 looks at communication studies in general.

11 The view that written language is secondary to spoken language appears in many recent works of linguistics. See in particular Lyons 1981a:11–17, and Ong 1982:7–8.

2 *Information and World 3*

1 The 'three worlds' are discussed in Popper 1972:Ch. 4, Popper and Eccles 1981: Ch. 2, Magee 1973: Ch. 4, and D. Miller 1983 (see subject index: 'world').

2 The opposition 'worldscape' and 'mindscape' is my own, although the single term 'mindscape' is used in a comparable way in Rucker 1982:35ff.

3 The term 'orature' is my own, and first appears in McArthur 1983:41 and 55. Cf. Ong's term 'orality' (Ong 1982).

4 For the historical development of the word 'information', see the *Oxford English Dictionary*.

5 The articles by Flood and Kronick are part of the series 'Information Processing' in the *Encyclopaedia Britannica* 15th Edition, 1976, Macropaedia 9. The specific quotation is from p. 568. The *EB*15 also contains two comprehensive articles relating to the organization of libraries, in Mac 10: 'Library', by Frank Francis, and 'Library Science', by Ralph Parker.

6 Sources that I have consulted with regard to the mind and brain include:

Asimov 1963 (the brain and senses generally)
Baddeley 1982 (the memory)
Borger & Seaborne 1966 (the psychology of learning)
Brown & Deffenbacher 1979 (perception and the senses)
Campbell, Robert 1977 (the mind generally)
Chomsky 1968 (language and the mind)
Edson 1975 (learning in general)
Gregory 1981 (the mind, logic, science and technology)
Hampden-Turner 1981 (various approaches to describing the mind)
Hofstadter & Dennett 1981 (views of the mind)
Jastrow 1981 (the evolution of mind and brain)
Jaynes 1976 (hemisphericity and states of consciousness)
Miller, George 1962 (psychology in general)
Miller, Jonathan 1983 (interviews with specialists)
Popper & Eccles 1981 (the self and the brain)
Rucker 1982 (infinity and the mind)

7 There is nowadays a dichotomy as regards 'words' between liberal humanists on the one hand (for whom 'words' are obvious things, hardly in need of

definition) and linguistic scientists on the other (for whom the difficulties involved in defining 'words' are a thorny problem). My remarks in this chapter derive from some 20 years of working professionally with words from both points of view.

Two typical recent humanistic works on words are Maleska 1981 and Safire 1980. Three typical linguistic works are Brown, R. 1958, Lyons 1981b, and Palmer, F. 1971.

From the strictly linguistic point of view, I have used the term 'word' fairly loosely in this chapter. To have entered, however, into technicalities and controversy with regard to words, lexical items, lexemes and morphemes (etc.) would only have clouded an already complex issue. (See also Ch. 17, on lexemes and lexical sets.)

8 The remarks on words being both sounds and images but also _beyond_ sounds and images relate to the fundamentally dual nature of language as medium and message simultaneously. For further discussion of this point, see Lyons 1981a: 11, from which I have adapted the term 'medium-transferable', and McArthur 1983:16ff. Further background can be found in Martinet 1960, which deals with the topic as 'double articulation'.

9 That linguistic science takes language seriously as a defining characteristic of being human is illustrated cogently in the titles of two recent books: _Homo Loquens_ (Fry, 1977), and _The Articulate Mammal_ (Aitchison, 1976).

The Ancient World

* The quotation from Herodotus is taken from _The Histories_, as translated by Aubrey de Selincourt (Penguin, 1954 p. 135).

3 Containers of knowledge

1 A good general description of Cro-Magnon Man is provided by Prideaux 1974: esp. Ch. 4, 'The Birth of Art', which discusses and displays both cave paintings and the smaller _art mobilier_ of the period.

2 Two standard works on the history of writing from prehistoric times onward are Gelb 1963 and Jensen 1935. I am indebted to Jensen for the remarks in his Ch. 1 on tally sticks, Maori genealogies, Australian aboriginal messenger sticks, etc.

3 Tally bones, etc., are discussed in Marshack 1972, a key source on prehistoric objects of reference, and in Claiborne 1974, esp. Ch. 1, which provides a good general resumé.

4 I was first set to thinking seriously about what we derive in our social conditioning from ancient Sumer by reading Parkinson 1963: Ch. 1, 'The Ancient East', which touches on the arithmetic of 60 that has given us our seconds and minutes, and the 360 degrees of the circle. Recent studies relating to ancient Mesopotamia and Egypt include:

Daniel 1968: esp. Chs. 2–4 (general)
Edzard 1976:963–99 (Mesopotamia)
Pfeiffer 1977: esp. Chs. 6–8 & 11 (general)
Sherratt & Clark 1980 (general and archeological)
Wente 1976:460–81 (Egypt)

5 A vivid description of life in an ancient scribal culture is provided in Claiborne 1974: esp. Chs. 3 and 4. This description is complemented by Hamblin 1973, on

the growth of the first cities. The series to which both volumes belong is the Time–Life *Emergence of Man* series, in which prose and the illustrative arts combine effectively to help recreate the past. The series is also a good example of a modern populist and thematic encyclopedia, even though it is not presented to the public as such. A graphic description of life in ancient Egypt is provided in Mertz 1964: esp. Ch. 9, which deals with hieroglyphs and the hieratic and demotic scripts.

6 The *Encyclopaedia Britannica* 15 carries a range of in-depth articles with a direct bearing on reference technologies and related matters. The following were particularly useful:

> 'Forms of Writing', Ignace J Gelb (Macropaedia 19:1033ff)
> 'Writing Implements', Forrest E Beck (Macropaedia 19:1045ff)
> 'Palaeography', William G Urry (Macropaedia 13:911ff)
> 'Calligraphy', Eric G Turner et al. (Macropaedia 3:645ff)
> 'Diplomatics', Peter Herde (Macropaedia 5:807ff)
> 'Paper & Paper Production', Kenneth W Britt (Macropaedia 13:966ff)
> 'History of Publishing', Philip & George Unwin (Macropaedia 15:221ff)
> 'Biblical Literature', Krister Stendahl & Emilie T Sander (Macropaedia 2: esp. 938–45).

4 Systems for knowledge

1 The sophistication of early scribal collections of words and facts is cogently displayed in Pettinato 1981, from which I derived the examples of syllabically-ordered words (p. 236). Pettinato, interestingly enough, describes such tablets of linguistic and general information as 'dictionaries' and 'encyclopedias' of the period.

2 The rivalry of Alexandria and Pergamon is described in the following:

> Dinneen 1967 (considering the linguistic controversies of the time)
> Francis 1976 (discussing the parchment/papyrus conflict)
> Gusdorf 1976 (esp. on the influence on culture of the librarians and text analysts of the time)
> McArthur 1983 (looking at the rivalry from the point of view of language teaching and the history of the concept 'grammar')

5 The taxonomic urge

1 My comments on stratification and social hierarchies date in some measure from observing the caste system while living and working in India (1964–7). Many works discuss caste and class, but one which I have found especially useful is Majumdar 1961: esp. Part III, 'Indian Social Organization and Problems in Applied Anthropology'. Two paragraphs in particular from Majumdar's work seem to me to sum up the taxonomic urge, the classical attitude, and social stratification:

> The functional classification of tribes makes it necessary to discuss another type of social stratification, *viz.* the caste system, which is a unique institution in India. India is generally known as the classic land of castes and creeds. Caste is said to be in the air, and even Muslims and Christians have not escaped infection. There are approximately three thousand castes and tribes in India, and there are probably as many theories of caste origins as there are writers on the subject.

The caste system is believed, not without good reason, to have been of immemorial antiquity. Many read a kind of caste structure in the Rigveda, as the Purusha-Sukta in describing the origin of the four Varnas, supports this view. Though doubts exist about the status of Purusha-Sukta being an integral part of the Rigveda, it is certain that a functional division of society was known at the time of the Rigveda.

2 The concept of 'hyponymy' was first discussed in detail, as far as I am aware, in Lyons 1968:453ff, as one of the 'sense relations' of language, along with synonymy, antonymy, etc.

3 The Chinese 'classics' are described succinctly in Tien-yi Li 1976:1050–2, from whose prose description I drew the basic material for my tabulation. I chose the framework of the Chinese classics for the purpose of exemplifying *post-facto* classicization because it is largely secular and the term 'classic' has traditionally been used in relation to the Confucian texts. The Vedas of India or the books of the Bible would have served equally well.

4 Lack of space prevented me from going into the background worldview of the Chinese classics. Works which discuss this worldview and which I have found useful include Reid & Croucher 1983: esp. Chs. 4 & 5, and Smart 1977: Ch. 8. (Both of these books are companions in print to BBC television documentary series, which represent a new development within the populist tradition of education and reference itself worthy of study.)

5 There are many books about Hindu attitudes to the Vedas, etc., which indicate that their canonization was a *post-facto* process comparable to the literal canonization of saints. My sources include:

> Renou 1961: esp. Ch. 2, 'Vedism'
> Sen 1961: esp. Ch. 8, 'The Vedic Age'
> Smart 1977: esp. Ch. 1, 'Hinduism'
> Zaehner 1966: esp. the introduction

6 There are many books about the composition, ordering, authenticity, etc., of the books of the Bible. Relevant essays on the original forms of the Old and New Testament materials and of the Apocrypha of the Old Testament can be found in *The New English Bible* (Oxford & Cambridge 1961), while the New Testament Apocrypha are discussed in Cameron 1983.

7 Concise reviews of the lives and works of the major Greek philosophers are widely available. A recent relevant biographical dictionary is Bowder 1982.

8 Grant 1982 provides comprehensive coverage of the Hellenistic world in terms of its general politics and culture, without however saying much about education or reference materials.

9 For my closing remarks on the *trivium* and *quadrivium* I am particularly indebted to Matoré 1968:46. For further brief but relevant comments on both, see also Collison 1964:44.

6 *Missionaries and monasteries*

1 For background information on Pliny the Elder I have drawn in fairly equal measure on Collison 1964 (my quotation from p.25), Stannard 1976 (my quotation from p. 572) and Whalley 1982.

2 Pliny's *Natural History* is available, with Latin and English on facing pages and translated by H. Rackham et al., in the Loeb Classical Library: Heinemann and Harvard University Press, 1942.

3 For the etymology of 'encyclopaedia', see the *Oxford English Dictionary*.
4 For a comprehensive and readable review of humanism, education, scholarship, Hellenism, the *trivium* and *quadrivium*, and the synthesis of pagan classicism with Christianity, see Gusdorf 1976.
5 Many works cover the development of early Christianity, the compromise with 'pagan' Greece and Rome, and the encounter with the 'barbarians'. Four that I have found relevant are:

> Bainton 1966: esp. Parts III to V, covering Jerome, Augustine, Cassiodorus, Isidore, the barbarians and the monasteries
> Chadwick 1967: esp. Ch. 15: 'The Development of Latin Christian Thought', and Ch. 17: 'The Church and the Barbarians', which discusses Cassiodorus.
> Smart 1977: esp. Ch. 3: 'Christianity'
> Trevor-Roper 1965: esp. Ch. 3: 'The Dark Ages'

The *EB*15 also has excellent articles on the main figures discussed in this chapter, and Cassiodorus now has a modern biographer in O'Donnell 1979, as well as numerous mentions in Kelly 1969. See also Collison 1964: Ch. 1.
6 How 'barbarous' were the barbarians, and how 'dark' were the Dark Ages? As Wilson 1980:10 puts it:

> The finger of accusation – if not of scorn – is levelled at the *barbares du nord*. The brutality of barbarians is an easy target; but it is well to remember the brutalities of the allegedly civilized. It is clear that the sophistication of the Mediterranean is missing from northern Europe . . . It is true that the Anglo-Saxons regarded the ruined masonry of Roman towns as 'the wondrous work of giants'; it is also true that the economic and political base of Germanic power was narrow. On the other hand, the technical achievement of the Germanic smith, the sophistication of the Scandinavian boat-builder, the engineering skills of the Slavs, the inventiveness of the Anglo-Saxon and Celtic historian and the brilliance and depth of the Germanic poet induce a consideration of these comparisons. As Rome destroyed itself and as Byzantine power faded the lacunae they left were filled quickly and imaginatively in the North.

In addition to Wilson et al., who discuss Northern Europe from AD 400 to 1100, I have found useful Foss 1975 (on the rise of chivalry, esp. Chs. 1 & 2), Herm 1975 (on the Celts), Laing 1979 (on the Celts and Dark Age Britain, esp. Ch. 4), and Scherman 1981 (on Ireland in the Dark Ages, esp. Part 4, 'The Flowering').
7 According to Gusdorf 1976:1173, the expression *en Khristō paideía* appeared as early as the first century AD, and 'avowed the possibility of a cultural conversion by which works of Hellenic inspiration could be subordinated to religious faith. The Christian church now took charge of the intellectual and aesthetic values of the past.'

The Medieval World

★ The quotation is a complete poem: 'Chaucer's wordes unto Adam, his owne Scriveyn', taken from *The Complete Works of Geoffrey Chaucer*, ed. Walter W. Skeat (Oxford University Press, 1912).

7 Faith versus reason

1 In addition to the works mentioned in Ch. 6, note 5, Benz 1976 provides a wealth of information on Augustine, the conflict between Christianity and Islam, Christian educational forms, and the rise of the universities (esp. pp. 514–15).

2 Many works cover the development of Islam into a world religion. Four that I have found useful are:

> Jansen 1979: esp. Ch. 1: 'The Totality of Islam'
> Rahman 1976 (esp. on religion and the secular sciences)
> Smart 1977: Ch. 5: 'Islam'
> Williams 1961 (general)

3 Collison 1964 and 1976 is probably the most detailed descriptive and bibliographical source of information on the history and nature of encyclopedias, reviewing many compilations and aspects of encyclopedism upon which I have been unable even to touch. Collison 1964, for example, contains a unique chronology of encyclopedic works from c. 370 BC to 1895.

4 The quotation is from Pieper 1976:353, the whole article a comprehensive and lucid review of Scholasticism.

5 With regard to Hugues de Saint-Victor I am indebted to Collison 1964 and 1976, and Ross & McLaughlin 1949, in the last of which Hugues's 'On Study and Teaching' appears in full, translated by McLaughlin. My quotation is from pp. 574–5 of that work.

6 Two twentieth-century renderings of the monumental *Summa theologiae* of Aquinas are:

1 an edition in five volumes issued between 1941 and 1945 by the Institute of Mediaeval Studies, Montreal

2 an edition with Latin text and English translation on facing pages, in 60 small volumes (Blackfriars in conjunction with Eyre & Spottiswoode, and McGraw-Hill, 1964).

The *Summa contra gentiles*, the other summation by Aquinas, which seeks to defend Christianity against the Muslims and other unbelievers, is available in a translation by Anton C. Pegis (University of Notre Dame Press, London, 1975, in 4 volumes; Doubleday, 1955 and Hanover House 1955, as *On the Truth of the Catholic Faith*, in two volumes).

7 Recent reviews of the life, times and significance of Aquinas include Copleston 1955 and Kenny 1980. My quotation is from Copleston, p. 10, and his objection to philosophers currently leaping straight from Aristotle to Bacon and Descartes, ignoring the Scholastics, is on p. 18.

8 *The élites of knowledge*

1 Detailed accounts of the sometimes surprising diversity and extensiveness of medieval education can be found in, among others, Orme 1973 (mainly as regards England), and Riche 1976 (generally). A brief but useful review can also be found at the beginning of Aldrick 1982.

2 The life, ideas and success as a teacher of Peter Abelard are described in many books. What has particularly interested me, and no doubt many others, is the intermingling of religion, scholarship and love in the lives of Abelard and Héloïse. Two particularly interesting works are now available on these topics:

1 *The Letters of Abelard and Héloïse*, Radice 1974

2 *Stealing Heaven: the Love Story of Héloïse and Abelard*, Meade 1979, a novel that recreates vividly the problems of an intelligent woman in medieval times.

3 The Scholastic educational system has left its mark on our civilization in a variety of ways. In McArthur 1983, I consider its impact on the teaching of

foreign languages, contrasting the 'monastery' with the 'marketplace' approach. The monastery tradition and the grammar-translation method as described there derive from Scholasticism, although I do not mention the Schoolmen by name in that book.

4 My etymology of 'faculty' is taken from the *Oxford Dictionary of English Etymology*, 1966.

The Early Modern World

★ The quotation from Shakespeare's *Love's Labour's Lost* is from Act I, Scene I, lines 192–3, taken from *The Oxford Shakespeare: Complete Works,* ed. W.J. Craig (Oxford University Press, 1905:146). The quotation on Shakespeare and an English dictionary is from the introduction to McAdam & Milne 1963.

9 *All knowledge for all men*

1 Vincent de Beauvais is discussed in Matoré 1968:48–9, and Collison 1964:60ff. and 1976:780 & 794. His work is also known as the *Speculum maius*.
2 The physical, social and political effects of the great plagues of the fourteenth century on Europe are described in Gottfried 1983 and Ziegler 1969.
3 For a discussion of 'the unacknowledged revolution', see Eisenstein 1979, esp. Ch. 1, which has that phrase as its title.
4 For biographies of Gutenberg, see Lehmann-Haupt 1976 and Scholderer 1963.
5 For a detailed history of printing, see Lechène 1976.
6 For the impact of printing on education, see Eisenstein 1970.

10 *Theme versus alphabet*

1 For a general background to the Schoolmen's approach to language teaching (and in particular grammar), along with discussions of the after-effects on the Western world of their ideas, see:

> Dinneen 1967: Ch. 5: 'Traditional Grammar'
> Kelly 1969: esp. Ch. 2: 'Teaching Grammar'
> McArthur 1983: Part 2: '25 Centuries of Grammar' and
>   Part 3: 'The Gift of Tongues?'
> Musgrave 1970: esp. Parts 2, 3 & 4
> Palmer, F. 1971: Ch. 2: 'Some Traditional Concepts'

2 Palmer, L.R. 1954 provides a history of the Latin language from its Indo-European origins to the development of 'Christian Latin'.
3 For a general background to the whole story of modern lexicography as it derives from the interlinear glosses and with particular concern for the alphabetic dictionary see:

> Hulbert 1955 (the origins of British & American dictionaries)
> Matoré 1968 (the origins of French dictionaries)
> Mathews 1933 (the origins of English-language dictionaries)
> Murray 1900 (European lexicography leading to the OED)
> Read 1976 (dictionaries generally)
> Whitehall 1958 (English-language dictionaries)

4 Whereas the historians of lexicography listed in the preceding note mentioned the *vocabularia* but saw them as a minor and relatively unimportant aspect of

their subject (because not alphabetical), Starnes & Noyes 1946 are much clearer in establishing two traditions, the alphabetic and the topical, although they do not set up a hard-and-fast typology for dealing with them.

5 References are made to the *Lexicon* of Suidas in Collison 1964:46 and 1976:788, Matoré 1968:43, and Read 1976:714, none of whom considers the work a major influence on future developments.

6 The esoteric quality of alphabetization right into Renaissance times is stressed in Eisenstein 1979:88–90, which also discusses the development of indexing (see her index to Vol. 2).

7 For the etymology and development of the English word 'dictionary', see the *Oxford English Dictionary*. For the origins of the word *dictionnaire* in French, see Matoré 1968:59–60.

11 *A blurring of languages*

1 I discuss the relationship between Latin and the vernaculars further in McArthur 1983: Part 2, especially with regard to the evolution of our ideas about, and attitudes to, the concept 'grammar'.

2 See also Baugh & Cable 1957:202ff, for a concise general account of the relationship between Latin and the vernacular languages.

3 The Renaissance stages in the development of dictionaries are also discussed in the sources listed in note 3 to Ch. 10. I have drawn variously on these sources for material in this chapter.

4 A particularly emotive condemnation in retrospect of the influence of Latin can be found in Matoré 1968:45–6.

5 For an important present-day analysis of the factors at work in the interplay of Latin and the vernaculars see Ferguson 1959:325–340, which proposes the term 'diglossia' to cover the duality that Matoré condemns. The concept 'diglossia' has proved fertile in modern sociolinguistics, and has been extended in a variety of studies. I have used the term 'bipolarism' to cover the same area, where a bilingual or bidialectal individual shifts from one end of a range of linguistic competences to another. For further discussions of such points, see Hymes 1964 and 1971, and Aitken and McArthur 1979.

6 For a concise discussion of multilingualism, diglossia, etc., see Peñalosa 1981: esp. Ch. 7. This source is particularly valuable in discussing di- and polyglossia in relation to the kind of 'high' and 'low' varieties that are important in this review.

7 The term 'classicization' as used here is my own. A related technical term of sociolinguistics is 'relexification', where the lexis of one language is seen as being absorbed wholesale into another. See Hymes 1971: esp. 77ff.

8 Histories of the English language almost invariably have chapters or parts of chapters devoted to such matters as 'borrowings' from Latin (although they seldom, in my own view, place a sufficient emphasis on the social process at work). A typical range of such histories is:

> Baugh & Cable 1957: esp. Ch. 8 (but see also index)
> Bradley 1904: esp. pp. 63–68
> Francis 1963 (see index)
> Potter 1950: esp. Ch. 3: 'The Revival of Learning'
> Strang 1970 (the only history I know that runs backwards from the present: see index, which allots the entry 'Latin' some 100 page references)

9 The battle of the innovators and the purists is presented very clearly in Baugh & Cable 1957, Ch. 8, which covers the effects of the printing press, the problems of the vernaculars, orthography, 'borrowing', inkhorn terms and the dictionaries of hard words.

10 I have drawn upon Potter 1950, Ch. 3, for part of my account of the arguments about inkhorn or inkpot terms, especially the quotation from Thomas Wilson, whom Potter quotes much more fully.

11 It is interesting to compare my observations on Latin as an international currency convertible into high local use with the following observations made by Henry Bradley, one of the editors of the *OED*, 1904:63, of which I was not conscious when writing those observations:

> The Latin element in Modern English is so great that there would be no difficulty in writing hundreds of consecutive pages in which the proportion of words of native English and French etymology . . . would not exceed five per cent. of the whole . . . And the Latin portion of the vocabulary is still constantly receiving additions. Until recently, the greater part of our literature was written by men who were classically educated, and for readers who were presumed to have more or less knowledge of Latin. Probably there are very few of our scholarly writers who are not responsible for the introduction of some new word of Latin derivation. It has come to be felt that the whole Latin vocabulary . . . is potentially English.

12 My list of words from Cawdrey and my quotation from Bullokar are taken from the original works. My comparative tables, however, showing 'plagiarism' from the Latin–English wordbooks, are adapted from the invaluable research of Starnes & Noyes 1946:21f., 31ff., the quotation giving their conclusions being from p.33.

13 As an example of an interesting experiment in teaching 'our hybrid heritage', see Hogben 1964. Such works are not confined to English, either, as can be seen from the Swedish work *De Internationella Orden* (International Words), a school textbook by Alvar Ellegård, 1966, which covers the Latin and Greek heritage in Swedish.

The Modern World

* The quotation is taken directly from the Preface to Samuel Johnson's *A Dictionary of the English Language* (1755). The complete text of the Preface can be found reprinted in both Bolton 1966:129–56, and McAdam & Milne 1963:3–29.

12 The legislative urge

1 The story of Thomas Cooper and his wife is well known in lexicographic circles, perhaps as a cautionary tale. Read 1976:714 re-tells it, quoting at some length from John Aubrey's *Brief Lives* (presumably the 1898 edition edited by Andrew Clark). As Aubrey noted of Cooper's stoicism: 'Well, for all that, that good man had so great a zeale for the advancement of learning, that he began it again, and went through with it to that perfection that he hath left it to us, a most useful worke.' The useful work was, in fact, Cooper's enlargement of Sir Thomas Elyot's Latin/English Dictionary, as the *Thesaurus Linguae Romanae et Britannicae*.

2 A useful background to the Renaissance, in terms of the eclipse of Scholasticism, the backward-to-the-classics and yet forward-to-a-better-future idea of 'renewal' and a new sense of human worth, is provided by three articles in

Wiener 1968: 'The Idea of Renaissance', Denys Hay; 'Renaissance Humanism', Nicola Abbagnano; and 'The Renaissance Idea of the Dignity of Man', Charles Trinkaus.

3 Read 1976:715 discusses the academies briefly in his historical review of lexicography.

4 For my description of Vaugelas and the Académie Française I have drawn heavily on the excellent review provided in Matoré 1968:70–87, which also describes the other major French dictionaries of the period. For Furetière, see also Collison 1964:4.

5 Even the title of Grevisse 1980 reflects the link with the legislators of the seventeenth-century: *Le Bon Usage: Grammaire française avec des remarques sur la langue française d'aujourd hui.*

My authority for linking Grevisse with Vaugelas directly is an article by Josette Pratte, entitled 'Une vie chez les mots', which appeared in the French Canadian periodical *Perspectives* (23 August 1980: Vol. 22, No. 34). This article, based on an interview with Grevisse, was a kind of obituary after his death on 4 July 1980 at the age of 84.

6 The original writings of the English 'Augustans' as regards 'fixing' the language include:

Daniel Defoe: 'Of Academies' (1697)
Joseph Addison: *Spectator 135* (1711)
Jonathan Swift: 'A Proposal for Correcting, Improving and Ascertaining the English Tongue' (1712)
Lord Chesterfield: Letter to *The World* (1754)

These pieces can all be found re-printed in Bolton, 1966, my Chesterfield quotation being from p. 125 and p. 126.

7 The contributions of Kersey and Bailey to English lexicography are discussed in Read 1976, Starnes & Noyes 1946, and Whitehall 1958. For a long time both compilers were very much in the shadow of Johnson, but are now generally seen as having played an important part in laying out the groundwork for Johnson. However, the exact role and ability of each is a matter of controversy, as can be seen from the following quotations:

The position of dictionary pioneer, commonly granted to Johnson or to Noah Webster, belongs in reality to one of the few geniuses lexicography ever produced: Nathaniel Bailey. (Whitehall 1958:159)

The spotlight of fame which has long been focussed on Johnson and has recently spread to his immediate predecessor, Bailey, has unfortunately thrown Kersey into the shadow. Kersey was, however, a notable pioneer, rejecting outmoded material and methods, working towards modern concepts, and in general playing his role of lexicographer with responsibility and intelligence. (Starnes and Noyes 1946:98)

My hope, however, is that this survey demonstrates how hard it is to find true initiators: everybody, however brilliant, owes so much to the one who went before, whether his is seen as a debt – or plagiarism.

8 The industry of the commentators on Johnson is large. My own indebtedness to these commentators is as follows (with pages quoted, where necessary):

Baugh & Cable 1957:270
Boulton 1971
Clifford 1955

Greene 1970:181
Hibbert 1971: Part I
McAdam & Milne 1963
Murray 1900:42
Roberts & Clifford 1976:147
Starnes & Noyes 1946:196

9 My quotation from the *Royal American Magazine* is taken from Baugh & Cable
1957/78:356, who suggest that the anonymous writer may have been John
Adams, future president of the United States. Baugh & Cable quote more
extensively than I have done from the original, and also from parallel views
expressed by Adams. Reference is made to the same magazine source in
Mathews 1933:36.

10 My sources on Noah Webster include:
Bolton 1966
Boulton 1971
Mathews 1933
Murray 1900
Whitehall 1958

11 My quotation of Webster regarding Johnson is from Webster's 1807 'Letter to
Dr David Ramsay', re-printed in Boulton 1971: 125–40, from p. 140.

12 My remarks in connection with Webster's changes in the orthography of
English relate to his 'An Essay on the Necessity, Advantages and Practicability
of Reforming the Mode of Spelling, and of Rendering the Orthography of
Words Consistent to the Pronunciation', the appendix to his *Dissertations on the
English Language*, 1789, as reprinted in Bolton 1966:157–73. Bolton also reprints
a letter from Benjamin Franklin to Noah Webster, congratulating him on his
Dissertations (pp. 174–9).

13 The use of the capitalized phrase 'High Mode' in contrast with such lower-case
phrases as 'low modes' and 'low varieties' is my own. It relates, however, both
to a traditional way of viewing styles of languages (as is implied in the
Shakespeare quotation that begins the chapters of 'The Early Modern World',
(p. XXX) and to current sociolinguistic usage (see Peñalosa 1981:115–17). I
have, however, extended the conventional sociolinguistic view of H (high) and
L (low) varieties to languages like English and French which have not generally
been considered to have such clearcut polarities, because it seems to me (from
both the diachronic and synchronic evidence) that they most definitely have.

13 Reference and revolution

1 Collison 1964 and 1976 presents the technical and universal dictionaries as the
forerunners of Chambers and therefore of all modern encyclopedias, whereas
Read 1976, dealing with the development of dictionaries 'proper', has relatively
little to say about them.

2 Matoré 1968:88–108 discusses the background to the *philosophes*, the reaction
against 'good taste' and 'good usage', the technical and universal dictionaries,
the Jesuits of Trévoux, the distinction between a dictionary and an encyclopedia,
Pierre Bayle, Ephraim Chambers, Denis Diderot and the *Encyclopédie*.

3 Chapter V of Collison 1964 provides a detailed account of the evolution of the
EB up to the 14th edition in 1929, while Kogan 1958 tells the story from the
point of view of the *EB* and the University of Chicago (its part-owner) up to

that date, and Einbinder 1964 provides a strongly critical assessment of what he sees as the 'myth' of the *Britannica*, its faults and its inaccuracies. For my own further discussion of the *EB*, see Ch. 18 and its notes 6 to 10.

4   The quotation is from Collison 1976:790. Collison 1964: Ch. 6 provides considerable esp. bibliographical detail about the *Brockhaus* tradition, while Collison 1976 devotes several detailed paragraphs to contrasting the *Britannica* and *Brockhaus* traditions.

5   Collison 1964 discusses in detail the human and commercial as well as the philosophical aspects of the failed *Encyclopaedia Metropolitana*. Collison 1964:238–95 provides a reprint of Samuel Taylor Coleridge's 'Treatise on Method', the essay justifying the thematic organization of the work.

6   Matoré's reference to Cassirer's remarks is on p. 97 of his work. The hint that the alphabetic mode might have been strengthened by the spirit of egalitarianism belongs in his remarks on the exiled radical *philosophe* Pierre Bayle (1647–1706). Bayle preceded Diderot in using the alphabetic format as a political tool, in his *Dictionnaire historique et critique*, a work which attacked traditional dogmatism, favoured freedom of speech and inclined towards atheism.

14   *Thematic lexicography*

1   I have found Paolo Rossi's article 'Baconianism' (in Wiener 1968:172–9) useful as a description of the lasting influence of Bacon and the various critical responses to his ideas. As regards Bacon's anti-scholastic approach to knowledge, Rossi notes: 'He understands knowledge not as a contemplation or recognition of a given reality, but as a *venatio*, a hunt, an exploration of unknown lands, a discovery of the unknown. Bacon wished to be the *buccinator* or herald of a new world, and his true greatness consists precisely in this function of his as a herald' (p.173).

2   Collison 1964 and 1976 devotes a significant part of his expositions on encyclopedias to the influence of Bacon. My specific diagram adapts his two prose descriptions. His own further comparisons of the classifications of knowledge of Bacon and Matthias Martini (*Idea methodica*, 1606), which I do not touch on, is also interesting, especially his comment that 'both philosophers were probably working from the same basic Platonic precepts' (p.795), which is intriguing when one considers Bacon's apparently anti-classical stance.

3   For references to the *vocabularia* and *vulgaria*, see the works cited in Ch. 10, note 3 (above), and also Starnes and Noyes (next note).

4   I am indebted to Starnes and Noyes 1946:197ff. for a general background to much of what I have been referring to as 'thematic lexicography'. Starnes is, from my point of view, a major figure in the assessment of this overshadowed area. The research work of Dewitt T. Starnes came to me as something of a revelation when, in the early 1970s, I was working on both my doctoral thesis and the foundation of what became the *Longman Lexicon of Contemporary English* (See Ch. 17).

5   For a concise biography and review of Comenius, see Sadler 1976 (my quotations from pp. 967–8).

6   Kelly 1969 has some 37 index references to Comenius and his contribution to language teaching, as well as a comprehensive bibliography. In a unique and useful survey, it is nonetheless interesting to note that Kelly can observe (p. 17):

> The first fully thought-out scheme of teaching vocabulary with pictures was that of Comenius, whose *Orbis sensualium pictus* first appeared in 1654. It was a development of his *Ianua linguarum reserata*, which was *merely a vocabulary ordered by centers of interest* (my italics).

This understatement of the significance of a thematic compilation like the *Ianua* typifies the kind of scholarly myopia that one finds quite abundantly in this area in the twentieth century.

7 The *Opera didactica omnia* ('Complete Pedagogical Works') of Comenius have been reprinted in six volumes by the Academia Scientiarum Bohemo-Slovenica, Prague 1957.

8 My thematic list is taken from the contents pages of the *English Duden: A Pictorial Dictionary*, edited in Mannheim and London and published by Harrap 1960. The English edition is an adaptation of the *Duden Wörterbuch* of 1958. A similar and more recent English work is the *Oxford–Duden Pictorial German–English Dictionary*, 1980.

9 My comments on a Pawnee or Martian observer relate to the Sapir–Whorf Hypothesis, which suggests that one's native language conditions one's way of thinking and seeing the world to such an extent that distinct cultures could not possibly come up with similar cosmic orderings. This topic is developed more fully in Ch. 17.

10 Bishop Wilkins's *Essay* is often referred to but seldom discussed in detail (perhaps because it is simply so abstruse). Even the *EB*15, a fund of information on macro-lexicographic topics, deals only in his founder-membership of the Royal Society and interest in such things as perpetual motion machines and human flight. My remarks derive in the main from my own examination of the original work and my speculations upon it.

11 For a detailed history of the 'synonymies', see Egan 1942. (See also note 15, below.)

12 Although the book has sold well for over a century, Roget's *Thesaurus* and its compiler have been neglected as subjects worthy of study in themselves. In recent decades, however, interest has been growing in both (possibly because of modern library science's interest in cataloguing by means of 'thesauri'). See notes 16–18 below.

13 My quotation of Roget in relation to Wilkins and a universal language is from p. xxxv of his introduction (1962 edition). In a related footnote, Roget draws our attention to two other antecedents to his work, the translation of a Sanskrit compilation, the *Amera Cosha*, whose contents bear (from what he lists) a marked similarity to the themes of Pliny, Aelfric, Bathe, Comenius and Wilkins, but which Roget dismisses as 'exceedingly imperfect and confused'; a *Pasigraphie*, a kind of multi-translator published in Paris in 1797, which is thematic and tabular but which he rejects as 'excessively arbitrary and artificial, and extremely difficult of application, as well as of apprehension'.

14 It is typical of the general approach to lexicography at present that, of the 18 encyclopedic columns taken up by Read's 1976 discussion of dictionaries, only the following lines refer to both Wilkins and Roget:

> The 'conceptual dictionary', in which words are arranged in groups by their meanings, had its first important exponent in Bishop John Wilkins, whose *Essay towards a Real Character and a Philosophical Language* was published in 1668. A plan of this sort was carried out by Peter Marc Roget with his *Thesaurus*, published in 1852 and many times reprinted and re-edited. Although philosophically oriented, Roget's work has served the practical purpose of another genre, the dictionary of synonyms.

(Compare with note 18, below.)

15 The only biography of Roget available at the date of writing is Emblen 1970, which fulfilled a longfelt need. According to Lloyd 1982, however, a second biography is currently being prepared by John Herkless. I have drawn on Emblen for my general background to the *Thesaurus*, and wish that there had been space for more on this remarkable polymath. In particular, Emblen's remarks on the place of 'thesauri' in modern information processing are particularly interesting. Certainly, attending various conferences in the 1970s of the Association of Librarians (ASLIB) informatics group I became aware of the importance of this area of taxonomic activity, although to my regret I have not been able to expand upon it in this study. We can note here, however, that Emblen sees modern information processing as owing much to Roget and the other great nineteenth-century classifiers.

  Longman as the original publisher and the inheritor of copyright has brought out two revisions of Roget in recent years: Dutch 1962 and Lloyd 1982. I have drawn here upon the introductory remarks of both editors. It is to be regretted that Dutch's essay will apparently die with the passing of the 1962 edition. Lloyd's general preface and her 'Dr Peter Mark Roget and his *Thesaurus*' are both readable and informative; indeed, the essays of both these editors are valuable contributions to the study of thematic lexicography.

  An interesting and sometimes acerbic critique of Roget's *Thesaurus* can be found in Egan 1942. A major point of dispute among synonymists is the degree to which the term 'synonym' should be defined narrowly or broadly so as to provide a criterion for including words in synonym groups in synonymic wordbooks. Lloyd argues with some justification that Roget greatly influenced the synonymists in widening their coverage, while Egan maintains that the *Thesaurus* is a mere 'word-finder'. She insists that the modern consultant of Roget 'has little knowledge of the original plan', which 'is obviously hard to use' (p. 14a).

16 My quotation of Roget as regards Natural History is also from p. xxxv (the footnote, first paragraph).

17 My quotation from Roget as regards the uniqueness of the *Thesaurus* is from p. xxiii from his introduction (1962 edition).

18 My quotation of Dutch on two points regarding the nature of a thesaurus and its relation to the human brain or mind is from pp. viii and xiv of his own introduction (1962).

19 For further observations on the thesaurus as an analogue of the human mind, see the closing paragraphs of Ch. 17.

15 Alphabetic lexicography

1 The following quotation from Crystal 1971:47 succinctly describes the effects that the Bibliocentric view of language origin had on the etymological studies of the time:

> Because of its prestigious position for religious studies, Hebrew was a firm favourite (as the original language of the human race). There were many elaborate 'proofs' proposed for this, for if Hebrew was the oldest language, then it had to be demonstrated that all living languages were descendants of, or variations of it. This led to the working-out of many complex permutations of letters between words of similar meaning in different languages, to try to demonstrate such a causal relationship. One justification for this letter-juggling (as it was sometimes called) was that Hebrew had been written from

right to left, whereas other languages went from left to right. Later, Voltaire was one who voiced his scepticism of such deductions: he defined etymology (the study of word history) as a science in which vowels count for nothing and the consonants for very little!

2 For descriptions of the rise of comparative philology and its general achievements, see:

> Dinneen 1967: Ch. 6
> Lyons 1968:21–38; 1981a: Ch. 6
> Robins 1964: Ch. 8

3 For a concise biography of the Brothers Grimm and a review of their works, see Denecke 1976:427–9 (my quotation from p. 428).

4 For my quotation of Read's negative opinion of Richardson, see Read 1976:717, where he also refers to him as 'a disciple of the benighted John Horne Tooke, whose 18th-century theories long held back the development of philology in England'. In the same passage, Read 1976:716 discusses Noah Webster's etymological misfortunes, the rise of comparative philology, Franz Passow, the Brothers Grimm, and the development of the *Dictionnaire de la langue française* (1844–73) of Maximilien-Paul Littré.

5 Works which discuss the fascinating history and complex nature of the *Oxford English Dictionary* include:

> Aarsleff 1962
> Baugh & Cable 1957:331–6
> Ehrlich et al. 1980
> Mathews 1933
> Read 1976
> Sutcliffe 1978
> Whitehall 1958

Reference should also be made to the general introduction to the *OED* itself, whose tone and quality are indicated by the first two sentences of the 'Historical Introduction':

> If there is any truth in the old Greek maxim that a large book is a great evil, English dictionaries have been steadily growing worse ever since their inception more than three centuries ago. To set Cawdrey's slim small volume of 1604 beside the completed Oxford Dictionary of 1933 is like placing the original acorn beside the oak that has grown out of it.

6 The seminal and radical work of Ferdinand de Saussure in the field of structural linguistics came out in 1916 (prepared by his students Charles Bally and Albert Sechehaye). For descriptions of De Saussure's work, see:

> De Mauro 1978 (Introduction to a revised De Saussure, 1978)
> Dinneen 1967: Ch. 7.
> Lyons 1968:38–52

16 *Universal education*

1 John Wesley's excursion into lexicography belongs among a variety of minor compilations of the eighteenth century in England, Scotland and Ireland, all of which aimed at improving general levels of literacy, and included the work of

Thomas Dyche, Benjamin Martin, Thomas Sheridan and William Kenrick.

2 The Chambers brothers are part of a Scottish tradition of lexicography that is in many ways distinct from that of England and more like the French and American. The tradition includes James Buchanan and William Perry in the eighteenth century, John Ogilvie and Charles Annandale in the nineteenth (who had considerable influence on American dictionary making), and the following Chambers editors of the nineteenth and twentieth centuries: Thomas Davidson, William Geddie, John Dickie and Miss A.M. Macdonald. The tradition also includes the wide-ranging lexicographical publications of the Collins family, of Glasgow.

3 Matoré 1968 provides detailed accounts of the development of academic-cum-popular reference books in France in the nineteenth century, from Littré through Larousse (pp. 124–8) and the Larousse books (pp. 138–51).

4 Funk belongs in what might be called the American counter-revolution against the Merriam–Webster reference books. In this, he is in the company of Joseph Worcester and William Dwight Whitney in the nineteenth century, and such compilers as Clarence Barnhart, William Morris, Jess Stein and Laurence Urdang in the twentieth century.

5 My remarks on the *COD* relate to the 5th edition, Oxford University Press 1964, although Fowler's original remarks about not learning to swim are actually from the preface to the 2nd edition, 1929. My general observations as to Fowler's plan relate, of course, to what he says in the preface to the 1st edition, 1911.

6 The position and progress of women in lexicography has not, so far as I know, been researched. Apart from the Abbess Herrad in the twentieth-century (Cf. Collison 1976:794), I am unaware of any major woman compiler apart from Hester Thrale-Piozzi in the eighteenth century – a friend of Johnson's who produced the *British Synonymy* in 1794. Elizabeth Jane Whately produced a comparable short synonymy in 1851, after whom the field appears to be empty until A.M. Macdonald of Chambers and Rose Egan of Merriam–Webster, in the mid-twentieth century. Since then, however, matters have greatly improved. Chambers, however, would appear to lead in this revolution, Macdonald having been replaced as general editor by Elizabeth Kirkpatrick, who edited the 1983 edition of the *Twentieth Century Dictionary*. Longman and Collins have also been progressive in this area, both having produced dictionaries in recent years in which women appear prominently in the editorial and managerial areas.

7 I am indebted for the American journalists' material on Webster's *Third International* to Sledd & Ebbitt 1962.

8 My references to Gove that specifically describe or relate to Webster's *Third International* are drawn from the introduction to that work: *Webster's Third New International Dictionary of the English Language, Unabridged* (London, G. Bell, 1966, two volumes).

17 *Semantic fields and conceptual universes*

1 'Semantics' since Bréal's day has become a complex area of study involving philosophers, logicians and sociologists, etc., as well as linguists and traditional philologists. Useful studies in this area include:

Black 1968	Ogden & Richards 1923
Leech 1969	Ullmann 1962
Lyons 1968, 1981a,b	

2 For the tradition that I describe as including Boas, Sapir, etc., see:

Boas 1911a,b; 1940
Hymes 1964, 1971
Leach 1970
Sapir 1921, 1941
Smith E. & Luce 1979
Whorf 1956.

I discuss the so-called 'Sapir–Whorf Hypothesis', that distinct languages serve to condition the thoughts and worldviews of their users, in McArthur 1983:14–16.

3 My quotations on the problems of conventional lexicography and Hanunóo plant names are from Conklin's 'Lexicographical Treatment of Folk Taxonomies', in Tyler 1969, esp. p. 42.

4 Linguistic studies of 'words', 'morphemes', 'lexemes', etc., that I have at various times found useful include:

Bauer 1983
Bloomfield 1933
Lyons 1968, 1981a,b
Marchand 1960
Martinet 1960
Matthews 1974
Sapir 1921
Tyler 1969
Vendryes 1923

For lexemes, lexical sets and lexical domains, see Tyler 1969:43–6 (in the Conklin paper). For the taxonomic structures, see Tyler's own introduction, pp. 7–20.

5 My quotation relating to the dinosauric nature of the *Third International* is from Weinreich's review of that dictionary (1964).

6 David Crystal's report to Longman is unpublished, but his support for the Lexicon project is acknowledged in the *Lexicon* itself (McArthur 1981).

7 The term 'macrostructure', used in a similar way to mine, interestingly enough appeared independently in Eikmeyer & Rieser 1981 (the same year as the *Lexicon*'s publication).

8 The Language Comprehender is described in Collins & Quillian, 'Experiments on Semantic Memory and Language Comprehension', in Gregg 1972.

18 *Tensions and trends*

1 The publishing details of the two alphabetized 'Roget' wordbooks that I mention are:

The New Roget's Thesaurus. 1961. Ed. Norman Lewis. Berkley: G.P. Putnam.
Roget's College Thesaurus. 1958. Ed. Philip D. Morehead. Signet, New American Library.

2 *The Thesaurus and Dictionary of the English Language* (Doubleday, 1902) of Francis A. March is in the tradition of the synonymy rather than the thematic wordbook *per se*; there is no cosmic framework or any philosophical concern for 'ideas'. Although March has never become a household name like either Webster or

Roget, Cousins observes (the 1968 revision, p. vi) that he has seldom met an owner of the work who did not 'express a devotion to the book verging on a literary mission to proclaim its virtues'.

3 Matoré 1968:153–5 and 170–2 discusses Paul Robert's contribution to French lexicography without enormous enthusiasm, noting that the idea of an analogical dictionary developed from such earlier enthusiasts as Boissière in the nineteenth century.

4 Further background details on the *Metropolitana* (1817–45) are provided at note 5 to Ch. 13.

5 The quotations of Coleridge regarding alphabetic encyclopedias is from Collison 1976:780. Collison's own remark as to the lasting influence of the *Metropolitana* is from p. 781. See also Collison 1964:178–81, 229–92.

6 The quotations from Warren Preece are taken from the *Propaedia* volume of the *Encyclopaedia Britannica* 15th Edition, Editor's preface, pp. xii–xviii. I have found this preface to be an admirable document, and would have liked to discuss it and quote from it more extensively. Suffice it, however, to add here Preece's virtual last word on the alphabetic and thematic modes:

> Though encyclopedists frequently debate the question of utility in terms of whether their works should be 'alphabetical' or 'topical' in organization, the fact is that the argument misses the point. In itself, knowledge does not exist in either a topical or an alphabetical form and knowledge can be organized only in a method that is both topical and alphabetical. By implication, then, what is at stake to the editors of encyclopaedias has to do only with the presentation of knowledge which traditionally has tended to be either topical or alphabetical.

No distinct 'third' mode has however developed, and we are left with my central question: what is or can be the relationship between the two modes in future?

7 The quotation relating to the *EB*15's neo-Thomism is from Quinton 1974:521. My further quotation regarding the organization of the *Propaedia* is from the same page.

8 Adler's description of the grand themes and the circle of learning is from the *Propaedia* volume of the *EB*15, 'Outline of Knowledge and Guide to the Britannica', 5–9 (the circle diagram on p. 6).

9 Despite their remarkable success in blending theme and alphabet, as well as the sheer range and comprehensiveness of their articles, the organizers of *EB*15 are curiously modest about the scholarly status of their work. They appear to see it as a work *of* scholars (which it clearly is), but not necessarily also a work *for* scholars. The *Britannica* Board have sought to provide in the *EB*15 a unique blend of the informational and the educational, and for this purpose have drawn on the expertise of numerous leading figures in many fields. Nevertheless, they have proceeded on the assumption that such a work has little to say of value to specialists in a given area. As Preece puts it: 'It was assumed, therefore, that although all readers of the *Britannica* might be specialists – or have the interests of specialists – in some area of knowledge, they will turn to a general encyclopaedia only as generalists interested in fields outside their own.' (p. xv). He blames present-day specialization for this state of affairs, and argues for the particular style of generalizing language developed for the *EB*15 as a kind of bridge among specialists who are not sufficiently able to communicate across their subjects. I am totally in sympathy with this aim and consider that the *EB*15 largely achieves it, but am intrigued by the assumption or fear that such a book

has nothing to say to people *within* a field. It seems to me that the remarkably high level of expertise offered in the *Macropaedia* volumes verges often on the truly specialized – to the point of baffling the general inquirer – and must be something for specialists to take into consideration. In my own case, I could not even have begun to write a book about works of reference, if I had ignored the *EB*15 contributions of three writers in particular whom I have frequently quoted here: Collison on encyclopedias, Read on dictionaries, and Gusdorf on humanistic scholarship. They are, in my view, not only useful for the interested non-specialist, but essential reading for anyone interested in those specific subjects.

Perhaps the history of *Britannica* has something to do with this failure to appreciate just how valuable the expert contributions in the *EB*15 are both within and across specialisms. The work began as a populist omnium gatherum that scholars could disdain and dismiss if they so wished. Too many first-rank scholars contribute today, however, for that to be any longer true. Additionally, as an inter-disciplinary source book for scholars in great need of extending beyond immediate specialisms – like myself – the *EB*15 is a valuable primary aid, and should be more widely recognised as such.

Pursuing the above point somewhat further, it is odd to find in the *EB*15 a rather clumsy hangover from a past in which macro-lexicographic contributors have tended to be read but not named. The sterling contributors to this work's in-depth articles are identified by their initials, and to the short articles are not identified at all – directly. Complicated lists of names are provided at the end of the *Propaedia* volume. In trying to be sure that I properly acknowledged whatever aid I have received from the *EB*15 I have had to become a juggler of volumes, and have found it frustrating. Future editions should certainly identify their contributors properly in the proper places: the articles themselves (certainly for the *Macropaedia*). This would probably serve to enhance the reputation of the *EB* further. One is constantly surprised on checking the initials to discover just who the contributors really are.

10 The quotations from the Mitchell–Beazley *Joy of Knowledge Library* are drawn from statements made on the covers. I was delighted to discover the use of the expressions 'alphabetic' and 'thematic' in relation to these books, which I regard as miracles of conciseness in terms of information and artistic organization.

Tomorrow's World

★ The quotation from the Revelation of Saint John is from p. 320 of *The New English Bible* (Oxford, Cambridge 1970), the first verse of the fourth chapter.

19 Shaping things to come

1 If space and time had allowed I would have expanded on the parallel histories of compilation and computation (just as I would have expanded on almost everything else in this survey), especially on the roles of Leibniz, Pascal, Jacquard, Babbage, Hollerith, and Turing. For a general informal introduction to the history of computation, see Evans 1979: Parts 1 & 2. For an account of Babbage, see Hyman 1982. For Turing's 'Computing Machinery and Intelligence', see Hofstadter & Dennett 1981:53ff. See also the general introduction to Barr & Feigenbaum 1981, on computers and artificial intelligence.

2 My basic description of the parts of a computer is adapted from Welsh & Elder 1979: Ch. 1 'Computers and Programming' (to which I have of course added my own analogies with past approaches to information processing).

3 Kent 1981 uses essentially the same technical language to discuss both human and machine 'brains', as can be seen from the following extract (p. 1):

> A great deal has been written about the similarities and differences between brains and computers . . . Most of what has been written on this subject is of a general nature and explores topics such as the possibility of artificial consciousness. Although I express my views on such subjects, the bulk of the present work is intended instead as a more detailed description of brain hardware for the person who is seriously interested in exploring new directions in electronic computer and control systems. In particular, it is addressed to those interested in designing machinery to handle tasks which are currently handled only by brains. This area is perhaps best described as being part of the emerging science of robotics.

Other works which I have consulted with regard to the brain/computer analogy include:

> Baddeley 1982 (human and machine memory)
> Barr & Feigenbaum 1981 (artificial intelligence)
> Hampden-Turner 1981 (cybernetics, etc.:158–78)
> Hofstadter & Dennett 1981 (various)
> Jastrow 1981 (brains, computers and the mind)
> Miller, J. 1983 (esp. the dialogue with Dennett, above, on artificial intelligence)
> Rucker 1982 (robot consciousness)

It is also worth noting that a discipline now exists which brings computers and the brain together: 'computational psychology' (*Dictionary of Computing*, Oxford, 1983:70).

4 My quotation on the *lingua electronica*, etc., is from 'The New Literacy', Benjamin Compaine, *Science Digest*, March 1983:18.

5 My quotations on 'living' computers are from Shu 1982: Ch. 20: 'Life and Intelligence in the Universe' (pp. 560 and 558), a most remarkable chapter to find in a textbook on astronomy, but indicative of the direction in which we are moving. Other indications come in large numbers in such periodicals as the popular science magazines, as the following sampling shows:

'Raising the Robot's I.Q.', Pamela Weintraub, *Discover*, June 1981 ('Scientists are devising machines that can see, feel, hear, walk, make decisions, and reproduce themselves')

'The Science of Deduction', Bruce Schechter, *Discover*, January 1982 ('A computer program at the Argonne National Laboratory radiates an AURA of machine intelligence')

'World Brain', Christopher Simpson, *Science Digest*, May 1982 ('After all computers are linked and capable of "intelligent interface", will they form a single superleader?')

'The Organic Computer', Natalie Angier, *Discover*, May 1982 ('Tomorrow's microchips may be built of proteins and manufactured by bacteria')

'The Thinking Computer', Robert Jastrow, *Science Digest*, June 1982 ('Get ready for a remarkable machine that . . . combines information and intuition, calculation and common sense')

'The Old Computers' Home', Natalie Angier, *Discover*, February 1983 ('A new museum near Boston brings alive the history of "calculating engines", from Napier's Bones to supercomputers')

I have unfortunately been unable here to go into the fascinating area of the computer use of natural human language. This began to interest me when I was involved intermittently with two different research areas at the University of Edinburgh in the 1970s: PAT (Parametric Artificial Talker), a speech synthesis machine in the phonetics laboratory, and the work of the pioneers of artificial intelligence.

For an 'early' discussion of machines analysing language, see Wilks 1972. For a comprehensive survey of the state of the art in computers and natural language, see Barr & Feigenbaum 1981: Ch. 4: 'Understanding Natural Language'.

6 The quotations from Urdang, Cassidy and Venezky are all taken from McDavid & Duckert 1973: 282, 341, and 290 respectively.

7 The *Chronological English Dictionary* of Finkenstaedt et al. is published by Carl Winter, Universitätsverlag, Heidelberg, 1970.

8 Ayto's remarks are taken from the Preface to the *Longman New Universal Dictionary* 1982.

9 Aitken's remarks are from 'Historical Dictionaries and the Computer' in Wisbey 1971:3–17, my quotations from pp. 15 and 16.

20 Knowledge, knowledge everywhere

1 The expression 'high technology' has not yet received much attention from lexicographers. The *Random House Dictionary of New Information Technology* 1982, for example, lists and defines 'high level programming language', 'high performance equipment', 'high speed printer', and 'high speed reader', but not 'high technology'. The *Longman New Universal Dictionary* 1982 lists 'high tech' and calls it an abbreviation for 'high technology', but does not see the need for further explanation. The *Chambers Twentieth Century Dictionary* (1983) lists the expression and says of it: 'advanced, sophisticated technology in specialist fields, e.g. electronics, involving high investment in research and development', while Webster's *Ninth New Collegiate Dictionary* (1984) defines the phrase as 'scientific technology involving the production or use of advanced or sophisticated devices especially in the fields of electronics and computers'.

2 So far I have encountered relatively few people in conversation or in my reading who have made explicit the contrast between 'high technology' and the 'low technologies' (and no one who has wanted to suggest a parallel with the 'high' and 'low' modes of language, etc). It seems to me, however, that the contrast in terms of technologies will be made increasingly, and that the parallelism with language is worth a little thought (especially when we go back again to thinking about kinds of literacy).

3 My quotation about newspapers and clay tablets, etc., is from Deken 1981:267. This work derives its title from a phrase used in Toffler 1980, and is a fairly informal guide on 'everyday living with your personal computers in the 1980s' (sub-title). A study which deals in great depth with the impact of the electronic age on newspapers is Smith 1980, a work which in many ways does for the newspaper what I have attempted to do here for reference materials.

4 My source for the information about grammar hotlines in the US and Canada is

a report in the *Montreal Gazette* of 3 February 1983 entitled 'Grammar Hotline an Idea to Really Learn From'.

5 The dial-a-translation-equivalent service to which I refer is a Quebec government service whose postal address is: Office de la langue française, Banque de terminologie du Québec, 700 boul. Saint-Cyrille est, Place Hauteville, Québec QCG1R 5A9.

6 My reference to medical patients in Glasgow derives from Evans 1979:113. The non-judgemental aspect may be more important than we currently suppose; certainly, as I have implied from time to time in this review, education and the use of the various modes of language have often been bedevilled by insecurities of one kind or another, as people are – or feel themselves to be – constantly judged by members of élites to which they do not belong: the priesthood, the teaching profession, the medical profession, and so forth. Computers may be much more welcome to such people than we suppose.

7 The only review that I am aware of concerning the lower East Side kids and their *Trictionary* is the source given in the text: *The New Yorker*, 10 May 1982. The publishers are: Art Resources for Teachers and Students (ARTS), New York.

Bibliography

I have made the bibliography as comprehensive as possible, but no list, however extensive, could hope to do justice to the amount of published material (current or in the last two centuries) on the kinds of topics discussed in the body of this book.

Aarsleff, Hans. 1962. 'The Early History of the Oxford English Dictionary'. *Bulletin of the New York Public Library* 66:417–39.

Abercrombie, David. 1967. *Elements of General Phonetics.* Edinburgh University Press.

Aitchison, J. 1976. *The Articulate Mammal.* London: Hutchinson.

Aitken, A.J. 1971. 'Historical Dictionaries and the Computer', in Wisbey.

Aitken, A.J. and McArthur, Tom, Eds. 1979 *Languages of Scotland.* Edinburgh: Chambers.

Aldrick, Richard. 1982. *An Introduction to the History of Education.* London: Hodder and Stoughton.

Asimov, Isaac. 1963. *The Human Brain: Its Capacities and Functions.* New York: Mentor (New American Library).

Baddeley, Alan. 1982. *Your Memory: A User's Guide.* UK: Multimedia. US: Macmillan.

Binton, Roland H. 1966. *The History of Christianity.* London: The Reprint Society.

Barber, C.L. 1964. *The Story of Language.* London: Pan.

Barnhart, Clarence C. 1968. 'Francis Andrew March: An Appreciation', in March 1902.

   1973. 'Plan for a General Archive for Lexicography in English', in McDavid and Duckert.

Barr, Avron and Feigenbaum, Edward A. 1981. *The Handbook of Artificial Intelligence:* Vol 1. Stanford and Los Altos, California: HeurisTech Press/ William Kaufmann.

Bauer, Laurie. 1983. *English Word-formation.* Cambridge University Press.

Baugh, Albert C. and Cable, Thomas 1957. *A History of the English Language.* New Jersey: Prentice-Hall.

Benz, Ernst Wilhelm. 1976. 'Christianity', *Encyclopaedia Britannica*, 15th Edition: *Macropaedia* 4:459–533.

Black, Max. 1968. *The Labyrinth of Language.* Harmondsworth and New York: Penguin.

Bloomfield, Leonard. 1933. *Language.* New York: Holt Rinehart and Winston; London: George Allen & Unwin, 1934.

Boas, Franz. 1911a. 'Linguistics and Ethnology', editorial introduction to the *Handbook of American Indian Languages.* Washington DC: Smithsonian Institution (reprinted in Hymes 1964).

   1911b. *The Mind of Primitive Man.* New York: Macmillan.

1940. *Race, Language and Culture*. New York: Macmillan.

Bolton, W.F., Ed. 1966. *The English Language: Essays by English and American Men of Letters 1490–1839*. Cambridge University Press.

Bolton, W.F. and Crystal D. 1969. *The English Language: Essays by Linguists and Men of Letters 1858–1964*. Cambridge University Press.

Borger, Robert and Seaborne, A.E.M. 1966. *The Psychology of Learning*. Harmondsworth & New York: Penguin.

Boulton, J.J. Ed. 1971. *Johnson: The Critical Heritage*. London: Routledge & Kegan Paul.

Bowder, Diana., Ed. 1982. *Who Was Who in the Greek World: 776–30 BC*. Oxford: Phaidon.

Bradley, Henry. 1904. *The Making of English*. London: Macmillan. (Revised in 1968 by Simeon Potter.)

Brantl, George. Ed. 1961. *Catholicism*. New York: George Braziller.

Bronowski, Jacob. 1973. *The Ascent of Man*. London: the BBC; USA: Little, Brown/Macdonald (Futura Publishers)

Brown, Evan L. and Deffenbacher, Kenneth. 1979. *Perception and the Senses*. Oxford University Press.

Brown, Roger 1958. *Words and Things: An Introduction to Language*. Macmillan.

Burling, Robbins. 1969. 'Cognition and Componential Analysis: God's Truth or Hocus-Pocus?', in Tyler.

Cameron, Ron, Ed. 1983. *The Other Gospels: Non-Canonical Gospel Texts*. UK: Litterworth Press.

Campbell, Jeremy. 1982. *Grammatical Man: Information, Entropy, Language and Life*. New York: Simon & Schuster.

Campbell, F. 1970. 'Latin and the Elite Tradition in Education', in Musgrave.

Campbell, Robert. 1977. *The Enigma of the Mind*. Time–Life.

Chadwick, Henry. 1967. *The Early Church*. Harmondsworth & New York: Penguin.

Chomsky, Noam. 1968. *Language and Mind*. New York: Harcourt, Brace, Jovanovich.

Claiborne, Robert. 1974. *The Birth of Writing*. Time–Life.

Clifford, J.L. 1955. *Young Sam Johnson*. New York: McGraw-Hill.

Collison, Robert L. 1964 *Encyclopaedias: Their History Throughout the Ages*. New York & London: Hafner.

1976. 'Encyclopaedia', *Encyclopaedia Britannica*, 15th Edition: Macropaedia 6:781–99. Chicago.

Conklin, Harold C. 1969. 'Lexicographical Treatment of Folk Taxonomies', in Tyler.

Copleston, F.C. 1955. *Aquinas*. Harmondsworth & New York: Penguin.

Cousins, Norman. 1968. 'Foreward' to March.

Crystal, David. 1971. *Linguistics*. Harmondsworth & New York: Penguin.

Daniel, Glyn. 1968. *The First Civilizations: The Archaeology of Their Origins*. London: Thames & Hudson.

Darlington, Philip J. 1980. *Evolution for Naturalists: The Simple Principles and the Complex Reality*. New York: John Wiley.

Dean, Leonard F., Gibson, Walker, and Wilson, Kenneth G., Eds. 1971. *The Play of Language*. Oxford University Press.

De Bono, Edward. 1969. *The Mechanism of Mind*. Harmondsworth & New York: Penguin.

Deken, Joseph. 1981. *The Electronic Cottage: Everyday Living with Your Personal Computer in the 1980s*. New York: William Morrow.

Delebecque, Edouard. 1976. 'Ancient Greek Civilization', *Encyclopaedia Britannica*, 15th Edition: Macropaedia 8:361–76.

Denecke, Ludwig. 1976. 'Grimm Brothers', *Encyclopaedia Britannica*, 15th Edition: Macropaedia 8:427–9.

De Saussure, Ferdinand. 1916. *Cours de linguistique générale* (1) published by Charles Bally and Albert Sechehaye. Paris: Payot (2) new critical edition by Tullio de Mauro. Paris: Payot, 1978 (3) translated by Wade Baskin, as *Course in General Linguistics*. New York: Philosophical Library, 1959.

Dillon, George L. 1977. *Introduction to Contemporary Linguistic Semantics*. New Jersey: Prentice-Hall.

Dinneen, Francis P. 1967. *An Introduction to General Linguistics*. New York: Holt, Rinehart & Winston.

Dutch, Robert A., Ed. 1962. *Roget's Thesaurus of English Words and Phrases*. London & Harlow: Longman.

Edson, Lee. 1975. *How We Learn*. Time–Life.

Edzard, Dietz O. 1976. 'History of Mesopotamia and Iraq', *Encyclopaedia Britannica*, 15th Edition: Macropaedia 11:963–79.

Egan, Rose F. 1942. 'Survey of the History of English Synonymy', in the *Merriam-Webster Dictionary of Synonymy*.

Ehrlich, Eugene, et al. 1980. *Oxford American Dictionary*. Oxford University Press/ Avon Books.

Eikmeyer, Hans-Jurgen and Rieser, Hannes, Eds. 1981. *Words, Worlds and Contexts: New Approaches in Word Semantics*. De Gruyter.

Einbinder, Harvey. 1964. *The Myth of the Britannica*. London: MacGibbon and Kee.

Eisenstein, Elizabeth L. 1970. 'The Impact of Printing on European Education', in Musgrave.

   1979. *The Printing Press as an Agent of Change,* Vols. I & II. Cambridge University Press.

Ellegård, Alvar. 1966. *De Internationella Orden*. Sweden: SÖ-forlaget:Skoloverstyrelsen.

Emblen, D.L. 1970. *Peter Mark Roget: The Word and the Man*. London & Harlow: Longman.

Evans, Christopher. 1979. *The Micro Millennium*. New York: Viking.

Ferguson, Charles A. 1959. 'Diglossia', in *Word* 15, reprinted in Hymes 1964.

Finkenstaedt, Thomas and Wolff, Dieter. 1970. *A Chronological English Dictionary*. Heidelberg: Universitätsverlag.

Finkenstaedt, Thomas, Leisi, Ernest, and Wolff, Dieter. 1973. *Ordered Profusion*. Heidelberg: Universitätsverlag.

Fisher, Helen E. 1982. *The Sex Contract: The Evolution of Human Behaviour*. New York: William Morrow.

Fiske, John. 1982. *Introduction to Communication Studies,* London and New York: Methuen.

Foss, Michael. 1975. *Chivalry*. London: Book Club Associates.

Francis, Frank C. 1976. 'Library', *Encyclopaedia Britannica*, 15th Edition: Macropaedia: 10:856–67. Chicago.

Francis, W. Nelson. 1963. *The English Language: An Introduction*. New York: W.W. Norton.

Fry, Dennis. 1977. *Homo Loquens: Man as a Talking Animal*. Cambridge University Press.

Gelb, Ignace J. 1952. *Von der Keilschrift zum Alphabet,* Stuttgart. Translated as
      A Study of Writing: the Foundations of Grammatology. Chicago University Press
      (revised, 1963).
      1976. 'Forms of Writing', *Encyclopaedia Britannica*, 15th Edition: Macropaedia
      19:1033ff. Chicago.
Goodall, Jane. 1971. *In the Shadow of Man*. London: Collins.
Gottfried, Robert S. 1983. *The Black Death: Natural and Human Disaster in Medieval
      Europe*: Macmillan.
Grant, Michael. 1982. *From Alexander to Cleopatra: The Hellenistic World*. London:
      Weidenfeld & Nicolson.
Greene, D.J. 1970. *Samuel Johnson*. New York: Twayne.
Gregg. L.W., Ed. 1972. *Cognition in Learning and Memory*. New York: John Wiley.
Gregory, Richard L. 1981. *Mind in Science: A History of Explanations in Psychology
      and Physics*. Cambridge University Press.
Grevisse, Maurice. 1980. *Le Bon Usage*. Paris: Duculot, Editions du renouveau
      pédagogique.
Griffin, Donald R. 1981. *The Question of Animal Awareness: Evolutionary Continuity
      of Mental Experience*. USA: Rockefeller University Press.
Grove, Victor. 1950. *The Language Bar*. London: Routledge & Kegan Paul.
Gudschinsky, Sarah C. 1982. *Literacy: The Growing Influence of Linguistics*. The
      Hague: Mouton.
Gusdorf, Georges Paul. 1976. 'History of Humanistic Scholarship', *Encyclopaedia
      Britannica*, 15th Edition: Macropaedia 8:1170–9
Hamblin, Dora Jane. 1973. *The First Cities*. Time–Life.
Hampden-Turner, Charles. 1981. *Maps of the Mind: Charts and Concepts of the Mind
      and its Labyrinths*. London: Mitchell-Beazley.
Hartmann, R.R.K., Ed. 1979. *Dictionaries and Their Users*. UK: Exeter Linguistic
      Studies, the University of Exeter.
Herm, Gerhard. 1975. *The Celts*. London: Weidenfeld & Nicolson.
Hibbert, Christopher. 1971. *The Personal History of Samuel Johnson*.
      Harmondsworth & New York: Penguin, 1984 (Longman, 1971).
Hockett, Charles. 1958. *A Course in Modern Linguistics*. New York: Macmillan.
Hofstadter, Douglas R. and Dennett, Daniel C. 1981. *The Mind's I: Fantasies and
      Reflections on Self and Soul*. New York: Basic Books.
Hogben, Lancelot. 1964. *The Mother Tongue*. London Secker & Warburg.
Householder, Fred W. and Saporta, Sol. 1962. Eds., *Problems in Lexicography*.
      Indiana: Bloomington; The Hague: Mouton (2nd edition, with additions and
      corrections, 1967)
Hulbert, James R. 1955. *Dictionaries British and American*. London: André Deutsch.
Hyman, Anthony. 1982. *Charles Babbage: Pioneer of the Computer*. Princeton
      University Press.
Hymes, Dell, Ed. 1964. *Language in Culture and Society: A Reader in Linguistics and
      Anthropology*. New York: Harper & Row.
      Ed. 1971. *Pidginization and Creolization of Languages*. Cambridge University
      Press.
Jansen, G.H. 1979. *Militant Islam*. New York: Harper & Row.
Jastrow, Robert. 1981. *The Enchanted Loom: Mind in the Universe*. New York:
      Simon & Schuster.
Jaynes, Julian. 1976. *The Origin of Consciousness in the Breakdown of the Bicameral
      Mind*. Boston: Houghton Mifflin.

Jensen, Hans 1935. *Die Schrift in Vergangenheit und Gegenwart.* VEB Deutscher Verlag der Wissenschaften, 1935; second edition, 1958. Translated as *Sign, Symbol and Script* by George Unwin. London: George Allen & Unwin.

Kelly, L.G. 1969. *Twenty-Five Centuries of Language Teaching: 500 BC–1969.* Massachusetts: Newbury House.

Kenny, Anthony. 1980. *Aquinas.* Oxford University Press.

Kent, Ernest W. 1981. *The Brains of Men and Machines.* New York: McGraw-Hill.

Kogan, Herman. 1958. *The Great EB: The Story of the Encyclopaedia Britannica.* Chicago: The University Press.

Laing, Lloyd. 1979. *Celtic Britain.* London: Routledge & Kegan Paul.

Leach, Edmund. 1970. *Lévi-Strauss.* London: Fontana/Collins.

Leakey, Richard E. 1981. *The Making of Mankind.* New York: Dutton.

Leakey, Richard E., and Lewin, Roger. 1978. *People of the Lake: Mankind and its Beginnings.* New York: Doubleday (Avon Books).

Lechène, Robert. 1976. 'Printing', *Encyclopaedia Britannica* 15th Edition: Macropaedia 14:1051–74. Chicago.

Leech, Geoffrey N. 1969. *Towards a Semantic Description of English.* London & Harlow: Longman.

Lehmann-Haupt, H.E. 1976. 'Johannes Gutenberg', *Encyclopaedia Britannica* 15th Edition: Macropaedia 8:505–6. Chicago.

Lloyd, Susan M., Ed. 1982. *Roget's Thesaurus of English Words and Phrases.* London & Harlow: Longman.

Lyons, John. 1968. *Introduction to Theoretical Linguistics.* Cambridge University Press.

    1981a. *Language and Linguistics: An Introduction.* Cambridge University Press.

    1981b. *Language, Meaning and Context.* London: Fontana/Collins.

Magee, Bryan. 1973. *Popper.* London: Fontana/Collins.

Majumdar, D.N. 1961. *Races and Cultures of India.* India: Asia Publishing House.

Maleska, Eugene T. 1981. *A Pleasure in Words.* New York: Simon & Schuster.

March, Francis A. 1902. *Thesaurus and Dictionary of the English Language.* New York: Doubleday.

Marchand, Hans. 1960. *The Categories and Types of Present-Day English Word-Formation.* Munich: Verlag C.H. Beck.

Marrou, Henri-Irénée. 1976. 'History of Education', *Encyclopaedia Britannica* 15th Edition: Macropaedia 6:322–9. Chicago.

Marshack, Alexander. 1972. *The Roots of Civilization.* London: Weidenfeld & Nicolson.

Martinet, André. 1960. *Elements de linguistique générale.* Paris: Armand Colin. English translation, *Elements of General Linguistics.* London: Faber 1964.

Mathews, M.M. 1933. *A Survey of English Dictionaries.* New York: Russell & Russell (re-issued, 1966).

Matoré, Georges. 1968. *Histoire des dictionnaires français.* Paris: Librairie Larousse.

Matthews, Peter H. 1974. *Morphology: An Introduction to the Theory of Word-Structure.* Cambridge University Press.

McAdam, E.L., and Milne, George. 1963. *Johnson's Dictionary: A Modern Selection.* London: Macmillan.

McArthur, Tom. 1981. *Longman Lexicon of Contemporary English.* London & Harlow: Longman.

    1983. *A Foundation Course for Language Teachers.* Cambridge University Press.

McDavid, Raven, and Duckert, Audrey R. 1973. *Lexicography in English.* New York: Academy of Sciences.

McLuhan, Marshall. 1964. *Understanding Media: The Extension of Man*. New York: McGraw-Hill.

Meade, Marion. 1979. *Stealing Heaven: The Love Story of Héloïse and Abelard*. New York: William Morrow.

Mertz, Barbara. 1964. *Temples, Tombs and Hieroglyphs: A Popular History of Ancient Egypt*. New York: Dodd, Mead.

Miller, David. 1983. *A Pocket Popper*. London: Fontana/Collins.

Miller, George A. 1962. *Psychology: The Science of Mental Life*. Harmondsworth & New York: Penguin.

Miller, Jonathan. 1983. *States of Mind*. London: BBC. New York: Random House (Pantheon).

Murray, James A.H. 1888. 'General Explanations', *The Oxford English Dictionary*. (Also in Boulton & Crystal).

   1900. *The Evolution of English Lexicography*. Oxford, 22 June: the Romanes Lecture.

Musgrave, P.W., Ed. 1970. *Sociology, History and Education*. London: Methuen.

Nicklaus, Robert. 1976. 'Denis Diderot', *Encyclopaedia Britannica* 15th Edition: Macropaedia 5:723–5. Chicago.

O'Connor, J.D. 1973. *Phonetics*. Harmondsworth and New York: Penguin.

O'Donnell, James J. 1979. *Cassiodorus*. University of California Press.

Ogden, C.K., and Richards, I.A. 1923. *The Meaning of Meaning*. London: Routledge & Kegan Paul.

Ong, W.J. 1970. 'Latin Language Study as a Renaissance Puberty Rite', in Musgrave.

   1982. *Orality and literacy: The Technologizing of the Word*. London & New York: Methuen.

Onions, C.T. 1966. *The Oxford Dictionary of English Etymology*. Oxford University Press.

Orme, Nicholas. 1973. *English Schools in the Middle Ages*. London: Methuen.

Palmer, Frank. 1971. *Grammar*. Harmondsworth & New York: Penguin.

Palmer, L.R. 1954. *The Latin Language*. London: Faber.

Parkinson, C. Northcote. 1963. *East and West*. London: John Murray.

Pattison, Robert. 1982. *On Literacy*. Oxford University Press.

Peñalosa, Fernando. 1981. *Introduction to the Sociology of Language*. Massachusetts: Newbury House.

Pettinato, Giovanni. 1981. *The Archives of Ebla: An Empire Inscribed in Clay*. New York: Doubleday.

Pfeiffer, John E. 1977. *The Emergence of Society: A Prehistory of the Establishment*. New York: McGraw-Hill.

Pieper, Josef. 1976. 'Scholasticism', *Encyclopaedia Britannica* 15th Edition: Macropaedia 16:353–7. Chicago.

Popper, Karl. 1972. *Objective Knowledge: An Evolutionary Approach*. Oxford University Press.

Popper, Karl, and Eccles, John C. 1981. *The Self and Its Brain: An Argument for Interactionism*. Revised edition. Berlin: Springer.

Potter, Simeon. 1950. *Our Language*. Harmondsworth & New York: Penguin.

Prideaux, Tom. 1974. *Cro-Magnon Man*. Time–Life.

Quinton, Anthony. 1974. 'The Organization of Knowledge'. London: *Times Literary Supplement*, May 1974: 521ff.

Radice, Betty. 1974. *The Letters of Abelard and Héloïse*. Harmondsworth & New York: Penguin.

Rahman, Fazlur. 1976. 'Islam', *Encyclopaedia Britannica* 15th Edition: Macropaedia 9:911–26. Chicago.

Read, Allen W. 1973. 'The Social Impact of Dictionaries in the United States', in McDavid & Duckert.

 1976. 'Dictionary', *Encyclopaedia Britannica* 15th Edition: Macropaedia 5:713–22.

Reid, Howard, and Croucher, Michael. 1983. *The Way of the Warrior: The Paradox of the Martial Arts*. London: Century.

Renou, Louis. 1961. *Hinduism*. New York: George Braziller.

Riche, Pierre. 1976. 'History of Education', *Encyclopaedia Britannica* 15th Edition: Macropaedia 6:333–9. Chicago.

Roberts, S., and Clifford, J.L. 1976. 'Samuel Johnson', *Encyclopaedia Britannica* 15th Edition: Macropaedia 10:244–52. Chicago.

Robins, R.H. 1964. *General Linguistics: An Introductory Survey*. London & Harlow: Longman; Indiana University Press; 3rd Longman edition, 1979.

Roget, Peter Mark. 1853. *Thesaurus of English Words and Phrases*. London & Harlow: Longman. (See also Dutch 1962, Lloyd 1982).

Ross, James B., and McLauchlin, Mary M. 1949. *The Portable Medieval Reader*. Harmondsworth & New York: Penguin. (First published in the USA by Viking, 1949; Penguin format, 1977.)

Rucker, Rudy. 1982. *Infinity and the Mind: The Science and Philosophy of the Infinite*. Boston, Basel & Stuttgart: Birkhauser.

Sadler, John E. 1976. 'John Amos Comenius', *Encyclopaedia Britannica* 15th Edition: Macropaedia 4:967–9. Chicago.

Safire, William. 1980. *On Language*. New York: Times Books.

Sapir, Edward. 1921. *Language: An Introduction to the Study of Speech*. New York: Harcourt, Brace & World.

 1941. *Culture, Language and Personality*. Menasha. Wisconsin: Sapir Memorial Publication Fund, 1941. Reprinted, University of California Press, 1956.

Scherman, Katherine. 1981. *The Flowering of Ireland: Saints, Scholars and Kings*. Boston: Little, Brown.

Scholderer, Victor. 1963 *Johann Gutenberg, The Inventor of Printing*. The Trustees of the British Museum.

Sen, K.M. 1961. *Hinduism*. Harmondsworth & New York: Penguin.

Sherratt, Andrew, and Clark, Grahame. Eds., 1980. *The Cambridge Encyclopaedia of Archaeology*. Cambridge University Press.

Shu, Frank H. 1982. *The Physical Universe: An Introduction to Astronomy*. California: University Science Books.

Skeat, Walter W. 1882. *A Concise Etymological Dictionary of the English Language*. Oxford University Press.

Sledd, James. 1972. 'Dollars and Dictionaries', in Weinbrot.

Sledd, James, and Ebbitt, Wilma R. 1962. *Dictionaries and THAT Dictionary*: A Casebook of the Aims of Lexicographers and the Targets of Reviewers. USA: Scott, Foresman.

Smart, Ninian. 1977. *The Long Search*. London: BBC. Boston: Little, Brown.

Smith, Anthony. 1980. *Goodbye Gutenberg: The Newspaper Revolution of the 1980s*. Oxford University Press.

Smith, Elise C., and Luce, Lousie F., Eds., 1979. *Toward Internationalism: Readings in Cross-cultural Communication*. Massachusetts: Newbury House.

Stannard, Jerry. 1976. 'Pliny the Elder', *Encyclopaedia Britannica* 15th Edition: Macropaedia 14:572–3. Chicago.

Starnes, Dewitt T., and Noyes, G.E. 1946. *The English Dictionary from Cawdrey to Johnson, 1604–1755* (including Starnes on various thematic compilations). Chapel Hill: The University of North Carolina Press.

Stendahl. Krister, and Sander, Emilie T. 1976. 'Biblical Literature', *Encyclopaedia Britannica* 15th Edition: Macropaedia 2:938–73. Chicago.

Strang, Barbara M.H. 1970. *A History of English*. London: Methuen.

Sutcliffe, Peter. 1978. *The Oxford University Press: An Informal History*. Oxford & New York: Oxford University Press.

Tanner, Nancy M. 1981. *On Becoming Human*. Cambridge University Press.

Tien-yi Li. 1976. 'East Asian Literature' (China), *Encyclopaedia Britannica* 15th Edition: Macropaedia 10:1050–9. Chicago.

Toffler, Alvin. 1970. *Future Shock*. New York: Random House, Bantam.
   1980. *The Third Wave*. New York: William Morrow, Bantam.

Trevor-Roper, Hugh. 1965. *The Rise of Christian Europe*. London: Thames & Hudson.

Turner, Eric G. 1976. (and colleagues) 'Calligraphy', *Encyclopaedia Britannica* 15th Edition: Macropaedia 3:645–70.

Tyler, Stephen A., Ed. 1969. *Cognitive Anthropology*. New York: Holt, Rinehart & Winston.

Ullmann, Stephen. 1962. *Semantics*. Oxford: Basil Blackwell. New York: Barnes & Noble.

Vendryes, J. 1923. *Le Langage*. Paris. Translated as *Language*. London: Routledge & Kegan Paul.

Webster, Noah. 1789. 'An Essay on . . . Reforming the Mode of Spelling' etc., appendix to *Dissertations on the English Language*, reprinted in Bolton: 157ff.
   1828. Preface to *An American Dictionary of the English Language*, reprinted in part in Sledd & Ebbitt.

Weinbrot, Howard D., Ed. 1972. *New Aspects of Lexicography*. USA: Southern Illinois University Press. London & Amsterdam: Feffer & Simons.

Weinreich, Uriel. 1962. 'Lexicographic Definition in Descriptive Semantics', in Householder & Saporta.
   1964. Review of Webster's Third, in *International Journal of American Linguistics* 30.

Welsh, Jim, and Elder, John. 1979. *Introduction to Pascal*. New Jersey: Prentice Hall International Series in Computer Science.

Wente, Edward F. 1976. 'History of Egypt', *Encyclopaedia Britannica* 15th Edition: Macropaedia 6:471–81. Chicago.

Whalley, Joyce Irene. 1982. *Pliny the Elder: Historia Naturalis*. London: Sidgwick & Jackson.

White, Edmund, and Brown, Dale M. 1973. *The First Men*. Time–Life.

Whitehall, Harold. 1958. 'The Development of the English Dictionary', in Dean et al.

Whorf, Benjamin Lee. 1956. *Language, Thought and Reality* (Selected writings, ed. by John B. Carroll. Massachusetts: MIT Press.

Wiener, Philip P., Ed. 1968. *Dictionary of the History of Ideas: Studies of Selected Pivotal Ideas*. New York: Charles Scribner's Sons.

Wilks, Yorick A. 1972. *Grammar, Meaning and the Machine Analysis of Language*. London: Routledge & Kegan Paul.

Williams, John A. 1961. *Islam*. New York: George Braziller.

Wilson, David M., Ed. 1980. *The Northern World: The History and Heritage of Northern Europe*. London: Thames & Hudson.

Wisbey, R.A., Ed. 1971. *The Computer in Literary and Linguistic Research.* Cambridge University Press.

Zaehner, R.C. 1966. *Hindu Scriptures.* London: Dent. New York: Dutton.

Zgusta, Ladislav. 1971. *Manual of Lexicography.* The Hague: Mouton.

Ziegler, Philip. 1969. *The Black Death.* London: Collins.

Index

NOTE Many entries in the index are conflations like 'topic(s) , etc.'; that is, they cover a range of related items such as *topic, topics, topical, topically, topic-related,* and so on. In addition, some entries with several meanings in the text are deliberately not sub-divided. Thus, although the term *tool* is used in two senses in the text ('physical' and 'mental' tools), it is listed here as one broad concept, which may help the reader to examine the evolution and relationship of the different kinds of tool more effectively. Other entries, however *are* sub-divided (as for example 'literacy' and 'technology'), the more precisely to show how they are used in the text.